Engine
of Inequality

Engine
of Inequality

*The Fed and the Future
of Wealth in America*

Karen Petrou

WILEY

For general information on our other products and services or for technical support, please contact our Customer Care Department within the United States at (800) 762-2974, outside the United States at (317) 572-3993 or fax (317) 572-4002.

Wiley also publishes its books in a variety of electronic formats. Some content that appears in print may not be available in electronic books. For more information about Wiley products, visit our web site at www.wiley.com.

Library of Congress Cataloging-in-Publication Data is Available

ISBN 9781119726746 (Hardcover)
ISBN 9781119727538 (ePDF)
ISBN 9781119730057 (ePub)

Cover Design: Wiley
Cover Image: ©P_Wei/Getty Images
Author Photo: courtesy of the Author

SKY10024165_012721

To Basil, whose tireless patience, encouragement, and critical rereading made this book possible along with so much more.

Contents

Acknowledgments

Grateful thanks are extended to Matthew Shaw, whose research helped to ensure that this book is as right as we can make it, and to Arezou Rafikian for her never-ending cheerful willingness to clean up all my typos. Space does not permit thanks also to the many bankers, policy-makers, industry critics, and friends who have read portions of the manuscript and provided both encouragement to be sure this story is told and constructive comments to make sure it's told correctly. Appreciation also to Leah Spiro, my bulldog agent; Bill Falloon, a very helpful editor; Ellen Kadin, who framed key parts of the initial proposal; Barbara Hendricks; and Mark Fortier and his crack advisory team. Finally, a pat on the head for Zuni, my German Shepherd guide dog. Her unflagging and enthusiastic presence got me to and from many meetings, speeches, and drinks with friends that honed my thinking.

About the Author

Dubbed by the *American Banker* "the sharpest mind analyzing banking policy today — maybe ever," **Karen Petrou** is one of the most sought-after financial consultants in Washington and one of the most influential experts on financial policy and regulation in the world. She is Managing Partner of Federal Financial Analytics, the Washington, DC, financial services consulting firm she co-founded in 1985. It does not lobby for anyone, providing strategic and policy analysis and advisory services to major financial institutions and global central banks. Her views can be found almost every day in the *Financial Times, American Banker, Wall Street Journal*, NPR, CNBC, and many other media. In addition to testifying before the US Congress, she has spoken before the Federal Reserve Banks of New York, St. Louis, San Francisco, and Chicago; the European Central Bank; the International Monetary Fund; and many other governmental, industry, and academic groups. She also provides strategic guidance to foundations on a pro bono basis in connection with work by her and her husband, Basil, to create new funding instruments to speed biomedical research. Winners of the Visionary Award in 2019 from the Foundation Fighting Blindness for this work, the Petrous live in Washington, DC, with Zuni, a German Shepherd guide dog.

Introduction

In 2008, the financial system collapsed suddenly and, to many regulators and central bankers, seemingly without warning. The "great financial crisis" that ensued wrought havoc, but by 2010 the financial system stabilized and stock markets began their upward climb. By 2013, the Federal Reserve was confident that the "Great Recession" that followed the great financial crisis had ended, with financial markets also well on their way to becoming bulletproof thanks to tough new banking rules. The US central bank thus proclaimed that all was right with the national economy and financial system even though only a tiny percentage of Americans benefit from rising financial markets, underemployment was endemic, and anyone who tried to save his or her way to a better life lost ground every day due to ultra-low interest rates.

The Obama Administration also congratulated itself on the sound economy and resilient financial system, Hillary Clinton campaigned on renewed prosperity, Americans knew more than economists about their own struggles, Donald Trump won, markets climbed higher, economic growth remained weak, and America grew ever angrier as economic inequality rose even higher. By 2020, COVID blew away every one of the foundations on which the Fed thought the economy and financial system so securely rested. A decade of rising financial markets atop acute economic and racial inequality made the US as vulnerable to an economic shock as an ill-kempt nursing home to the coronavirus.

I'm among the Americans who got angrier and angrier from 2010 to 2020 as America became increasingly unequal while well-intentioned policy-makers assured us that, as the Fed likes to say, the US economy was in a "good place." In my day job, I analyze monetary and regulatory policy to assess its strategic impact on financial-services companies and markets, doing so for major corporations, central banks, and those elsewhere in the financial market who make or lose money based on what policy-makers do. This isn't exactly a job in the inequality trenches, but it does afford a unique perspective on the totally perverse effect of post-2008 financial policy: acute inequality and resulting risks to both growth and financial stability.

As the 2016 campaign began, I also saw another consequence of post-crisis financial policy: voter fury about the deaf ear most financial decision-makers gave to the warp-speed disintegration of the American middle class, economic despair in communities of color, and profound distrust across what was once the US's manufacturing and agricultural heartland. Calls resonated for policies founded on populism, nativism, and even racism – calls that turned out to be clarion to all too many because vast swaths of the US were in acute economic distress no matter the aggregate growth and employment numbers with which the Federal Reserve comforted itself.

Because my nature is one of an analyst, not an advocate, I dove into the data. As you'll see from all of it in this book, the more one knows the hard facts of financial policy's inequality impact, the angrier one becomes. I thus switched into advocate mode.

In 2016, I told a group of global central bankers that income inequality is the battlefield casualty of post-crisis reform,[1] urging them to clean up their own mess, not count on changes to taxation, spending, technology, or other policies somehow to do it for them. The central bankers were receptive, but none acted. Inequality then climbed higher as post-2008 monetary and regulatory policy continued unchanged, leading me in another speech to central bankers in 2018 to make a still more forceful case for rapid financial-policy reform.[2] Again, central bankers listened but did no more.

This book is my answer to all that inaction, an answer made still more angry and urgent by America in the wake of the pandemic. If more small businesses had been able to access sound credit before COVID, then many fewer would have closed and many more lower-income jobs would have survived. If most Americans had been able to put aside some savings, then families wouldn't have run to food pantries in still-untold numbers. If policy-makers had seen the extent to which the Fed's vaunted recovery stopped far short of people and businesses of color, then the fury following George Floyd's murder would have focused solely on racial justice, not also on demands to "eat the rich." If financial institutions – not just banks – had been properly regulated, then Americans wouldn't have been so deeply in debt and the financial system wouldn't have crumpled the first day COVID's force was felt. And if the Fed hadn't immediately rushed in to rescue all this risk-taking, then Americans of wealth wouldn't have become so much richer so much faster even as US unemployment numbers reached heights not seen since the Great Depression.

Economic inequality is not a curse that afflicts America because some people just don't try hard enough or even because some politicians just don't care enough. This book – the first to do so – will show that US income and wealth inequality grew worse faster than ever before after 2010 due to the one thing that dramatically changed that year: the way the Federal Reserve set monetary and regulatory policy. As you will see, there is a clear and causal connection between financial policy and economic inequality and breaking it is desirable, feasible, politically achievable, and meaningful as a near-term equality remedy.

It might seem fanciful to target financial policy – after all, most of us don't even follow financial policy, let alone feel its impact in our daily lives. However, the interest rates we get at the bank or pay on our debt, the returns some of us achieve in the stock market, the financial companies we choose or are forced to do business with, and even the wages we get are the result of financial policy. As a result, financial policy controls key turbines in the inequality engine.

Financial policy is the combination of the monetary policy dictated by the Federal Reserve Board and the rules written by the Fed and financial regulators. Although ignored by most assessments of economic inequality, financial policy sets the speed and direction of the inequality engine because the inequality engine's fuel is money and no policy moves money with more force than financial policy. When the US economy largely depended on manufacturing and agriculture, financial policy moved the inequality engine, but only a little in comparison to other causes of American economic inequality such as tax or trade policy. But when an economy is "financialized" – i.e., when growth depends in large part on financial activities, not real production – financial policy is an inequality engine unto itself. The US is a financialized economy and financial policy is thus a potent inequality force.

In the US, money thus moves where monetary and regulatory policy drives it. And ever since the great financial crisis, policy drove money to take ever more speculative bets in financial markets that know neither risk nor bounds thanks again to financial policy. How could it have been that, the day in April 2020 that the US announced then-record COVID deaths, the S&P 500 finished its best week since 1974? As this book will show in detail, one need look no farther than the Fed, which that day also stepped in with trillions to backstop even the riskiest investments.

It's thus clear that money determines an economy's haves and have-nots, but how does the inequality engine powered by money work? First, the engine analogy encapsulates the lesson in the Gospel of St. Matthew: "For unto every one that hath shall be given, and he shall have abundance: but from him that hath not shall be taken away even that which he hath" (Matthew 25:29).

This scriptural injunction is in a parable some scholars read as an assessment of spiritual growth, but it aptly describes the critical finding in Thomas Piketty's magisterial analysis of economic inequality:[3] when financial rates of return are above that of broader economic growth, inequality speeds up in a cumulative way, just like a gassed-up engine driven by someone with a heavy foot on the pedal.

The second reason to think of inequality as a financial-policy engine is that it helps us reckon with the critical importance of taking actions that put it into reverse or even turn it off. Letting an engine continue on its course even though the course is wrong only gets us farther from our goal at speeds set ever faster by the engine's cumulative force. To make a difference in inequality, we thus need to pick policies that make a difference as quickly as possible.

This book thus not only details how financial policy made America increasingly unequal faster and faster, but also lays out changes we can make to the engine under current law with remarkably little controversy that will quickly slow the engine and recalibrate its direction toward renewed economic equality.

Much inequality thinking proposes far grander repairs, but most are controversial, costly, and – most importantly – slow-acting. For example, reforming the nation's educational system is indeed an important inequality fix, but it will take years before kids in a better primary school graduate from institutions of higher education and decrease family inequality. We can't wait that long.

Because inequality is an engine with cumulative force that chews up low-, moderate-, and even middle-income families, meaningful solutions must not just be fast-acting, but also politically plausible. Changes to US fiscal policy – i.e., to taxation and spending – such as a "wealth tax" or "guaranteed income" are appealing to some in macroeconomic and social-justice terms but face long, long political odds. Financial-policy fixes to the inequality engine aren't always optimal, but practical policy solutions to income and wealth inequality slow down the inequality engine and give us time also to make more profound structural repairs.

So, what are these fast-acting, politically plausible, and high-impact financial-policy fixes? The first recrafts US monetary policy so it sets interest rates at levels I call a "living return" and retracts the Fed's safety net from beneath financial markets. Ever since the mid-2000s, the prime directive of US monetary policy is what the Fed calls the "wealth effect," which as its name clearly implies assumes that the wealthier a few people get, the more money trickles down to the rest of us. The wealth effect worked in one sense – wealth has grown to prodigious heights in fewer and fewer hands – but it's done nothing for broader, shared prosperity. This book thus posits a set of monetary-policy actions premised on an equality effect derived from ground-up Fed interventions, not top-down largesse.

You'll see that one reason the Fed thought the "wealth effect" created a "good place" is because the Fed measures America as it was decades ago, not as it now is. When it measured employment, the Fed missed the millions holding only part-time jobs or those out of the workforce due only to lack of hope, not lack of desire to work. The Fed said that American households had growing wealth, but it ignored the fact that most of this wealth was held in fewer and fewer hands. Wage gains in which the Fed took pride resulted from more people in more families having to work more jobs, not from higher wages allowing one wage-earner to support his or her family in reasonable comfort as many of us assumed when we were kids.

And the Fed missed the fact that most American families lived paycheck to paycheck, making ends meet only via high-cost debt. The central bank touted its ultra-low interest rates as a boost to the wealth effect, but all they meant to the vast majority of American households was no hope of saving for the future. Most of the debt they used to get by also remained very, very expensive.

As we'll see, this high debt burden, combined with the challenges to robust employment, hit America hard when COVID pulled the rug out from under all the Fed's mistaken expectations. Still, when the pandemic struck, the Fed created two huge facilities to backstop giant corporate debt and opened a "Main Street" bank that in fact did business with companies able to repay loans greater than $250,000 because their annual revenues were as much as $5 billion. The Fed could and should instead have opened a Family Financial Facility that provided ground-up – not trickle-down – emergency economic support.

However, it's not enough for the Fed first to fix monetary policy based on a true reading of America's unequal economy and also to aid those truly in economic need under acute stress. We cannot have shared prosperity if the US financial system crashes disastrously every decade or so.

The third fix to the inequality engine in this book thus redesigns US financial regulation not by removing all the costly rules imposed on banks after 2010, but instead by realigning rules so that like-kind financial activities come under like-kind rules. When only banks are under tough safety-and-soundness and consumer-protection rules, finance moves outside banks and thus outside a lot of equality-critical regulation. This it did from 2010 to 2020 and we know what happened then.

Fixing the financial system means not just new rules, but also new institutions. We can fix the unequal allocation of affordable credit in part by fixing how financial institutions are constructed. Equality Banks are thus among my fixes for a more equal financial system.

Finally, we can't forget the inequality engine's fuel: money. Companies such as Facebook and Amazon aren't just dominant in social media and retailing – they plan to issue new forms of money on a redesigned payment system. This could give them control not only over with whom we associate, what we buy, what we read, and even how we vote, but also over how much money we have and to whom it goes how. We are used to thinking about money as the bills in our wallets or the numbers in our bank accounts, but a quiet revolution redefining money is well under way. If it proceeds without appropriate controls, then the inequality engine's fuel will go still faster and in even larger amounts to those who need it least.

Thus, the last fix I detail crafts a new, digital money system under Fed control along with controls on the Fed to ensure that its new money enhances equal access and secure transactions, not just for the wealthy but also for the rest of us. Much in this book lambasts the Fed, but I still trust it with my money more than Facebook.

In the sixties, a social philosopher said, "In the same way as men [sic] cannot for long tolerate a sense of spiritual meaninglessness in their individual lives, so they cannot for long accept a society in which power, privilege, and property are not distributed according to some morally meaningful criteria."[4] When so much wealth is in so few hands, its morality is elusive and the fury this engenders becomes widespread.

To address the defining economic, social-justice, and moral questions of our time requires a fast-acting, targeted, and politically-plausible action plan aimed at the policies that exert the most force in the inequality engine. This book will prove that financial policy is this inequality engine and also that it can first be reversed and then shut down. If we fail in the 2020s as badly as we failed in the 2010s to fix financial policy, fury will indeed be loosed and financial policy-makers will deserve it. The rest of us, not so much.

Chapter 1

Inequality: Why It's So Much Worse and What to Do About It

Nobody had our backs in office, not Democrats or Republicans. I'm tired of being sugarcoated and being robbed in the process. ... [Politicians] are so out of touch with reality and real people. All of them.
  – *An autoworker who voted twice for Barack Obama and then for Donald Trump**

This bitter sentiment was voiced by an autoworker in May 2019. One month later, the US achieved a seemingly remarkable milestone: the longest economic recovery ever, at least as tallied by economists.[1] The Federal Reserve's chairman took comfort from this milestone, spelling

---

* Sabrina Tavernise, "With His Job Gone, an Autoworker Wonders, 'What Am I as a Man?'" *New York Times*, May 27, 2019, available at https://www.nytimes.com/2019/05/27/us/auto-worker-jobs-lost.html.

out the broad benefits of this putative recovery – it was good for all Americans, not just the wealthy – or so he said.[2] But the Fed was wrong, and the autoworker and hundreds of millions of Americans just like him were right: the economic recovery after the 2008 "great financial crisis" was extraordinarily unequal. When the COVID-19 pandemic hit in March 2020, the shared-prosperity facade disintegrated – unemployment ravaged millions and millions of households and millions of Americans also took to the streets not just to protest George Floyd's murder, but also to mark a decade of extraordinarily unequal growth. No wonder.

If more Americans had had more savings with which to buffer the shock of sudden unemployment and had the American financial system been more equitable, then COVID's economic cost would still have been dear, but not disastrous. But as the US headed into the pandemic, it was the most unequal of all advanced economies, becoming far more unequal far faster after 2010.[3]

It's no coincidence that 2010 also marks the start of massive changes to US financial policy due to the monetary and regulatory response to the 2008 financial crisis. The powerful link between financial policy and our far more unequal economy is the topic of this book; breaking it is its goal.

You might think that monetary and regulatory policy are far afield from economic inequality given the usual focus on factors such as tax and education policy. Economic inequality results from many causes, but who gets the money how is the most important element in each of them. Money doesn't just fall from trees (would that it were so). The job of central banks such as the Federal Reserve is to control who gets the money, with the Fed the only agency of the US government expressly responsible for allocating money not just for stable growth, but also for shared prosperity. It and other central banks around the world use their own money and the reserves banks hold to encourage markets to rev up or slow down a nation's economy. Starting in 2010, the Fed threw the money into the increasingly ample laps of the wealthiest households. In 2020, it redoubled those efforts with still more trillions for still fewer millions. Thanks to the Fed,[4] the period immediately after the COVID pandemic struck was "one of the greatest wealth transfers in history."[5]

Financial regulators also control who gets the money by opening or closing the money spigots to discipline banks or to protect borrowers. After 2010, bank regulators inadvertently turned off funding for affordable loans to average Americans and cut off the bank accounts that households once used to earn living returns on hard-earned savings. Some hard-luck families found financing from high-flying, unregulated financial companies, but this often came at great cost and long-term equality risk. As the last decade closed, new forms of unregulated financial institutions were increasingly powered by new forms of money, much of it formulated by giant tech companies such as Facebook, which over the same years digitalized both economic and everyday life to their own considerable advantage.

What the Fed called a robust recovery was in fact the slowest since the Second World War and the most inequitably shared one ever, as this book will prove. The economy was also very fragile because gains were in large part derived from high-flying financial markets with no staying power beyond the wind the Fed put beneath their wings. Ultra-low interest rates not only failed to stimulate growth, but also made most Americans even worse off because trillions of dollars in savings were sacrificed in favor of ever higher stock markets. Even families with a bit put aside and those with a strong case to start a small business couldn't get loans at reasonable rates on safe-and-sound terms. In short, the economic-equality divide got bigger – a lot bigger – due to all of these financial policies. Capitalism is working fine, but only for capitalists.

Federal Reserve chairs and other financial policy-makers clearly understand what's happening. They see that economic inequality has wrought havoc in American political consensus,[6] household well-being,[7] and even mortality rates.[8] As COVID decimated the nation, the chairman of the Federal Reserve noted that it was an inequality "increaser."[9] However, at the same time and often in the same speech, Fed chairs eschew any responsibility for inequality, preferring to ascribe it to unavoidable innovation, an aging population, long-term problems in the US educational system, unaffordable housing, or fiscal policy. All of these are indeed potent inequality drivers, but that there are other causes of US inequality doesn't absolve financial policy-makers from fixing the ones readily within their own reach.

One reason financial policy-makers dismissed suggestions about their anti-equality effects is that they and the economics theorists on whom they rely failed to anticipate how financial markets responded to all of these reforms. More than a decade after 2008, stock markets rode higher and higher at ever greater risk due to a new set of incentives created by Fed policy. Banks are indeed safer, but now also so different that Facebook is ready to replace them – hardly a comforting thought.

Fixing monetary and regulatory policy won't on their own bring back the "glory days"[10] many of us expect in America. But fixing financial policy will have fast impact, meaningfully improving equality and buoying hope for a "kinder and gentler"[11] nation and shared prosperity. Unlike many other causes of income and wealth inequality, financial policy is remarkably easy to fix and quick-acting afterwards. All it takes is the will to act.

What We Know about Inequality that Economists Don't

Decades before today's economists reached their conclusions based on complex models that only more or less have anything to do with real life, Harry S. Truman observed, "An economist is a man who wears a watch chain with a Phi Beta Kappa key at one end and no watch at the other."[12] The Federal Reserve and the economists on which it relies have been clutching fancy chains, but most Americans know what economic time it is and many are not the least bit happy about it.

Americans once proudly thought – and many economists still believe – that the US is a middle-class nation. However, the middle class has been hollowed out. Now the US consists of a large majority of folks barely getting by plus a tiny sliver of wealthy households.[13] In fact, just three Americans – Bill Gates, Jeff Bezos, and Warren Buffett – own more of the nation's financial wealth than the bottom half of the country combined.[14] Even what's left of the middle class isn't what it was – 23 percent of families that are still considered middle class skipped medical treatments they could no longer afford even before the COVID crisis left many more Americans without employer-provided health insurance.[15] Despite sharp spikes in the cost of medical and child care, education, and housing, middle-class median income in inflation-adjusted terms was about the same in 2019 as 2001.[16]

In fact, income inequality in 2019 was even worse in the US than it was during the Great Depression.[17] Reflecting this, 37 percent of the US was at grave financial risk after only a $400 unexpected expense.[18] Clearly, unexpected expenses poured down in waves after COVID hit, increasing the percentage of Americans who couldn't pay their monthly bills in full by 12.5 percent between just late 2019 and April 2020.[19]

The younger you are, the worse it gets. In the "theft of a decade" characterizing the years after 2008 for younger citizens, Americans entering the workforce were mired in student debt, struggled to find jobs, and generally owned nothing more than a car that they could call their own.[20] In 2019, the average net worth of millennials was still just $8,000, far less than earlier generations at their age.[21] When COVID hit millennials yet again, some called them the "unluckiest generation ever."[22] This might not be historically true, but anger across the entire US political spectrum tells us that it's how millions feel. Even relatively wealthy Americans said that their financial position was a cause of acute stress, and that was before COVID.[23]

Cut these data down to see how African Americans and Hispanics are doing and one sees still sharper divides – racial economic-equality disparities are as bad as they were before the civil rights era promised Black Americans a better, fairer deal. There is now a bigger homeownership gap between Black and white Americans than before 1968, when critical fair-housing legislation was first signed into law.[24] In 2016, white household average wealth was seven times that of Black households and five times that of Hispanics.[25]

The Economic-Recovery Mirage

The Federal Reserve touted a robust US economy starting in 2015[26] and then up to and even after COVID hit in March 2020.[27] President Trump cited stock prices, gross domestic product (GDP), and "record" employment numbers when it suited him. When it didn't, he blamed the Fed, arguing that big economic gains on all of these counts would have continued were it not for a miserly central bank or, after COVID, unduly cautious public-health officials. Mr. Trump had a far better sense of the electorate's mood and how to move it than the Fed. But each of their statements nonetheless portrayed a prosperity remote from the lives of many, including large percentages of those who voted for Donald Trump in 2016.

The Fed and President Trump make the same mistake: they measure the economy by across-the-board indicators. Most of these matter only to the wealthiest Americans who own most of the assets in the stock and bond market. Unemployment may have looked as if it was at record-breaking lows before the pandemic, but that's only if you ignore labor-participation rates, which also show who wants to work or work more. At the height of the seeming boom in 2019, one-third of Americans reported that they were not working as much as they wanted. This is a far more telling number than the aggregate employment dot on the Fed's chart. It proves just how many Americans struggled. Indeed, even this number underestimates the struggle – far more Americans worked more jobs and/or more hours than ever before in late 2019, but their wages barely budged.[28]

From 1989 to 2018, middle-class, real (i.e., inflation-adjusted) wealth increased about 1 percent a year;[29] over the same period, real gross domestic product went up about 2.5 percent a year.[30] Clearly, someone was getting a lot richer as the US economy prospered, but it was not the middle class.

It's not just numbers that obscure the economic reality confronting most Americans. Many economists also firmly believe that capitalism ensures that those who try are those who win. For economists, this conclusion is cloaked in "efficient market" theory – that is, markets reward skill and talent. Conservative politicians concur, but also believe that wealth accumulated ultimately trickles down to lower-income workers, who then get their chance to compete for capitalism's rewards. Some have even said that it's not actually all that bad that almost 40 percent of Americans can't handle a $400 expense since most of them have friends or willing creditors.[31] It goes unsaid that such assistance impoverishes families and loads them down with debt in an endless, debilitating cycle of deepening impoverishment.

Some go beyond aggregate data or supply-side theory to say that America is only unequal because a lot of Americans are indolent, sometimes renewing attacks on "welfare queens" to argue that folks would get back to work if government benefits such as disability payments to veterans were curtailed.[32] Others quibble with various statistics illustrating income and wealth inequality on grounds that this or that data point ostensibly fails to include one or another additional or different data point such as receipt of food stamps that a particular pundit prefers.[33] None of these inequality dissenters notes that, even if one adjusts data points up or down to reflect refinements, trend lines are inexorable: America is clearly unequal no matter how one measures income or wealth and became far more unequal far faster after the financial crisis. After 2008, middle-class wealth collapsed, but the wealth of the top 10 percent grew 19 percent in the following decade,[34] resulting in the largest wealth-share increase – 6 percentage points – since the Second World War.[35] At the same time, middle-income family wealth was still below its 2008 level, and lower-income families lost 16 percent of their pre-crisis wealth (not much to start with, of course).[36]

Why So Unequal So Fast?

Something happened after the 2008 crisis ebbed that turned inequality into a faster and still more corrosive force running through the fabric of American social and political thought. This book will show that this something wasn't the great financial crisis itself – painful though it was, the years between 2008 and 2010 were actually more equalizing than those that preceded them due in large part to the short-term decrease in the value of assets held by the wealthy. What happened starting in 2010 is that federal financial policy-makers tried to boost the economy and redesign American banking through a series of unprecedented market and regulatory interventions. All were well intentioned but most were nonetheless still directly and demonstrably destructive to US income and wealth equality.

Is it really plausible that financial policy on its own could make the US so much less equal at such speed? Yes. Economic equality is determined by who has the money and financial policy sets the terms on which markets allocate money to whom as dictated by the inexorable forces of profit maximization. Indeed, as we will see, financial policy now even defines what money is as well as who gets it. "Profit maximization" sounds like a textbook term, and indeed it is. But its meaning is anything but academic: profit-maximizing companies (and that's virtually all of them) set corporate strategy to satisfy the investors on whom corporate survival – not to mention senior-management bonuses – depend. Scrupulous companies will not violate law or rule to maximize profits, but they will find a way to align profits and compliance, no matter the cost to economic inequality. Once, investors were tolerant of long-term strategies that sacrificed a bit of near-term return in favor of long-term profitability. Now, not so much.

This profit-maximization construct is so common that it has characterized American corporate life for the half-century and more since Milton Friedman first pronounced:

> There is one and only one social responsibility of business – to use its resources and engage in activities designed to increase its profits so long as it stays within the rules of the game, which is to say, engages in open and free competition, without deception or fraud.[37]

Many dispute the economic wisdom and even the morality of this corporate edict, but it has nonetheless defined US business behavior before, during, and after the 2008 great financial crisis and again after COVID struck in 2020. Indeed, the profit-maximization, quarter-over-quarter ethos is one contributing crisis cause. However, unless or until investors relent, it prevails.

As a result, corporations through their actions convert economic theory into financial-market reality – and a very hard reality it became after post-crisis financial policy redesigned finance. The Federal Reserve bought trillions of dollars of assets from the banking system starting in 2009, ultimately growing its portfolio to $4.5 trillion. Although these purchases effectively countered the crisis at the start, they did not jump-start the economy as the Fed hoped. Indeed, over time, the Fed's huge portfolio made inequality even worse because the long-term impact of this unprecedented policy was to boost equity prices in the stock market, not long-term, job-producing growth.[38]

In 2020, the Fed repeated this playbook, this time throwing still more trillions into the financial market. As a result, stock markets bounced back from the brink in record time even as American unemployment continued to skyrocket to levels not seen since the Great Depression of the 1930s, if then.

As the Federal Reserve sucked trillions of safe assets from the financial system, investors looked desperately for places to put their funds. Starved of Treasury obligations and even of the chance to earn a reasonable rate of return by putting money in the bank, investors had little choice but to head to the stock market or to high-risk assets promising returns above the Fed's low rates. All this demand boosted equity prices, which led to more demand and still higher stock prices. The more financial markets go up, the still better off the wealthy become, at least for as long as markets go up or the Fed prevents them from coming back down.

If all Americans owned stock, then all Americans would benefit from rising markets, but all Americans don't own stock; the bulk of household stock ownership – 86.5 percent – was in the hands of the wealthiest 10 percent of households, and the top 1 percent owns more than half of all US stock.[39]

To be sure, many Americans owned stock in 401(k) plans and mutual funds. But wealth doesn't come from just owning stock; it's of course due to how much you own. The percentages showing that the rich benefit most from rising financial markets of course reflect the fact that stock ownership is best measured by the value of the shares each person owns, not by the number of people who own them.

As a result, Fed asset purchases stoked stock-market rises that dramatically increased the wealth of those able to invest in the stock market. From 2007 to 2019, the S&P index for stocks rose 77 percent; that is, an investor with $10,000 in the market at the start of the crisis would have $17,700 to show for it after these twelve years. As shown below, small savers who were not also stock-market investors were worse off than ever before. Wealth inequality was thus even worse than it was before 2008, and the Fed is to blame for at least part of it.

Even worse, the Fed's portfolio also increased income inequality. Looking out for themselves and working hard to comply with tough post-crisis rules, banks didn't just take the money and lend it out as the Fed's economic theories expected. More loans would have likely led to more jobs. Instead, banks took the money and then allocated it not to suit the Fed's monetary-policy theories, but rather to maximize profitability. Fearful of losing money if they made the growth-boosting loans predicted in Fed models, banks used the cash to buttress their reserves as higher capital requirements kicked in. Capital requirements demand that shareholder equity stand behind bank lending, making the cost of lending higher because investors have lots of places to put their funds to use if stock prices at banks fail to suit them. Whatever capital banks had to spare thus went into dividends or stock repurchases that made investors richer or, if market conditions didn't allow, then to backing "excess reserves" – that is, into deposits at the Federal Reserve instead of into loans to hard-pressed households trying to refinance their mortgages, put kids through school, or just make ends meet.

Of course, banks also lend to corporations. One might thus have thought – the Fed surely did – that banks wary of consumers would still lend to companies that then built plants and bought more equipment, stimulating the recovery as conventional thinking dictates. However, companies that got loans didn't boost economic growth; nonfinancial companies maximize profits at least as assiduously as banks. As a result, there was a giant spree of stock buybacks and other capital distributions that made shareholders richer, but kept the overall US economy in first gear. That's better than reverse, of course, but still nowhere near good enough to enhance equality.

To make matters even worse, wealth gains at the top 1 and 10 percent came largely at the expense of what we once quaintly called the middle class. Homes are supposed to be the bedrock of middle-class wealth, but they in fact do far less for wealth than owning stocks and bonds. As we'll see, house-price appreciation and equity free of debt is principally a rich household's reward.[40]

And the Fed did more than stoke stock-market booms by stripping the financial market of trillions of dollars of assets once held by private investors. It also drove real (inflation-adjusted) interest rates below zero. Interest rates close to and sometimes even below zero on either a real or nominal (i.e., the rate on the posted sign) basis reverse the normal relationship between debtors and creditors. When rates fall below zero, the depositor pays the bank for the privilege of holding his or her money.

Conversely, a borrower will actually owe less than he or she borrowed when paying back a loan with a negative interest rate.

When the Fed began to raise rates in 2015, these were still at or below real positive territory, with interest rates ever since hovering at just about a sliver above or below inflation. Rich investors can borrow cheaply at rates such as these and then invest in rising markets to make their returns still greater (if also riskier due to all this leverage). Average households don't play in the complex "carry-trade" or high-leverage arenas that benefit from ultra-low rates. They also often lack access to mutual funds or other investment vehicles that beat the Fed's low rates.

Instead, these households put whatever money they may have – and as we've seen it's not much – in the bank. Interest rates of 0.25 percent – not counting fees for bounced checks and other costs – made money in the bank a losing proposition for anyone without $10,000 or so to put aside.

A simple example shows why. Assume a parent saving for a child's education puts $2,000 a year in a savings account paying a 5 percent compound rate of interest for 20 years. At the end of 20 thrifty years, he or she has $69,438 to show for this in nominal terms. After accounting for 2 percent annual inflation, he or she has $49,598. As a result, $40,000 has earned an additional $9,598, or 24 percent. Now take that same $2,000 for the same 20 years – $40,000 – and the same 2 percent inflation. But instead of a 5 percent interest rate, the parent earns only the half of one percent interest rate paid on small savings since the financial crisis. Instead of $69,438, this parent has only $42,168. After accounting for inflation, that is only $30,120, almost 25 percent less.

Clearly, the Fed's long-term, low rates quashed the chances that an average household can save for a financial cushion against adversity, to fund a mortgage down payment, or to secure their retirement. A generation ago, it took only three years for a young family to fund a mortgage down payment. Before COVID set younger households still farther back, it took at least nineteen years, due in part to very low interest rates.[41]

After 2008, the Fed expected that low interest rates would make low-cost loans available to lower-income households, but Fed policy instead made the rich a lot richer and left everyone else still farther behind. One study estimated a total loss across the US economy of

$2.4 trillion in savings accounts due to the very low interest rates that prevailed from 2008 through mid-2017.[42] The longer there are low rates, the farther most families fall behind.

Had the Fed "normalized" rates – that is, brought them closer to a rate with a sizeable positive edge over inflation – the dynamics of high-risk markets and hard-pressed families would have begun to correct to a more stable, equitable economy before COVID hit in 2020. Further, if rates had been higher, the Fed would have had more tools with which to confront renewed crisis. Since they weren't, it didn't, and the Fed threw still more trillions into the financial market, leading to record gains even as US unemployment ravaged one in four working households.[43] Monetary policy after 2008 directly contributed to post-crisis inequality; post-COVID policy made the inequality engine hurtle over average Americans in a race to save financial markets.

Regulatory Wreckage

Financial policy subsumes more than monetary policy. It also includes all of the tough new rules bank regulators imposed since the crisis. It makes a lot of sense to make banks safer. But the inexorable nature of profit-maximization means that, when rules make lending to lower-income families unprofitable, banks don't make loans to lower-income families. Only higher-income Americans with stellar credit histories need apply.

Post-crisis rules may well have made US banks safer, but they have also changed the bank business model to one focused on wealth management, corporate and commercial real-estate lending, and other activities with little equality impact. Given the depth of the great financial crisis in 2008 and how close we then came to another Great Depression, it's easy to say that banks deserve every rule they got. But no matter how justified all of this regulatory retribution, quashing the capacity of banks to take deposits, make loans, and to operate the overall financial system leaves America with two choices: do without banks and the economic growth that depends on them, or rely instead on nonbanks, including giant technology companies such as Facebook and Amazon.

These tech giants are quickly filling the vacuum left behind by departing banks. They do a great job handling our demand for next-day sneakers and getting us messages from the boy next door in what seems like a nanosecond, but this doesn't necessarily mean that tech companies should be allowed to use the huge troves of personal data amassed in these businesses to provide equality-essential financial services. In the absence of safety-and-soundness rules and in light of all the privacy, conflict, and security problems at giant tech companies, a bank-free consumer-finance system could be a very high-risk consumer-finance system.

One doesn't have to look far to see the grand ambitions tech companies harbor in the financial-services arena. These huge companies already derive 11 percent of their revenue from financial services,[44] but many want to do more – lots more. For example, Facebook announced "Libra" in June 2019.[45] Libra combines the 2.6 billion or more users Facebook counts on its social-media platform with a "crypto-asset"-based currency. Libra touts all the lower-income households it would include in the financial-services marketplace. Yet crypto-assets are not just secret, but also very high risk. Who bears this risk? In Facebook's plan, customers – not Facebook – take the fall.

The ability of tech companies to know where you live, with whom, and so much else about us may encourage them to make you a loan a bank wouldn't touch. But all of this personal information also gives these companies the power to price financial services based on data stockpiles that differentiate the rich from everyone else. Given that these companies are at least as profit-hungry as banks, will they still make loans to lower-income people once they are sure which of their customers buys high-markup products? Will financing costs go up for even essential financial services because the big-tech company has enough data to charge higher-risk customers instead of cross-subsidizing transactions across the entire customer base? Will artificial intelligence really secure fair lending when it still can't even read the faces of people of color? How will tech companies cross-sell checking accounts and sneakers? That is, might we get a loan from a tech company, but only if we buy the products it produces at prices it demands under terms no federal regulator can control? One former US regulator has observed:

> Today's economic activity is built on digital code. Digital information is the most important capital asset of the 21st century. Typically, Gilded Age assets were hard assets: industrial products that ended up being sold. Today's economy runs on the soft assets of computer algorithms that

crunch vast amounts of data to produce as their product a new piece of information. The business of networks like Comcast, AT&T, and Verizon, and of platform service providers like Google, Facebook, and Amazon is not just connections or services, but the digital information about each of us that is collected via those activities and subsequently reused to target us with specific messages.[46]

What if all this power to send us messages combines with the power to hold and manage, transfer, and even create our money?

Banks are barred from commerce because of manifest conflicts of interest and risks when a lender is also a manufacturer, advertiser, publisher, and retailer. Big-tech platform companies have no such constraints and can thus condition financial-product access on the purchase of other goods or services, alter pricing based on personal financial information or relationships, and otherwise transform financial services with far-reaching inequality impact.

How to Fix Financial Policy

The first fix is for the Fed to see America as it is, not as it was. Top Fed officials came of age in the 1970s and 1980s when America was among the most equal nations in the world. At that time, monetary-policy theory could rightly assume that aggregate data about income and wealth represented the vast majority of Americans.

Now, due to American inequality, the country as a whole no longer buys goods and services or invests as old models predict.[47] Vast differences in US educational levels have resulted in large numbers of low-skilled, low-wage workers who do not move where jobs are plentiful or otherwise respond to economic signals as conventional monetary-policy models anticipate.[48] We will see in Chapters 6 and 7 how antiquated analytics have been destructive not just to Fed thinking, but also to its ability to transmit monetary policy. Mistaken analytics have also done irreparable damage to equality because policy inadvertently but all too effectively benefits only the wealthiest among us.

The second fix goes to the heart of this mistaken monetary-policy construct, requiring the Fed to stop rescuing financial markets in trickle-down giant programs and instead to support ground-up growth.

This starts with stepping back and letting markets function normally instead of rushing in to save them each time a little stress shows itself in a bad day on Wall Street. We will see in Chapter 6 that the Fed has mistakenly made policy since the early 2000s based on an expectation that market rescues lead to a "wealth effect" that then benefits the rest of us after the wealthy have had their fill. Unprecedented inequality ever since is clear proof that the wealth effect is all too effective for the wealthy, but an accelerant to economic hardship for everyone else.

As we will also see, the wealth effect has made markets prone to another risk. Known as "moral hazard," it occurs when investors take high-risk bets, insouciant in the knowledge that the Fed will always bail them out. It did in 2008 and again in 2020, making financial markets rise ever higher even as unemployment rose to unprecedented heights. The Fed readily admits it doesn't know how to normalize the trillions now on its hands in the wake of all its post-COVID rescues, suggesting very slow normalization should anything like normal ever again be possible. We will see in Chapter 11 how to take the Fed's heavy hand off the market as quickly as possible without overturning the market at the same time.

The third fix needed for an equality-focused policy reckons not only with the anti–wealth equality effect of the Fed's giant portfolio, but also the anti–income equality impact of ultra-low interest rates. The lower these go, the less companies spend on investment, the harder it is for lower-skilled workers to find jobs, and the farther behind family savings fall from any hope of buying a home, going debt-free to college, or securing retirement. Equality will advance with a smaller Fed portfolio and higher interest rates. These are counterintuitive to traditional thinking, which assumes that the bigger the Fed and the lower the interest rates, the better it is for bottom-up growth. Since 2008, the Fed followed this traditional playbook and became by far the biggest it's ever been, driving rates below zero after taking even a little bit of inflation into account. The result was inequitable, slow growth and a fragile financial system that crumpled virtually in minutes when markets realized how dangerous the pandemic would prove. As we will see, it's simply impossible to have a stable financial system without economic equality no matter the trillions the Fed deploys to stabilize markets. Trickle-down monetary policy has proven disastrous to both equality and stability. The Fed indeed must quickly remedy this not just by normalizing its portfolio, but also by gradually raising interest rates to provide for what I call a "living return" – that is, a rate enough above that of inflation to give small savers growing nest eggs from which to start families, buy homes, or retire in comfort.

And, federal financial regulators should redesign post-crisis regulation so that its burden is borne equitably by all financial companies, especially those companies that offer higher-risk financial products to vulnerable households. This would expand the supply of equality-essential financial services beneath an umbrella of regulation that protects at-risk consumers. It would also ensure that privateering financial companies die by their own hand instead of receiving the trillions of dollars in bailouts proffered during the great financial crisis and again as COVID struck. We'll see how asymmetric regulation creates equality and financial-system risk in Chapter 8, with solutions laid out in Chapter 10. These include new ways to apply like-kind rules to like-kind companies, changes to key rules to increase credit availability for low- and moderate-income (LMI) households, and new financial institutions focused solely on economic equality dedicated to under- and unserved communities, including those of color.

Finally, the Fed and bank regulators must reckon quickly with the new, digital forms into which money is quickly being transformed. Financial policy builds the engine of economic inequality, but money is its fuel. If it joins financial policy in revving up the most powerful – i.e., the wealthiest – parts of the engine by flooding them with gas, the US financial system will quickly become still more inequitable and thus even less stable. We will see in Chapter 9 how a new central-bank digital currency that harnesses the fuel in a newly designed equality engine would set us quickly on a more level, tranquil road.

We will also see in Chapter 10 how to ensure that new rules or institutions aimed at equality actually do what they're told. Purpose and profit do not rest easily within private-sector financial companies. So it's also time for the federal government to step in with targeted financial products and newly designed financial institutions. There must also be tough rules to ensure that those given lucrative benefits to serve the less well-off do not repeat past instances in which financial companies hid behind do-good charters and did all too well only for themselves. Classic cases in point are the $5.5 trillion US government–sponsored enterprises Fannie Mae and Freddie Mac. In the lead-up to 2008, they invested millions in advertisements echoed by nonstop lobbying touting the "American dream of homeownership" and how they made it real. In 2008, both of these companies' failures initially cost taxpayers $187.5 billion,[49] but their former executives to this day enjoy posh retirements funded by the enormous salaries and lush pension plans doled out before the crash.

Polarized like so much else in American discourse, the current financial-policy debate contrasts two ends of the policy extreme: government intervention in the financial market or a wholly market-driven financial system. This is indeed the contrast between socialism in full flower and capitalism red in tooth and claw. John Kenneth Galbraith once observed, "Where the market works, I'm for that. Where the government is necessary, I'm for that."[50] This is insightful, but of course also facile – it's not hard to be for working markets and an effective government; it's hard to know which is which.

The rest of this book is an effort to determine when markets work well for equality-enhancing finance and when the government needs to step in with monetary policy, regulation, and even government-backed programs such as new "Equality Banks" that provide vital financial services when the private market falls short.

Chapter 2

How Unequal Are We?

For the first time in decades, we are no longer simply concentrating wealth in the hands of a few. We're concentrating and creating the most inclusive economy ever to exist. We are lifting up Americans of every race, color, religion, and creed.

*– President Donald J. Trump**

If President Trump is right, then the rest of this book is a waste of time. Why bother to show that post-crisis financial policy has made Americans even more unequal or devise ways to fix it for equality's sake if we aren't unequal?

The answer lies in the data deluge that is to come in this chapter. Normally, loads of numbers are many numbers too many. However, when a president and many of his advisers and supporters insist that America is equal and then some, it is vital to demonstrate that America

---

* President Donald J. Trump, "Remarks by President Trump at the World Economic Forum" (January 21, 2020), available at https://www.whitehouse.gov/briefings-statements/remarks-president-trump-world-economic-forum-davos-switzerland/.

has been increasingly unequal since 1980, that it was at levels of income and wealth inequality not seen since World War II before COVID hit, that many other nations are more equal than the US, that African Americans were even more unequal in 2019 than before the civil rights era, and that all of these underlying trends skyrocketed to unprecedented inequality when post-crisis financial policy changed the distribution of wealth in the US starting in 2010. It will take some time to count COVID's long-term impact on American economic inequality, but the ravages it wrought on household wages and employment show irrefutably that the pandemic made inequality worse along with pretty much everything else it touched. Reforming financial policy is thus a still more urgent equality priority.

Economic Inequality Fundamentals

Throughout this book, I refer to "economic inequality" even though much popular discussion focuses on "income inequality." The reason to focus more broadly on economic inequality is that there are at least two key components that determine the have-a-lots, have some, and have-nots in the US and across the globe.

First indeed comes income. This is what you and others in your household earn from the fruits of your labor (i.e., from your job), the benefits you get from the government minus the taxes you pay, and what you earn from your savings accounts and investments (including pension income and capital gains). Although different ways to count "income" in the Tax Code have different statistical effects, income is often and I think rightly measured after taxes to capture the equality impact of changing taxation policy.

Most income measures also and again rightly capture "transfer payments" – welfare, tax credits for purposes such as child care or education, public pensions such as Social Security, and other government income. Income equality is also affected – a lot – by capital income – that is, how much we earn on investments such as stocks, bonds, and savings accounts and whether we realize a profit when we sell our home or any of our investments. Very few measures of income equality look also at how far our income goes to maintaining a comfortable life – what we used to call being middle class. However, in this book, I'll look not only at what you earn, but also at what you have left over to spend on day-to-day essentials without going still more deeply into debt.

In short, income is what you earn and wealth is what you keep. Wealth is usually measured as net worth – i.e., the value of owned assets minus any debt needed to accumulate them. This is the right way to assess equality since debt burdens not only chew up income to make us poorer, but also expose us to the acute risk of personal bankruptcy or home foreclosure. Because the value of the assets wealthy households own – stocks and bonds – soared since 2010, and these households have little to no debt, they have done very, very well.[1] Wealthy households that depend on financial assets are also more resilient households than lower-income ones for whom the main source of wealth is a home. It's of course far easier to sell a few stocks or bonds to tide one over a hard patch or even a crisis such as COVID than to sell one's abode.[2]

Worse, the real inflation-adjusted value of the most important asset for many Americans – our homes – stayed flat after 2010 even as markets soared.[3] Putting many of us farther away from any hope of wealth accumulation, homeownership was increasingly out of reach because of the debt burdens that rose sharply after 2010. This is now record-breaking,[4] due in part to the huge cost younger Americans bear to fund their educations. Before COVID created its own economic catastrophe, student debt exceeded 100 percent of income for US millennials with student debt and is an astounding 372 percent of income for the least well-off.

Failing to combine both income and wealth into considerations of economic inequality quickly leads one astray. Working these income and wealth drivers into specific cases, one can see that thrifty retirees with large real-estate holdings able to leave a large inheritance look relatively poor based on "income" but quickly show up among America's most prosperous once wealth is considered. Conversely, two young people beginning their working careers might look similar in terms of income, but the one given a large house down payment by his or her parents is a good deal wealthier and has far better long-term equality prospects than the other, who not only lacks parental support, but may well also pay large student-loan bills that cut deeply into consumption capacity and long-term wealth accumulation. Affluent parents are a great comfort to their relatively wealthy millennial offspring, with 63 percent of them saying that their own retirement security depends on inheritance from parents, grandparents, and even friends.

Looking only at income also masks the inability of low- and moderate-income (LMI) households to amass the wealth needed to move into the middle class through capital-income-generating savings accounts or growing home equity. Having a small or even no cushion against the unexpected means that households can quickly lose what little they have after something as minor as a blown tire, let alone an event as eviscerating as the economic shutdown due to the novel coronavirus. Data from the Federal Reserve show just how close many of us with relatively robust incomes were to the edge even if our income pushed us into the nominal middle class – 37 percent of American adults (almost 100 million) feared that they could not handle an unexpected bill of only $400 no matter the seeming prosperity of late 2019.[5] Even a small rainy-day fund is essential for household resilience, but as COVID hit in April 2020, almost one-third of Americans lacked a rainy-day fund of more than three months.[6]

Income and wealth may also not tell the whole inequality story. Conservatives disputing that America is in any way unequal avert their gaze from income and wealth to look only at what we own regardless of how much debt we took out to get it.[7] I do not use this approach because consumption is distorted by many factors, not least the fact that the richer one is, the more one saves rather than spends in proportion to income and the less debt is needed to fund consumption.[8] Further, measuring equality by how many cars, televisions, or air conditioners a household owns (as is sometimes done) confuses the often-larger numbers in lower-income households – two cars may well mean two earners are needed to maintain the same income found in a higher-wealth household with just one (probably more expensive) car.

However, one approach to "multidimensional" economic equality incorporates consumption data with income and wealth in a very interesting way. A Federal Reserve study examined households with the largest amounts of income, wealth, and consumption to see how households along these three dimensions fare from an economic-equality perspective.[9] Using this three-dimensional approach shows an even more unequal America after 2008 well ahead of COVID.

In 2007, half of all households that were in the top 5 percent of income were also in the top 5 percent of households in consumption and wealth. By 2016, 60 percent of the households with top 5 percent wealth were also in the top 5 percent of consumption or income. These gains for the top 5 percent in income, consumption, and wealth came at the expense of almost everyone else – the bottom 80 percent of households saw their share of income, consumption, and wealth fall still farther.

Who Has How Much

Unsurprisingly, economists have many ways to study income, wealth, distribution, and even how many households or individuals should be counted.[10] Still, I've found no objective, time-tested data to suggest that the United States is anything like the equality powerhouse President Trump asserted.

First to income and some hard numbers that make inequality all too real. One could of course assess the US in COVID's wake to make a strong inequality argument, but this might be countered by those saying it's unfair to take a snapshot of the US at the worst of times. So let's look instead at the end of 2019, the best of times since 2010. This is compelling evidence that Mr. Trump was wrong and the need to repair the inequality engine is urgent.

According to the Fed,[11] 26 percent of adults in 2019 had a family income of less than $25,000, which was just about the federal poverty level for a family of four in the contiguous US. Another 10 percent had a family income above $25,000 but below $40,000. Thus, more than one-third of Americans had family income below middle class as many define it.[12]

The top 20 percent had an average pretax income of $234,000 in 2018 (the most recent data available).[13] Even in this group, income is segmented – the top 5 percent had pretax incomes exceeding $416,000 on average in 2018.[14] At the same time, the bottom 20 percent made an average of $13,775[15] and as a whole earned only 3.1 percent of US pretax income.[16] Working-age adults in the bottom 50 percent group earned no more in 2014 than they did in real terms in 1980.[17] By contrast, the average income for the top 1 percent rose more than 200 percent between 1980 and 2014 to more than $1.3 million.[18] Put another way, the average earnings differential between the top 1 percent and bottom 50 percent was 27 times in 1980 but rose to 81 times in 2014.[19]

What of the vaunted American middle class? Using the "Gini coefficient" – an established equality measure – the middle class disappears into a void left by far more wealth at the top and far less sliding down to the bottom. Simply put, a Gini index of zero means that everyone earns or owns the same amount of income or wealth – perfect equality; a Gini of one means that one person earns or owns it all. The Gini coefficient thus helps to tell us if America's long-cherished image as a nation of middle-class households is still true. Sadly, it isn't.[20]

The Gini coefficient and survey data used by the Congressional Budget Office (CBO) show that the middle class took home a smaller slice of the income pie – i.e., it was "hollowed out" – by large income gains at the very top of the income distribution and by the descent of many once middle-class earners into lower-income groups from 1979 to 2016.[21] In 1970, middle-class families earned 62 percent of national income; in 2018, this was 43 percent.[22] Over the same period, the upper-income share grew from 29 percent to 48 percent,[23] and lower-income share fell from 10 percent to 9 percent.[24]

The Federal Reserve Bank of Cleveland in 2020 looked at all of the most recent studies of the US middle class,[25] comparing the 2018 middle class to the far more vibrant one in the US of 1980 before inequality began to accelerate. Looking at real median household income for working-age adults and recalculating it to reflect higher consumption costs, this study corrects for problems such as US demographic shifts and oversimplified income measures that do not reflect recent hikes in the cost of living. It finds "fairly flat" real income growth for the working-age middle class as a whole, but much of this is due to the growth of two-income households and all of it is eviscerated when the cost of health care and housing are taken into account. These costs increased more than nominal middle-class income from 1980 to 2018, with the cost of education alone over this period increasing an astonishing 600 percent.

What of Wealth?

Unsurprisingly, wealth inequality has gone up as inexorably as that of income. In 1989, the top 1 percent of Americans had 24 percent; by the end of 2019, their share was 33 percent of US wealth, with top 1 percent wealth growing nearly $3 trillion in just the first half of 2019.[26] The bottom 50 percent did grow its infinitesimal share of the national wealth pie, bringing it up to 1.5 percent,[27] a negligible share and a tiny increase highlighted by President Trump and the Fed even as the wealth of the top 1 percent and the 90 to 99 percent group each grew over the first half of the year by more than the total wealth of the entire bottom 50 percent.[28]

Before COVID, households in the bottom 50 percent of US wealth had about as much debt as assets, with the bulk of what wealth they have often to be found parked on the street.[29] In 2016, the bottom half of the US had less real wealth than it did in 1971.[30]

The Inequality Engine

As these data demonstrate, the fundamental engine of economic inequality is that the more you get, the more you keep unless gigantic market downturns or fiscal policy (e.g., inheritance taxes) takes it away. Wealthy households earning high returns on financial assets buoyed by rising market prices that are not purchased with debt acquire larger and larger shares of national wealth. In fact, 2 percentage points in wealth share equals 14 percentage points of total annual household income – it's a lot harder to get equal by earning your way to the top.[31] Given this, it's no wonder that economists honor F. Scott Fitzgerald's memorable get-rich-quick hero, using the "Great Gatsby Curve" to describe the relationship of income to wealth and resulting economic inequality.

The inequality engine also works in reverse. Just as the more you have, the more you keep absent policy intervention, so it is also that the less you have, the less you retain. Once set on a downward path due to lost wealth or income, it is increasingly difficult to recover lost momentum. For white male workers in the bottom half of the US income distribution, lost working hours may have been the primary source of income inequality over the past 52 years.[32] Working hours generally decline during recessions but then fail to recover when economists believe prosperity has returned. Often, white men who lose hourly wages also exit the workforce, making them disappear from traditional counts of the unemployed but of course heightening their own economic distress as well as that of their families. As the authors of this study conclude, "The cycle drives the trend."

Although the US is renowned for its economic optimism, before the pandemic only about a third of Americans believed that their children would do better than they did.[33] They have a reasonable hope of seeing this come true if they're white and already doing well. Being non-Hispanic white, over forty, and having college-educated parents boosts the next generation's income by three times and its wealth is six-fold more than less demographically advantaged families. About half of these differences are due to a wealth-generated head start, not the natural advantage in the second generation of also being college educated.[34]

In Denmark – one of the world's most equal nations – it takes only two generations for low-income families to enter the middle class; in the US before COVID, it took five. Post-COVID, it's likely to take still more unless policy solutions – including the financial ones I lay out in this book – restore realistic hope of doing well by working hard.[35]

Worse Than That

President Trump made much of unusual equality criteria – "creed" and religion – but his racial and color criteria are far more relevant to many Americans. Here, as with overall American equality, the president was mistaken. As I said, African Americans are often now worse off than before the "Great Society" of the 1960s and subsequent anti-discrimination laws presumably afforded fair and free access to financial services.[36] In 2016, the average wealth of white households ($933,700) was seven times the average wealth of Black households ($138,200) and five times that of Hispanic households ($191,200).[37] In 2017, Black household median income ($38,183) was less than two-thirds that of median white households, with about one-third of Black households earning less than $25,000 compared to only 18 percent of white households.[38]

Before COVID, only 41 percent of Black households owned their own homes, the lowest rate since the 1960s.[39] White homeownership was below its highs, but still stood then at 73 percent.[40]

As of June 2019,[41] white Americans owned 85 percent of US household wealth. That of African Americans was 4.4 percent. Hispanic wealth share was 3.2 percent, and others held 7.4 percent. To put this into context, non-Hispanic whites were only 60.4 percent of the US population at the time.[42] In terms of hard cash, whites held $91 trillion; Blacks owned $4.7 trillion.

A qualitative view of racial equality comes from the Urban League, a US advocacy group. Its "Equality Index" assigns ratings based on economic and qualitative factors. In its most recent analysis,[43] African Americans had an index of 72.5 percent versus the benchmark 100 granted to whites; the Hispanic index was 79.3 percent.

These inequality data are depressing enough, but they still do not show the real extent of underlying income and wealth distribution. A French scholar, François Bourguignon, has developed an interesting concept: intangible economic equality.[44] He styles this the "inequality of opportunity." This covers inequities not captured by bottom-line data because results on income and wealth may seem the same, but be substantively different due to household circumstance. For example, differences in the way a family might grow its income – getting one large pay raise versus working twice as hard – do not show up in total household labor income data. Similarly, wealth from inheritance has different market, social-welfare, and policy effects than wealth derived from one's own invention. Housing may seem available and affordable based on aggregate loan balances and costs. However, inequality occurs if the home is purchased in an undesirable neighborhood with poor schools or at a significant distance from the place of employment. As I will show later on, the Federal Reserve and US bank regulators often rely on averages or bottom-line totals to assess policy results, a methodology that masks unintended effects on shared prosperity in the glow of how well the overall system seems to be doing.

The Most Inclusive Ever?

Having addressed President Trump's assertion that America now is awash with shared income and wealth that knows neither race nor color, let's see if the US is, as he also says, the most inclusive in the world.

In the most recent global-equality analysis,[45] the Middle East was again the most unequal part of the world due to decades of tribal and similar wealth-distribution practices. Russia and China interestingly became strikingly more unequal as their communist past has faded into capitalist-oligopolistic wealth distribution. In Russia, the ratio between private wealth and national income grew three times as the state economic regime changed; in China, this ratio actually quadrupled even though overall wages in China also grew dramatically for lower-income workers.[46] Although overall global inequality has gone down slightly, the very top of the income distribution in emerging economies still receives far more of growing national income than most of the rest of the population. In many nations, the very top and the lowest income groups gained share, but what was once the middle class is as hollowed out as that in the US.

From the US perspective, the most interesting aspect of the global data is the divergence between Western Europe and the US. Although both were about equal from 1950 to 1980, the income divide has grown dramatically and differently ever since.[47] As Figure 2.1 shows, in 1980, the top 1 percent in both regions controlled about 10 percent of income. By the latest data from 2016, the 1 percent's share in Western Europe was 12 percent. In the US, it was 20 percent.

Look below the numbers and it's even clearer how much of a difference policy decisions make to equality results. Western European nations are institutionally structured to ensure equality to the greatest extent possible through higher taxes, universal health care, inexpensive higher education, and generous state retirement benefits – just to mention a few equality-policy distinctions. Critics counter that these same policies constrain growth and, in the most recent period, innovation. However, US economic growth was at best lackluster before COVID and the "full" employment about which the Fed was wont to brag was in fact far less impressive when labor-participation rates and other factors are carefully considered.

Figure 2.1   Diverging Income Inequality: Changes to Income Distribution
1980-2016, U.S. vs. Western Europe

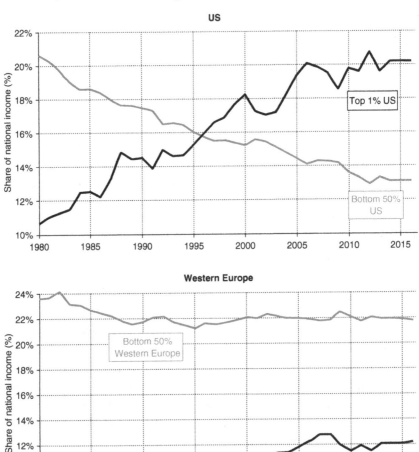

Source: WID.world (2017).

Labor-participation rates measure not who has a job, but who wants
a full-time job but has yet to find one. This rate has declined over the past
twenty years, a sharp contrast to other industrialized nations in which
men and women between 25 and 54 steadily joined the workforce.[48]
Also, having a job is no guarantee that the job is good enough to ensure

household sustenance – in late 2019, nearly one in five Americans had a job but still wanted and many also needed to work more to make ends meet.[49]

All told, Western Europe remains more equal than the US even if one gives the US the benefit of the doubt due to somewhat greater growth and employment since the great financial crisis and overlooks the enormous macroeconomic cost of COVID that reversed all these gains in as little as two weeks. And, no matter all the cost to high-income households of all its equality and social mobility, Sweden still had more billionaires as a percentage of its population than the US.[50]

The Great Financial Crisis and Its Equality Aftermath

I have already established that the US is not only far less equal than President Trump said or many of us would like, but also on a downward trajectory that sharply differentiates America from many advanced democratic nations. However, this downward trajectory took a dive not during the 2008 Great Financial Crisis – when it might have been expected – but after 2010 when post-crisis financial policy kicked in. We shall see later why this was so and how financial policy made us so much more unequal so much faster than underlying trends would have forced. Now, I show that it was so.

In 2019, the wealth of the top 10 percent was 19 percent higher than it was before the crisis, even taking stock-price declines in late 2018 into account. Middle-income family wealth was still below where it was before the financial crisis and lower-income families lost 16 percent of their pre-crisis wealth (not much to start with, of course).

From 2010 to 2016, the median income of the highest-earning Americans grew 14.7 percent[51] and their median net worth grew 24.3 percent in real terms.[52] During the same period, middle-class median income grew only 4.2 percent[53] and their wealth rose 12 percent.[54] In fact, the middle class's recovery from the financial crisis was so tepid – particularly when compared to that of the most well off, as shown in Figures 2.2 and 2.3 – that middle-class median income in 2016 remained 2.6 percent below its 2001 level and median wealth was 5.5 percent less.

Figure 2.2   Growth in Real Income for Select Income Groups, 1989–2016

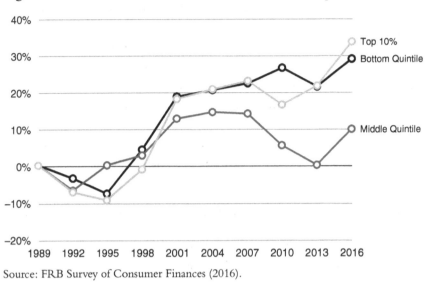

Source: FRB Survey of Consumer Finances (2016).

Figure 2.3   Growth in Real Wealth for Select Income Groups, 1989–2016

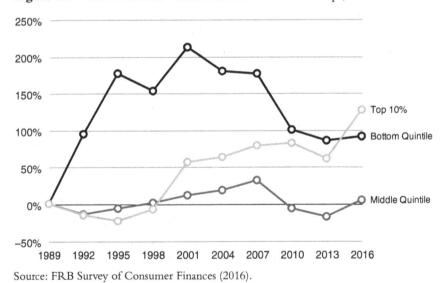

Source: FRB Survey of Consumer Finances (2016).

Things are even worse for those further down the income distribution – both of the bottom two quintiles' median wealth in 2016 was less than two-thirds what it was in 2001. Being upper-middle class is no respite either; median wealth of this group in 2016 was almost 14 percent lower than it was in 2001.

Nothing else changed that much so fast with so much impact on money and thus on who gets how much of it. Why, what's next, and how to avert it are the subject of the rest of this book.

Chapter 3

What Makes Us So Unequal

So why is income inequality such a problem? The reality is that some people work harder, learn more skills, risk more and are more intelligent than others. That is why there is income inequality. And that is not a negative outcome.

> — *Dave Majernik, Vice Chairman of the Allegheny County, Pennsylvania, Republican Committee**

The views above are not unusual. They are most often spoken or thought when the parlous economic plight of many African-American households is considered,[1] but racism is not the only reason some believe

---

* Dave Majernik, "Letter to the editor: Reason for income inequality," Trib Total Media, LLC (January 2, 2018), available at http://triblive.com/opinion/letters/12975908-74/letter-to-the-editor-reason-for-income-inequality.

that inequality is inevitable. As another commentator said, "The white American under-class is in thrall to a vicious, selfish culture whose main products are misery and used heroin needles."[2] A bit more charitably, some attribute American inequality to "organic capitalism," which is said to determine success by skill and then to reallocate wealth when rich people are foolish enough to squander it.[3]

When inequality is put this way, then the only way to read all the data in Chapter 2 is to conclude that anyone who earns or owns less does so because they're pretty much no good. Thus, the indolent in one generation breed slackers in the next, women are inherently less equal than men, Blacks are similarly and personally inadequate, and pernicious thinking then validates regressive policy that allows the prosperous to keep what they have and then to amass still more.

If inequality is indeed endemic, then a radical solution far afield from my financial-policy solutions might do the trick. One scholar has even suggested that war would do wonders for economic inequality – everyone down in the bunker together and all that. Those tempted to deal with economic inequality through nuclear war – the only option one recent book says might flatten the distributional curve[4] – should, though, expect that capitalists then even more "sauvage" than French theory postulates will find a way as long as there's something left to keep for themselves.

There is no arguing with these perspectives because they are based on belief, not data, and happily they are also not widely held. Thus, this chapter will proceed to an analysis of constructive solutions to economic equality, sizing each up on its own terms and then in relation to a financial-policy fix. If any of these other equality-enhancing policies work as well, better, and/or faster, then they should be our national priority with or without financial-policy enhancements.

However, as we'll see here, none of these other, more widely discussed policy solutions has the power to fix economic inequality as quickly, with as little political division, or as decisively. The reason financial policy works so well is not that none of these other solutions is unnecessary – many would be very constructive indeed – but that none can directly and immediately alter the fuel that powers the equality engine – money – or redirect its flow across the economy.

The Mechanical Engineering of Economic Inequality

The economic-inequality engine works like this: the more income you have, the less you need to use for consumption; the more you invest, the more you receive in wealth-accumulating assets; and the more non-wage income you can divert to still more wealth-enriching assets that make you so much richer that neither you nor your descendants need to work anymore. This engine could also make most everyone better off, rebalancing income and wealth distribution based on merit or luck. But to obtain this happy result, nations, including the US, have to start from a far more equal place. If they wait, then wealth accumulation will continue to move from generation to generation at ever-larger benefit to a smaller and smaller number of very wealthy families blessed not to have had profligate ancestors who spent the family fortune just having too much fun.

The way the inequality engine works also means that long-term solutions – essential though many are – won't slow it down much, if at all. They will remedy a bit of economic inequality – for example, by improving primary-school education – but so much equality ground is lost by then that advances come only at the margin in the still more unequal economy two decades away. This is not to say that primary education and equal advancement across the entire spectrum of educational achievement should not be enhanced and encouraged – of course they should. It's rather to point out that policy attention to this well-known problem will benefit many children in the near term but take generations to affect economic equality. Even then, it will do so only if other impediments to equality are reduced or eliminated – getting more kids qualified to go to college will still not increase equality if college in the future is still funded only by crippling debt.

To slow or even reverse inequality, you have to press the brakes as fast as possible as hard as possible without creating a tailspin. This means that policies need to be selected not only for their short-term impact, but also for their political plausibility. As a result, well-intentioned solutions such as a global tax on capital charged by every single nation around the world on every oligarch's proceeds may satisfy economic theory, but flunk the pragmatic plausibility criterion. Too many tax-haven nations that owe their prosperity to being havens for tax-avoiding proceeds will join with too many oligarchs and just plain old billionaires to block any such idea. Even the European Union (EU), with an avowed policy of tax equality, has been unsuccessful in getting its member states to agree to an EU-wide capital tax even though EU law binds all nations to do what they are told. In the US, years of work to get states to change "shell" corporations that permit wealthy households to hide income failed year-in, year-out despite bipartisan agreement about the urgent need to shut them down.[5]

Financial policy changes are considerably easier to execute because many are fully and immediately possible under US law and none I propose packs the anti-capitalist punch some attribute to wealth taxation. Even if wealth taxes are politically plausible no matter these controversies, monetary-and-regulatory policy reform short-circuits the rich-get-richer engine without the politically toxic side effects sure to follow confiscatory wealth or inheritance taxes or other schemes that would take money immediately away from those who already have it. Financial policy instead alters financial-market incentives in ways that take nothing away, but still make it easier for lower-income households to do well without the taxpayer costs of a guaranteed national income or other overtly redistributive proposal that some fear would harm what's left of the US middle class.

Further, financial policy in a "financialized" economy such as the US is a far bigger economic force than widely recognized. The value-added of financial activity to GDP has almost doubled from 1970 to 2018.[6] When an economy depends so much on how the money moves, not on who builds or grows what, the financial policies that drive money flows pack a powerful equality punch.

Death and Taxes

Fiscal policy is often cited as a major inequality engine, and so it is. Like financial policy, fiscal policy is totally about money and it thus directly affects economic equality. However, fiscal policy moves the money in ways often far distant from the economy and thus with far less impact on US income and wealth distribution than comes from realigned monetary and regulatory standards. As I said, money is the inequality engine's fuel, and money moves first and with the most force at order from financial –

not fiscal – policy-makers. As we'll see, this is not just due to the way the Federal Reserve dramatically changes economic winners and losers at the moment it issues a press release, nor the immediate restructuring of US financial services once a major rule hits the books. Even our understanding of money is set by financial policy. Our newly digital economy has even led to calls for digital currency, a concept that fundamentally changes the very nature of what money is and who controls it for whose benefit.

The reason for financial policy's power is straightforward. Fiscal policy is set in the US by Congress and each president's administration, raising or lowering taxes or federal spending as political imperatives dictate. Fiscal policy thus has a direct impact on economic equality by changing who pays how much in taxes, but it is only one part of US fiscal policy. Tax burdens are also set by state and local standards – for example, states, counties, and cities have higher or lower property and income taxes with larger or smaller equality impacts combined with federal taxes. Further, effective taxes for those in the middle class and below are also unlikely to drop much absent massive federal reform because payroll taxes are the bulk of the federal taxes paid by those below the 50 percent threshold. Payroll taxes account for about 11 percent of the bottom 50 percent's pretax income.[7]

As a result, a lot more than most realize would have to change to make US taxation even a little less regressive. Fiscal policy also has many objectives separate and unrelated to the economy – funding America's armed services, for example – making it an even blunter tool in the effort to repair the equality engine. Massive infrastructure programs that instead increase employment opportunities for lower-income workers might help do the fiscal-policy trick – after all, the Great Depression was initially reversed due to massive economic-infrastructure spending. However, even here the power of monetary policy is clear. The Federal Reserve was spooked by the growing recovery due to the New Deal, stepping in in 1937 to slow it down. Instead, the Fed actually reversed much of the New Deal's benefits, throwing the US into another deep recession that ended only when World War II spending created demands even the Federal Reserve could not resist.[8]

The Role of Transfer Payments

Fiscal policy has two sides: gathering revenue through taxes on the one hand and spending or saving national resources on the other. A considerably happier way to reduce economic inequality than death or taxes is to ensure that a significant share of national income is transferred to the have-nots through payments for retirement, health care, food, housing, education, child care, and similar costs of living. In general, all of these transfer programs are more generous in Western Europe than the US, and often considerably more so in other nations such as the Nordics. Furthermore, larger transfer payments in these other countries usually come in tandem with more progressive taxation policies, increasing the equalizing benefit of fiscal policy outside the US in many nations with truly market-based economies and democratic governments. Like new taxes, new transfer payments could be progressive; indeed, that's largely their goal. However, as it turns out, US transfer payments are remarkably regressive.

US transfer payments come in the form of income-based payments (e.g., food stamps, welfare, and Medicaid) and entitlements paid to eligible recipients generally regardless of income and wealth (e.g., Social Security and Medicare). Looking at federal pre- and post-tax income shows that the balance of transfer payments received by lower-income earners is generally equal to the amount of taxes paid by transfer-payment recipients.[9] In essence, there were no net federal transfers to lower-wage workers because their pre- and post-tax incomes were roughly the same. This does not mean, though, that lower-income people are at least holding their own. Taking transfer payments into account, the lifetime marginal tax rate for lower-income households can exceed 70 percent, almost double the comparable median lifetime rate for the nation as a whole.[10]

The only significant exception to this tax/transfer equilibrium depends on how old you are. Average pretax income in the lower 50 percent income group has fallen 20 percent for those aged 20 to 45 and 8 percent for those between 45 and 65 – the working-age population. However, pretax income – which as noted includes transfer payments such as Social Security and Medicare for older households – has risen. On an after-tax basis, older Americans have received 70 percent more in transfer payments than in 1980, growth that in fact accounts for all of the increase in post-tax income for those in the below-50-percent income group.

Still, are older Americans more equal thanks to transfer payments? In 2016, the top 20 percent of older households had annual incomes of $398,000; those in the bottom quintile had only $14,000.[11] Wealth disparities are also acute because higher-income older Americans have retirement accounts and home equity on which to rely in addition to all the transfer payments they receive. White households in all earnings groups hold more wealth than minorities in each income bracket.[12] Indeed, older Americans are among the least equal in the advanced economies.[13] Rising bankruptcy rates for older Americans grimly attest to these hard facts.[14]

Transfer payments such as Social Security and Medicare are designed to be equalizing; they ensure certain social-welfare goals are met regardless of an individual's ability otherwise to pay for them. These programs are known as "entitlements." However, entitlements largely benefit those in the middle class and above. Even the top 10 percent of earners receive about 8 percent of per-adult national income in transfers through entitlements, largely in the form of Social Security and Medicare.

A Supply-Side Solution?

Advocates of low tax rates for the well-to-do often believe that upside-down tax rates will ultimately prove progressive based on what is often called the "trickle-down" approach of supply-side economics. Lower corporate tax rates are, it is said, likely to lead to greater investment that then spurs employment and wage growth even as lower tax bills for upper-income households increase consumption, employment, and growth in consumer-facing enterprises.

So far, these supply-side rewards are scarce to be found each time they are tried. This was particularly true for the Trump tax cuts, which came in concert with sharp spikes in US economic inequality. As I will discuss in more detail later on, the more affluent you are, the less you are likely to spend because you don't need all that much anymore. Instead, upper-income households save added income due to tax breaks, increasing their wealth without boosting growth because, as we will also see, savings are no longer converted into growth- and employment-boosting lending. Instead, ultra-low rates divert savings into investments in stock and other financial markets, hiking asset prices, not shared growth. The less the nation spends for overall consumption of goods and services, the less need for businesses to invest in new plants and infrastructure to meet demand. The lower the incentive for companies to use their tax breaks to invest, the more capital they simply redistribute to shareholders who are principally the wealthiest among us.

Further, even with some reductions in the Trump tax cuts for middle- and lower-income households, what was once growth-generating spending is now powered by equality-destroying debt. Lower-income and -wealth households were so stretched before the pandemic in 2020 that they cut consumption wherever possible and went into far more debt than ever before; see student debt as just one case in point.[15] The middle class that responded to prior tax cuts to boost economic growth was too hollowed out before the pandemic to support shared prosperity via additional consumption. Health-care spending increases in tandem with tax refunds, demonstrating that low, moderate, and even middle-income households experience no "wealth effect" from lower tax rates.[16] Instead, any extra money goes to urgent needs such as taking a child to the dentist.

Because low-, moderate-, and middle-income households were all in so much debt in a seemingly prosperous time, they had few resources on which to rely in adversity and huge amounts of debt many had difficulty paying when COVID struck. This is always true under stress, but it was never so true as it was in 2020 because the US economy had never in modern times been anywhere near as unequal.

Public Wealth: A Sputtering Part in the Equality Engine

If one is an adherent to "modern monetary theory" – that deficits don't really matter for a strong nation with low interest rates[17] – then we could theoretically increase tax cuts, transfer payments, and entitlements all at the same time without constraining new spending, especially under stress. However, a larger US deficit creates a still bigger divergence between public wealth – government-owned assets that are often dedicated to social-welfare – and private wealth – the resources individuals and households control for their own purposes. The more the deficit grows, the less net wealth US taxpayers collectively own and thus the less there is not only to go around, but also to devote to progressive policies other than those that can be accomplished by private philanthropy or financial policy (which does not rely on public-wealth assets because US central-banking and bank-regulatory agencies are self-funded).

Figure 3.1 shows public sector assets and liabilities in the US since 1945. As you will see, public wealth (also known as public sector net

Figure 3.1   The Rise and Fall of U.S. Public Wealth, 1945–2015

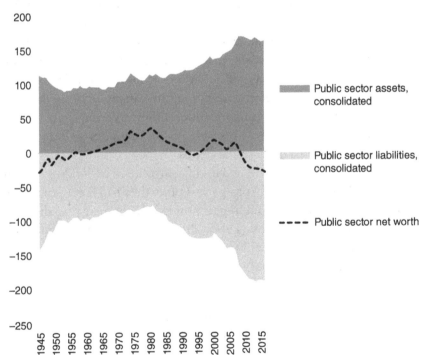

Source: Fabien Gonguet and Klaus-Peter Hellwig, "Public Wealth in the United States," *IMF Working Paper 19/139* (July, 2019), available at https://www.imf.org/en/Publications/WP/Issues/2019/07/02/Public-Wealth-in-the-United-States-46834.

worth) increased from 1945 through the 1970s, reflecting all the years of public investment in infrastructure after the Second World War. Peaking at 35 percent of GDP in 1980, public wealth has since decreased to −27 percent of GDP; i.e., public wealth is now negative. This is due to a combination of infrastructure depreciation, lower domestic spending, and increased federal deficits that destroyed public wealth even as lower taxes for higher-income households powered up the inequality engine.

Is Education the Answer?

Educational inequities play a clear role in economic inequality and indeed exacerbate it. However, solutions here depend first on having enough public wealth to fund them and then on political consensus and the many years it takes to reverse profound and negative US trends in intergenerational mobility.

Many studies have shown that education is directly linked to economic advancement,[18] but public education by definition depends on public wealth. The less there is, the worse public schools and universities become and the harder it is also for students and their families to find tax-subsidized sources of educational financing that do not result in record, unsustainable debt for borrowers and a still larger deficit for taxpayers. Although the 2017 tax changes included several revisions to enhance educational savings, these are of most value to the wealthiest households.[19] Lower-income households finance higher education largely through student debt at growing cost to them and the economy. Once, lower-income children, especially if they were white, were often able to obtain high-quality primary, secondary, and higher education without any direct cost to students and their families; now, this is virtually impossible, especially as one ascends to college and post-graduate education.

In fact, student debt now exceeds all other forms of US debt other than mortgages,[20] due in large part to the fact that the cost of higher education rose 63 percent from just 2006 to 2016.[21] No wonder that, of 100 children with parents in the bottom 10 percent of income earners, only 30 go to college; the number of kids in college rises to 90 when parents are in the top 10 percent bracket.[22] No wonder too that student-loan defaults are skyrocketing.[23]

This sad side effect of shrinking public wealth also affects another factor often cited as a cause of global and US economic inequality: technological innovation. Innovation per se is not a deciding inequality force – global data show that very innovative nations (e.g., the Nordics, Germany) can also be considerably more equal than the US. However, technological innovation demands high-skilled workers – the same highly educated ones who must now finance their skill acquisition from the private resources that are so hard to find below the top of the economic-equality ranking. Opinions differ on whether poor education leads to less equal innovation or if less equal innovation spurs greater educational inequity, but either way the two forces are intertwined, very damaging, and not easily remedied any time soon.

Is Trade Policy a Problem?

"Globalization" – a phenomenon comprised in various parts of free trade in goods, open financial markets, tax evasion, regulatory arbitrage, different rates of technological innovation along with resulting market efficiency, and immigration – is also often seen as a cause of economic inequality. It is for this reason that populists and progressives are generally united in demands for barriers to open markets in manufactured and agricultural goods, and often also for insulating financial markets from global forces. Liberal and free-market thinking has countered protectionism by arguing that efficient global markets ultimately reward both workers and consumers, but a study of 147 countries over 45 years in fact finds that globalization has diminishing equality returns, with the most closed nations – e.g., China – benefiting the most from other nations' openness.[24] In already-globalized countries, more globalization does not lead to statistically significant income improvement. Indeed, the study finds a "robustly positive and statistically significant effect" from economic globalization on income inequality, with this strongest in highly globalized, advanced economies – i.e., in nations such as the United States.

One reason for this in the United States appears to be the interaction between a drop in manufacturing jobs and a rise in economic inequality;

a recent study finds that the US is the lone economy in which workers who lose manufacturing jobs in one sector generally can't find them in another.[25] Instead, US workers who lose manufacturing jobs migrate to the service sector (e.g., flipping burgers, delivering packages) and make far less than they used to.

Open-market advocates weren't wrong then – the giant study noted above also finds that globalization would have been good for economic equality had the study stopped 10 years ago.[26] A meta-analysis of 123 peer-reviewed, relatively recent papers confirms these results, finding that globalization over time has indeed increased income inequality around the world.[27] This effect is found in both developing and advanced economies, although nations with advanced technology and high educational levels are less adversely affected by globalization.

Based on both popular sentiment and these rigorous analyses, it might seem that closing our borders would quickly boost economic equality. However, the solution here is as complex, slow, and politically fraught as many other high-profile causes of American economic inequality. Simply closing borders would increase US consumer costs, a consequence that is no longer just theory in light of experience since the Trump trade tariffs came into effect.[28] Inequality might thus be better addressed with barriers to job exports such as bans on moving plants to Mexico. However, in the absence of barriers to imports of low-cost goods from foreign manufacturers, domestic employers unable to reduce costs by relocating plants might simply uproot their operations altogether to third countries or just close down. Open immigration would reduce home-country labor costs and related incentives to move jobs to low-cost nations, but at considerable cost to political consensus and strain on public wealth due to heightened calls for social services. Still more jobless Americans would demand a lot of help, either draining already scant public wealth or making income inequality considerably worse or both.

Global Policy Reform?

Global policy-makers increasingly recognize that economic inequality is getting worse not so much because they read a lot of data, but due to what constituents tell them, sometimes quite rudely. Economic inequality thus poses an increasing threat not only to geopolitical stability, but also to the electoral prospects of the policymakers adding equality to their to-do list.

However endearing this commitment, its impact is at best uncertain because national and international policy statements are often as unachievable as many of the recommendations crafted by high-minded economists. In 2015, the United Nations (UN) agreed to a set of "sustainable-development goals,"[29] many of which were echoed in the 2017 statement by the Group of Twenty (G20) heads of state[30] and the 2018 pronouncement of the Group of Seven (G7) heads of the world's largest advanced nations.[31] All of these high-level global statements were stratospheric in their ambitions – e.g., "reducing inequality," but totally nonbinding with regard even to the few specific goals they contain (e.g., "monitoring"). And, when global equality forums get specific, they can also get unhinged – in 2019, a United Nations' Secretary-General Task Force called for an end to private-sector finance through regulated channels – i.e., through banks.[32] The UN preferred financial intermediation through giant technology companies said to ensure that consumers could direct their funds to sustainable activities such as reducing climate change, although why big tech would want to do this any more than banks is not exactly clear. The UN Task Force did, though, have a fallback: total government takeover of private finance.

All of these concepts are not only up in the clouds, but also usually so long term in their deadlines (where there are any) as to be safely kicked down the road to the next group of aspiring politicians sure to espouse still more fervent equalizing ambitions as long as nothing binds any of them to anything plausible in the near term or politically painful back home.

Efforts to ensure an end to global warming bear sad evidence to the challenges confronting any global equality proposals striving to go beyond rhetoric to practical and political plausibility. Many nations only reach for politically challenging climate goals when the air in their capitals gets too bad to breathe – that is, when it's too late. This is not to say that international organizations should ignore economic inequality – far from it. Given the critical importance of cross-border trade, money flows, and taxation, harmonized regimes designed to enhance progressive taxation, encourage sound fiscal policy, and prevent tax evasion are all to the good. And rhetoric may make a difference – heads of state who agree to equality goals in global forums may be held accountable back home. Even so, global solutions are no substitute for national action, as the climate-change crisis also proves all too definitively.

What to Do?

Clearly, many inequality "solutions" either won't make a difference or won't do so anywhere near fast enough. Do we just sit back? Of course not. We can and should turn to equality repairs that, even if they do not completely and quickly build a just economic system, make it as fair as possible as fast as possible. Because monetary and regulatory policy turn money flows on and off almost instantaneously and have profound power over who gets the money as it moves through the engine, financial policy can and should be reformed to make a major dent in US inequality.

We'll turn shortly to the how-to of equitable financial policy; first, though, we turn to the why we have to act. As the next chapter will show, US income and wealth inequality does even more damage than you might have thought.

Chapter 4

Why Does Economic Inequality Matter So Much?

[D]angerous and growing inequality and lack of upward mobility has jeopardized middle-class America's basic bargain – that if you work hard, you have a chance to get ahead. I believe this is the defining challenge of our time: Making sure our economy works for every working American.

– President Barack Obama*

Not everyone, including President Obama's successor, agrees with this statement. However, Mr. Obama has at least one prominent backer. Aristotle said, "It is manifest that the best political community is formed

---

* President Barack Obama, "Remarks by the President on Economic Mobility," THEARC, Washington, DC (December 4, 2013), available at https://obamawhitehouse.archives.gov/the-press-office/2013/12/04/remarks-president-economic-mobility.

by citizens of the middle class, and that those states are likely to be well-administered in which the middle class is large, and stronger if possible than both the other classes, or at any rate than either singly; for the addition of the middle class turns the scale, and prevents either of the extremes from being dominant."[1]

With the extremes increasingly dominant in the US, this chapter will show that Aristotle is being proved right all over again about the importance of economic equality. Even worse than the Greek philosopher prophesied, inequality also exacerbates personal misery and stunningly but irrefutably even hastens early death and vulnerability to the novel coronavirus. This chapter will also describe a less well-understood but insidious inequality effect: its destructive impact on the ability of economic policy-makers to craft post-crisis recoveries and ensure long-term, sustainable growth.

In fact, the more unequal we get, the higher the risk of financial crises such as those in 2008 and 2020 due solely to great wealth seeking still more in speculative markets combined with the growing inability of financial and fiscal policy to restrain them. As a result, inequality threatens not just constitutionality and even mortality, but also the ability of financial policy makers to restore the prosperity that could avert these awful consequences. This is yet another reason that inequality is an engine – the faster inequality increases, the harder it is for drivers to control its destructive force.

Inequality and Mortality

The impact of economic inequality on society as a whole is so profound and personally intense that it actually predicts crime and the risk of dying young. A World Bank study[2] found stunning differences between nations in terms of violent criminal behavior correlated with and apparently even caused by economic inequality, excluding other national factors. It has, of course, always been true that wealthier individuals with greater comfort, access to health care, and the leisure to protect themselves are generally at less mortality risk than those suffering from an array of health risks sparked by economic disadvantage. However, it is striking how closely inequality and mortality risk stride hand in hand to a grim end.

Prior to the pandemic, US life expectancy since 2010 had already taken a sharp turn for the worse for younger Americans regardless of race, gender, or education.[3] We knew that opioids were devastating, but this study confirmed others showing also that the overall reversal in US life expectancy was due to more profound and mysterious afflictions. Doctors flummoxed by why US mortality is so much higher than that in other advanced countries where life expectancy continues to increase for younger citizens concluded that something endemic is going on behind the epidemic of "diseases of despair."[4]

Breaking down life expectancy by income confirms the causal link between economic equality and mortality. At the same time that deaths associated with diseases of despair were increasing, life expectancy for men increased by 2.3 years between 2001 and 2014 and by 2.9 years for women in the top 5 percent of the income distribution; for the lowest 5 percent, these improvements were only 0.3 years for men and 0.4 years for women.[5] Research[6] also demonstrates that an increase in deaths associated with diseases of despair – those due to drug overdoses, suicides, and alcohol – among men with a high school education or less negated any benefit to life expectancy associated with reductions in deaths from cancer and heart disease (the two biggest killers in middle age) among this group. In short, despite fewer white men with a high school education or less dying from cancer and heart disease, this group's overall mortality rate has increased in tandem with reduced income and wealth and, quite likely, hope.

The 2020 pandemic finally forced the interaction between economic inequality and mortality onto public attention. In city after city, African Americans died at far higher percentages of COVID-related deaths than they were in the population as a whole.[7] In just one state – New York – African American mortality as of June 2020 was 26 percent of COVID-related deaths even though African Americans were only 14 percent of the state's population.[8] The reasons attributed to this are not only preexisting conditions that led to the overall mortality increases cited above even before COVID, but also the inequality in education, housing, and financial access that led African Americans to hold a disproportionate share of frontline jobs and to live in close-packed housing affording no refuge from the pandemic. COVID is of course color-blind – income or the lack of it appears to be the most telling indication of likely COVID mortality.[9]

Political Polarization

The easiest way to reduce inequality and its grim mortality would be for the nation to agree that it must be done and for policy-makers then to concur on constructive solutions. Unfortunately, economic inequality eviscerates consensus.

The sharp difference of opinion between Presidents Obama and Trump makes it clear that views about inequality are politically divisive on their own. However, it's worse than that – inequality itself is extremely divisive, contributing to the political polarization that led to such different outcomes in the 2008 and 2016 elections. US politics is also increasingly aligning as it did at the start of the 20th century, when populists and progressives first squared off. In 2016 and 2020, US political debate was dominated by democratic socialism on one side and free-wheeling capitalists on the other. As I noted in Chapter 1, these populist and progressive views were voiced the loudest by each political party's base, but President Trump nonetheless characterized his economics platform as a defense of capitalism against socialism.[10] The demonstrations sparked first by George Floyd's death and then by so much else in 2020 focused principally on police brutality and social justice, but economic inequality also figures prominently, with "eat the rich" and "end capitalism" slogans sprayed across the nation's downtown business districts.

With a hollowed-out middle class, US constitutional government is clearly being pulled apart. Many analyses of the impact of the 2008 great financial crisis cite populism and polarization as among its costliest lasting effects,[11] with some claiming that polarization on its own explains President Trump's 2016 victory.[12] Bernie Sanders's popularity in 2016 and still more support for him in 2020 were also testament to the strong feelings leading millennials across the entire US political spectrum to reject capitalism[13] and drive overall US faith in the federal government to record lows.[14] Even views about inequality are polarized. In late 2019, 43 percent of Republicans thought the US was about as equal as it should be; only 7 percent of Democrats agreed.[15]

US political history is not unique. A study of financial crises from 1780 to 2014 in advanced economies[16] validates this intuitive conclusion. It finds that "far-right" parties tend to increase their vote shares by 30 percent within five years of a financial crisis, with the study defining far right by factors such as anti-democratic and pro-ethnicity or pro-nationalist ideologies. Ten years after a crisis, voting totals tend to revert back to country norms, although this is a weak effect across all the times and nations studied yet to show itself in many post-crisis advanced economies. Political protests and violent riots – 2020 in the US? – also pick up after financial crises, with none of these effects found following business-cycle recessions.

The sum total of all of these social-welfare factors, often combined with polling data on less tangible indicators such as contentment and consensus, tells us a lot about inequality's impact through a "happiness" index. The most equal nations, generally found in Scandinavia, are the happiest. The US came in 18th in the most recent ranking[17] when it comes to happiness even though Americans had the highest per-capita income among major countries and most Americans consider themselves middle class.[18] Finding that inequality is "immiserating," a research survey concluded that, even for the seemingly prosperous in a wealthy but unequal country, "gains in national income can decouple from well-being."[19]

Inequality's Eviscerating Cost

Inequality's cost goes beyond its damage to constructive decision-making of the sort that might have averted at least some of the economic and health inequality that exacerbates mortality risk for lower-income Americans. However, the Fed was blind to this in all but rhetorical terms before COVID forced a reckoning and, even then, the Federal Reserve stoutly maintained that the US economy was in a "good place" well into 2020.[20] In fact, the head of the Federal Reserve Bank of New York said in May 2020, "We are kind of in a really good place."[21] He said this because he thought the US then was bouncing along the bottom of the COVID crash, but the idea that unprecedented unemployment and widespread macroeconomic devastation then seemed a happy place is still hard to fathom unless you are a graph.

The reason for this dauntless optimism lay in myopia, myopia that blinded the Federal Reserve to why a decade of unprecedented monetary-policy stimulus did so little for all Americans save a very few at the very top. As a Nobel Prize–winning economist has observed, the more unequal an economy, the less likely it is that policy efforts to simulate macroeconomic growth – monetary and regulatory ones again very much included – will take hold.[22] When the Federal Reserve thinks about the US economy, it – like all too many economists – looks at aggregate or average data, rarely breaking them down to go beyond how well the US is doing in general to see who is doing more or less well thereby.

Averages hide all too many critical changes in a nation that, like the US, has a hollowed out middle class in which income and wealth are heavily concentrated in a small minority of US households. For example, the Fed joins many others in using gross domestic product (GDP) data to determine if the US economy is growing. But, as another Nobel Prize winner, Paul Krugman, notes in calling for new ways to think about GDP, "If Jeff Bezos walks into a bar, the average wealth of the bar's patrons suddenly shoots up to several billion dollars – but none of the non-Bezos drinkers has gotten any richer."[23]

In fact, whatever US GDP growth there has been has been unequally shared. The International Monetary Fund (IMF) has found that post-crisis gains in real US GDP largely benefited only the wealthiest households,[24] as the data referenced in Chapter 2 sadly confirm. Another IMF study separates the overall relationship between equality and growth – which often averages out over lengthy periods of time – to determine which countries support the most sustained, stable recoveries.[25] The best performers are the most equal nations. Even when external shocks are added to the duration over which growth is assessed, equality still determines growth, a finding corroborated in a global study of developed countries including the US up to 2014.[26] Another IMF study examining the growth/equality trade-off across many nations over a 50-year time span finds that "slow or fragile growth and high inequality seem to be two sides of the same coin, and durable growth at a healthy pace will only be possible if growth itself becomes more inclusive."[27] Thus, if the US had been more equal, the country would have recovered more quickly and resiliently after 2008. Now that the US is even more unequal after a decade of financial-policy misfires and COVID's eviscerating equality cost, the odds of shared prosperity are even smaller, with the need for equitable financial policy thus even greater.

Looking at 141 countries from 1995 to 2011, the World Bank goes beyond GDP as the measure of national prosperity to examine national balance sheets to separate the impact of human and physical-infrastructure and natural-resource, and financial assets subsumed within aggregate, unadjusted GDP numbers.[28] Countries that invest in human and financial assets in physical infrastructure or resource development gain in wealth while those who use proceeds for consumption and financial investment get poorer regardless of how aggregate GDP data calculate income and production.

Why? GDP is flawed because a simple GDP figure such as 2 percent means no per-capita growth if population growth is also 2 percent. If demographic growth is faster than GDP growth – which it has been over the past decade – than real, per-capita GDP growth can still be lower – sometimes a lot lower – than the nominal percentage increase. Further, GDP is by definition "gross." As a result, when a disaster strikes, its cost is not subtracted from growth but rebuilding counts to GDP in ways that suggest prosperity even if we're just treading water. Sharp increases in GDP after the late 2017 hurricanes were touted as proof of policy success, but in fact GDP owed much of its strength to reconstruction that, once it was complete, no longer buoyed the economy or employment.

The "inclusive development index"[29] attempts to capture the interplay between growth as measured by GDP and economic equality along with environmental sustainability. The latter is a particularly subjective measure, but the index's results are still instructive: the US ranks only 23rd.

Inequality and the Long Recession

The IMF has calculated that, in inflation-adjusted terms, more than half of the US population in 2017 earned less than it did in 2000.[30] And, as I said, more than ten years out from the great financial crisis, almost one hundred million Americans have no buffer against even a minor economic setback, let alone against an economic shock as crippling as COVID.[31] No wonder savings rates for lower-income households are proportionately far less than those for wealthier families,[32] a tremendous obstacle to long-term equality due to the inexorable workings of the inequality engine at a time of ultra-low interest rates on small-dollar accounts.

Had the US been more equal before the great financial crisis, then the climb out of the crash would have been easier because households would have responded more quickly to the Fed's monetary-policy signals. If the US were not still more unequal before the pandemic, the seeming prosperity of the "good place" measured by GDP numbers would have been more evenly distributed across the US population and the nation would have handled COVID with the resilience evident in some more equal nations such as Germany.[33] And, if income and wealth were better distributed, then enough households would have been able to borrow and spend more, enough companies would have invested in new employees, and considerably more growth would be the happy result.

Financial-Crisis Risk

Inequality and slow growth not only go hand in hand, but financial crises tag along. A literature survey of the link between inequality and financial crises uncovered extensive empirical and theoretical research demonstrating a clear linkage that is not only a result of correlation, but also causation – crises are often directly attributable to inequality.[34] Most of these studies are posited on the instability resulting from large populations of low-income households who must sustain consumption with debt – i.e., countries all too much like the United States. Notably, this paper also found that the length and depth of recessions after financial crashes are also worse than more run-of-the-mill recessions over the business cycle.

A study from the Federal Reserve Bank of San Francisco[35] expands on these structural points to show still more clearly the link between economic inequality and financial-crisis risk. This paper deploys exhaustive research across decades in 17 countries based on statistical correlations of inequality, productivity, credit growth, and crises. Although productivity has a strong impact on crisis risk, a widening income share for the top 1 percent is the most predictive antecedent to a crash even when controlling for an array of other possible causes, including the asset-price bubbles when the prices investors pay for homes, stocks, bonds, and other assets are well above acknowledged measures of the risks they run. No wonder the US had one massive financial crisis in 1929 and then decades of relative economic stability in concert with remarkable middle-class resilience until 2008 and – even worse – the 2020 crash.

Another study from the Federal Reserve supports the equality/crisis nexus with a comparison of data in the US to an econometric model.[36] The model – always the construct of the economists who craft them – finds that income inequality stokes secular stagnation (i.e., the slow growth described above), deflation, asset bubbles, and financial crises. The combination of data and theory is at least worrisome, if not also conclusive: economic inequality is not only polarizing and deadly, but also an endless and downward loop unless it's short-circuited.

In the next chapter, we'll turn to the US institutions established as the economy's electricians. These include not just the Federal Reserve, but also financial regulators that, while obscure, importantly decide to whom banks can lend and which nonbanks offer what products to whom at what cost or risk. We've seen in the past few chapters how unequal America has become, why it's so unequal, and how much inequality costs even those who are economically equal or still better off. Now, to who's in charge and, thereafter, not just to what they can and should do, but also to how they can quickly make a meaningful, immediate difference redesigning the US inequality engine.

Chapter 5

Following the Money

We "finance people" see the world very differently from the way economists do.

— Ray Dalio*

As this hedge-fund billionaire observes from much experience, economists do not understand money with anything like the unblinking ferocity of financial-market traders. Economists often flatter themselves by calling economics a "hard" science. But, no matter the dizzying plethora of complex mathematical models on which financial policy is premised, economic data aren't quarks. GDP, inflation, and all the indicators on which economists rely are not impermeable manifestations of the forces of nature; they are the end result of the asset prices and market valuations anticipated and created by finance people and, when finance people follow the money with acumen, also a source of wealth

---

* Ray Dalio, *Principles: Life and Work* (New York: Simon & Schuster, 2017), 83.

so vast that many economists needed new categories for it after the great financial crisis.

Given the stakes, finance people are not only inexorable realists, but also short-term actors. They measure success or failure by the minute, hour, day, month, or quarter regardless of whether they sit at a trading desk, make loans, sell services, or reside in plush corner offices where they are beset by demands from investors looking at their own profit-and-loss clocks. Economists measure success or failure not by how much money they make, but by what a thesis adviser says, at which university they teach, how many books they publish, and whether anyone important or rich asks for their views. This is a subjective incentive system – models that make the masters happy are those rewarded when economists seek advancement. Models that make money are the ones that reward finance people and it is the decisions that finance people make – not those that economists urge – that drive the economy and the financial markets on which it depends.

Thus, if you want to understand what happens when the Fed changes interest rates or regulators impose a new restriction, you have to follow the money, not the model. Money knows instinctively and mercilessly where inequality lies and how monetary and regulatory policy affect it regardless of what big-picture data tell policy-makers. Even as the Fed said repeatedly that the US economy was in a good place after 2015, Mr. Dalio not only highlighted US inequality as a looming threat,[1] but even forecast violent insurrection if it was not quickly reduced.[2]

To be sure, money may be inexorable, but those following it aren't infallible. Markets were caught more than off-guard in the 2020 coronavirus pandemic, the 2008 financial crisis, the 2001 dot-com bust, and many other market downturns across the course of history. Short-term thinking isn't the same as long-term vision, as Mr. Dalio's own hedge fund found out the hard way in 2020.[3] However, Ray Dalio still has billions to protect him from the economic wolves, as do most of his fellow big-money Wall Street denizens. Not so much for the rest of the nation.

Financiers can and should lose money, but financial policy-makers cannot pursue policies that stabilize money-makers at the expense of the rest of the nation. Confusing markets for the economy as a whole is the Fed's signal failure because markets without risk are markets without discipline and markets without discipline always end very, very badly.

As we'll see in the next chapters, the Fed's focus on market profit, not on fixing widespread inequality, set the US up for the historic crash of March 2020. The Fed couldn't have seen the pandemic coming, but it shouldn't have engineered financial markets so that a crash when it came was as hard, as fast, and as devastating to low-income households.

Money fuels the inequality engine propelling financial markets based on where finance sees a win, whether that win comes from ingenuity and perseverance or, as has often been the case since the Federal Reserve decided to manage the markets, from central-bank decisions. As we will see, monetary and regulatory policies each exacerbate inequality in their own right, but also make matters worse in a little-recognized way due to the sum total impact of the interaction between monetary and regulatory policies and real-world financial market. As we'll also see, financial markets premised on policy are also political markets, making them even more unstable and risky to those without a voice in the corridors of power.

Thus, reversing the inequality engine depends on following the money not just through the markets, but also through the political process. Model-driven solutions such as global wealth taxes or still more profound transformations of national and global social priorities may well have considerable equality and even moral benefit. But they won't happen fast, if at all, given the political power of the same unblinking financiers bent on protecting themselves no matter the risks they let loose upon the land.

Fixing financial policy to enhance equality is far less controversial and requires few changes in US law. It won't ensure a truly just society, but we'll be more equal and that's more than enough for starters.

How Central Banks Work

Starting with the first central bank, the Bank of Amsterdam in 1609, central banks have been banks, bank-like public-private entities (the Federal Reserve), or government-owned banks, all of which then work through banks to exert their will. This "bank-centric" monetary-policy model is premised on the long history in which the major private movers of money were banks, not individuals, finance companies, stock brokers, or other money-lenders.

The confluence between central banking and private banking results from the fact that banks long performed essential "financial-intermediation" services – that is, banks were the only entities that gathered deposits and, by transforming these funds in terms of different liquidity and/or maturity characteristics, converted them into the credit and funding flows on which macroeconomic growth depends.

Each time you place a deposit in the bank, you power up financial intermediation. Before modern banking, a $100 deposit locked into the bank for one year would have been converted by a lender into a $100 loan for the same one-year period, with the depositor hoping to get his or her money back with interest at the end of the year and the lender hoping to get repaid with enough interest not just to give back the depositor's money with the promised interest payments, but also to make a profit. Because depositors took the most risk in these transactions, they often required lenders to put the lender's own funds into a reserve account backing the deposit (e.g., to put aside $100 worth of gold or other impregnable asset to give the depositor confidence that he or she will see $100 come sliding back across the table in a year).

This model of banking secured savings and made loans, but at considerable cost and risk. Economies with traditional, fully reserved finance grow slowly, if at all, because the lending that powers growth is all in relation to the economy and grows only slightly faster than the amount of currency immediately on hand and the assets readily to be found to secure it.

Modern banking is founded on financial intermediation because a $100 one-year deposit is turned into $1,000 or more in loans of various maturities (one year, six months, whatever). Banks expect to fund loan commitments a few years out with deposits coming in then rather than having all the money in the bank each minute for each loan every day of every year. More loans are made than the deposits on hand to fund them and economies grow more quickly. This is called "fractional reserve" banking because only a bit of a bank's reserves (its own hard assets such as cash and gold) back each loan. The bank's owners – now usually shareholders – are also supposed to have their own money (i.e., capital) invested in the bank to create an additional risk buffer and establish better incentives for prudent finance. As we will see later on, financial institutions without capital are financial institutions that take undue risk secure in the knowledge that someone else will pay for it.

Fractional banking fires up growth because some money creates more money and more money powers employment and capital expenditures (e.g., building factories). Or, at least this is how fractional banking once worked. Now, due to regulatory incentives we'll discuss later on, money in fractional-reserve banking has contributed not only to growth, but also to the development of complex financial instruments that power speculation, not productivity.

Fractional-reserve banking also accelerates financial instability – if depositors fear that they can't get their money back, they may stage a "run," literally pulling as much money out of the bank as fast as they can, leaving the bank with no funds and thus no ability to honor its commitments. The bank thus fails at cost not just to itself, but also the depositors who couldn't run fast enough. As we will see, the entire construct of modern financial regulation is aimed at balancing the growth potential of fractional-reserve financial intermediation with rules to reduce risk and still more safeguards – e.g., Federal Deposit Insurance Corporation (FDIC) insurance and central-bank liquidity – to prevent runs when rules aren't enough.

In theory, tightening up financial intermediation reduces the money flow into the economy; conversely, loosening it opens the spigots to promote lending and accelerate growth. In practice, this works less and less well when a nation's financial system is financialized (i.e., when it serves itself, not the economy as a whole) or if it ceases to rely on regulated banks to provide credit and liquidity. In financialized economies, interest rates can – and, as we will see, did – spur speculation, not investment for structural and shared growth. Traders using low-cost loans for leveraged (i.e., high-risk) trading take bets on markets instead of making loans companies use to build factories. Nonbanks do not have access to the Fed and thus their rates are only indirectly influenced by changes to monetary policy. Eventually, lower or higher interest rates may affect nonbanks, but monetary-policy transmission is slowed and, if nonbanks are the principal source of a nation's financing, far less effective.

As we saw in Chapter 3,[4] the US is a financialized nation in which money moves for money's sake, not for ours. The US financial system is also the least dependent on banks of any advanced economy; "bank dependency" in the US is only 20 percent, with the most-dependent advanced nation (New Zealand) coming in at close to 80 percent.[5] As we will see, US monetary policy and equitable financial intermediation is increasingly short-circuited because many lenders other than banks are critical to credit flows across the spectrum of individuals, households, small businesses, and giant corporations. Post-crisis rules also short-circuit financial intermediation by imposing costs on deposit-taking and lending that lead banks to do less financial intermediation to focus instead on trading, wealth management, and other profitable activities with little growth impact and considerable, adverse equality implications.

The Modern Monetary-Policy Construct

Economists love data and many completely cherish theories about how to use it to define the macroeconomy – i.e., the sum total of nitiatives - rule and market actions. There is an enormous literature about different ways to conduct monetary policy in which floors, corridors, ceilings, and other architectural images are deployed to describe different techniques. But, while economists can build monetary policy, they can't make anyone come – since 2010, trillions of once-unthinkable Fed intervention led only to the slowest economic recovery in modern memory, a bloated financial system, inequality growing faster and fiercer than ever, and, in 2020, a tremendous crash that made vulnerable households even worse off.

Very simply put, US monetary policy prior to 2008 is called "conventional" monetary policy. As discussed in more detail in the next chapter, the Federal Reserve before 2008 largely relied on revisions to its "open-market" position (i.e., how it traded government securities) and/or on changes to requirements governing the reserves it demands of banks. The Fed uses these techniques to set the "federal funds" rate, thus determining the cost of bank funding provided to other banks that long defined the overall financial market's pricing of credit. According to hallowed theory, the cheaper loans become due to lower interest rates, the more generous (i.e., "easier") the monetary policy and the greater the contribution to growth. Conversely, the "tighter" the policy, the more the Fed tries to constrain growth, crimp inflation, and otherwise cool down macroeconomic activity hotter than the Fed thinks fit and proper.

"Unconventional" policy goes beyond these relatively narrow changes in the federal funds market in hopes of making a far bigger difference – i.e., reversing the forces that the Fed in 2008 feared could drive the US and then the globe into a repeat of the Great Depression. Compared to that risk, unconventional policy was a success, but this is faint praise for slow, inequitable growth after the crisis ebbed and the Fed plowed still more trillions into the economy and kept interest rates below zero after taking inflation into account. From 2008 to 2020, the Fed used ultra-low interest rates, trillions of Fed asset purchases, and direct market interventions never before seen in US monetary policy-making. This policy was "unconventional" in terms of the tools it used – the giant Fed portfolio, for example – and how low interest rates dropped.

However, unconventional policy is at its heart still completely conventional; the Fed counted on banks to transmit its policy even though banks don't drive national finance, expected a middle-class nation to respond to its signals even though the US is no longer a middle-class nation, and believed that the lower interest rates go, the stronger the US economy will be. We will see shortly how these policies badly backfired not only to make the US far less equal, but also to increase the risk of the 2020 financial crisis. It is sadly ironic that a bold policy that at its outset reduced the cost of the 2008 crisis made the next one more likely and more costly by dint of increased inequality and distorted financial markets.

To be fair, the Fed knew it had a problem before the 2020 crash laid it bare because growth was anemic no matter what it did. It thus decided in early 2013 to step back. However, when then-Chairman Bernanke made a faint-hearted hint about a portfolio reduction, financial markets flew into what came to be called the "taper tantrum." Focused as ever more on markets than on economic equality, the Fed was so frightened by the market's conniptions that it only began very gradually and very tentatively in late 2018 to ease back. By then, markets had become so used to measuring prices by Fed policy – not underlying growth or profitability – that the Fed was wholly uncertain how to conduct monetary policy. It launched a 2018 project in which economists across the US filled the Fed's suggestion box,[6] but by September 2019 the Fed went back to holding a huge portfolio. In the 2020 crisis, its only monetary-policy tool was its printing press churning out dollar after dollar. It revved this up to more and more trillions, but the money moved only to banks, money-market funds, huge "primary dealers," and other giant companies. The Fed printed money headed for mid-sized businesses and municipalities only when Congress affirmatively ordered the Fed to do so.

The awful irony of modern monetary policy is that the Federal Reserve used its formidable power backed by trillions of dollars to make Americans far more unequal faster than ever, but still couldn't avert the financial crisis that accompanied the 2020 COVID pandemic. Future chapters will describe each of the Fed's monetary-policy tools in more detail and show why they did so much damage instead of all the good the Fed proclaimed from 2008 through 2020. Suffice it to say here that results speak for themselves.

The Fed's Bailout Buckets

Making monetary policy is not, though, all that central banks do. In the US and most other nations, central banks are also providers of seasonal funding to support banks with temporary liquidity shortages and, demonstrated with hundreds of billions during the great financial crisis and again in 2020, also of emergency liquidity and even solvency support across the entire US and even global financial system.

Seasonal or even short-term liquidity support to banks is a traditional central-bank function. It is not a bailout because banks are heavily regulated in return for access to these "discount windows" and post high-quality collateral to reduce the Fed's risks. However, when the Fed eases discount-window terms or opens up lots of new windows with far fewer restrictions, then it moves beyond short-term liquidity support, abandoning the traditional central-bank role as a lender of last resort and instead becoming a market-maker for all comers and even, as in 2020, a lender of first resort to giant financial and nonfinancial companies.

An array of emergency-liquidity and direct aid to insolvent companies joined other hastily constructed programs during the 2008 crisis to prevent another Great Depression. However, the trillions poured into the financial system in 2008 also made what came to be called the Great Recession worse, longer, and more unequal over the ensuing decade. In 2020, the Fed outdid itself – establishing facilities of hundreds of billions for the highest-risk corners of the financial market and even becoming a lender of first resort to companies that often use Fed backstops not to create jobs, but to increase payouts to shareholders. The Fed persuaded itself that it was taking no risks unbecoming a central bank because the US Treasury provided hundreds of billions of upfront risk-absorbing dollars. However, all this did was to make the Fed still more of an agent of fiscal (i.e., political) power. None of its facilities helped families facing financial ruin due only to the pandemic and the only one backing truly small businesses did so only via banks and even then only thanks to Treasury's guarantee for all the loans involved. When it came to "junk" bonds, the Fed stepped in and took risks; when it came to hard-pressed families and small businesses, it demurred.

All of these Fed bailouts create vicious cycles in which risks grow higher, bailouts seem even more essential to the Fed, and financial markets become even more assured that, the next time stress rolls around, the Fed will open its bailout windows all over again. Emergency-liquidity and solvency protections reinforced market expectations that some companies – and especially the very largest ones – are too big to fail (TBTF). The Dodd-Frank Act of 2010 includes regulatory and orderly resolution provisions designed to end TBTF financial companies in the US.[7] This actually worked reasonably well for the largest US banks.[8] However, as we will see, the Fed skirted the hard edges of the 2010 law to find ways to provide all the bailouts it rushed through in 2020, ratifying the pre-2008 TBTF construct Congress tried to end in 2010 because all the Fed could think to do in 2020 was again to bail out the nation's largest financial companies. In fact, in 2020, the Fed went farther and made even giant nonfinancial companies TBTF by virtue of hundreds of billions of corporate-loan rescues.

TBTF finance sows both systemic risk and economic inequality. Following the money, finance people naturally move money into institutions at which they think they take no risk. This is called "moral hazard" because investors reap rewards at taxpayer risk in ways that encourage undue risk-taking. Following the money before 2008 and again ahead of 2020 shows that much of it moved into the riskiest, highest-yielding investments, which investors expected – correctly, as it turned out – came with a TBTF backstop. In 2008 and again in 2020, this moral-hazard bet paid off handsomely; fearing market collapse, funds moved at warp-speed from investments they hoped would have a TBTF stamp into those they knew came with one – Treasury securities and big-bank deposits. This put still more stress on those still hoping for safety in unguaranteed investments so that the Fed felt compelled to do what it did in 2008 all over again in 2020. It established one after another trillion-dollar facility backing money-market funds, high-risk investment funds, and speculative asset-backed securities.

Economic efficiency combines with economic morality to argue against moral hazard. However, if there are to be any TBTF borrowers, then economic and even social justice demand that they be not the high-flying financial companies and investors the Fed backs crisis-in, crisis-out, but households struggling to make ends meet due to no fault of their own for whom sudden unemployment is a devastating event they could neither have predicted nor prevented.

The Fed's Payment Powers

Finally, the Fed has a major role in the US payment system. It not only regulates the flow of checks and other cash-like transactions across the US, but also provides an array of payment services that were the sole purview of the private sector until 1980. The Fed is even contemplating a still larger payment-system role as technology changes the way cash is used and which companies have access to which parts of the payment process. Again, significant potential conflicts arise because the critical step in many payment transactions – transferring a deposit to another account – is no longer solely a function provided by regulated banks. Fed ownership of the payment system adds TBTF protection across its many players. This makes sense when it comes to each of us hoping a check will clear; it's far less clear that Amazon, Google, or other unregulated consumer-finance companies should also get TBTF protection by way of Fed clearing and settlement.

However, the asymmetry embedded in a payment system owned and operated by the central bank and payment systems still outside it also poses challenges to monetary and regulatory policy. Various proposals – some aimed at improving economic equality – even suggest "digital" money through which the Fed would replace banks as deposit-takers, payment-makers, and perhaps even lenders. Amazon, Google, and Facebook might see their own digital-money efforts preempted by the Fed or they might be able to ride along, gaining still greater TBTF cachet. This question and its equality impact are addressed in Chapter 9.

Rules of the Financial Road

Together, the Fed and three other federal agencies also regulate different aspects of the banking system, but – with just a few exceptions – none of the other parts of a financial system that is increasingly dependent on nonbanks. How bank regulators do this job in the US and the relationship they have to the Fed's monetary policy operations and to regulators of nonbank financial institutions – when there are any regulators to speak of – is complex, but also critical to financial policy's equality impact.

When essential financial functions are fulfilled by nonbanks under light-touch safety-and-soundness regulation or none at all, this interaction becomes still more complex. As I said, financial institutions are led by finance people with ample ability to follow the money. This means that function follows form into the least-regulated, least-costly corners of the US and global financial system. It doesn't take much to move a transaction from a regulated market to one with little to no prudential, tax, money-laundering, terrorist-sanction, or other scruples. Push a button, move the money.

This lowest-common-denominator market preference not only vastly complicates monetary-policy transmission, but also moves key parts of the financial-intermediation chain outside regulated firms. Bank rules are meant to ensure continuing service under even acute stress and vital protections (e.g., FDIC deposit insurance) also protect the most vulnerable consumers. Consider that $1,000 of hard-earned wages in a bank is safe in the US even if the bank fails; the same $1,000 in an online venture is decidedly at far greater risk, as are funds housed in largely unregulated asset managers under stress scenarios unless, as in 2020, the Fed bails them out. These nonbanks can and often do offer higher returns for what would otherwise be deposits, but only the most affluent and best educated customers understand these risks and are able to withstand them. Too-big-to-fail expectations spawned by the 2008 rescues have also led many individuals and households to think that their money is safe wherever it is stored instead of understanding that only FDIC insurance is a full-faith-and-credit US guarantee.

A brief overview suffices to show the complexity of the US financial-regulatory framework and why the US has ceased to be a bank-dependent financial system.

First, there are four federal regulators: the Federal Reserve (backed up by 12 Federal Reserve Banks with regional supervisory duties); the Office of the Comptroller of the Currency (OCC), which regulates banks that choose a national charter; and the FDIC, which both provides deposit insurance and regulates state-chartered banks that are neither OCC-regulated nor "member" banks subject to Fed regulation and supervision. The fourth, the Bureau of Consumer Financial Protection (CFPB), has overlapping duties with these agencies for consumer-protection and, while this is separate from safety and soundness, issues often overlap and conflict. Unlike the federal banking agencies, the CFPB has limited jurisdiction over large nonbanks.

Who governs whom is more than slightly complicated. Savings-and-loan institutions (often called thrifts) do much of what banks do and are regulated by the OCC or FDIC for federal purposes based on whether the company chooses a national or state charter. State-chartered banks come under rules that are sometimes different than those for national banks and sometimes preempted by overarching federal standards.

The federal framework is further complicated by the existence of bank holding companies (BHCs), savings-and-loan holding companies (SLHCs), depository institution holding companies (DIHCs), financial holding companies (FHCs), and parent companies that own insured-depository institutions (IDIs) outside the reach of direct holding-company regulation by anyone. Each of the holding-company options governed by the Fed comes with its own activity restrictions and safety-and-soundness requirements, which, to make things still more complex, also vary by the size of the holding company and/or subsidiary insured depository institution.

And, it's worse than that – foreign banking organizations and even some foreign nonbanks are allowed to operate different types of banking ventures under differing state and federal rules or, sometimes, almost none at all. Many exemptions – e.g., from capital requirements – apply to even very large foreign banking operations in the US based on expectations of parent-bank support, but these parent banks operate under very different rules than US BHCs. As a result, foreign banks can often get an edge over US ones and, if the parent company isn't a bank, operate with still greater freedom in the US.

And this complex federal system for banks is just for starters. As the distinctions above for federal charters suggest, IDIs can elect a state-run charter. Some states – e.g., Utah – provide these with considerable enthusiasm, meaning that insured depositories can be owned by companies that do not need to register with the Fed and thus may evade activity restrictions. BHCs and other entities under the Fed may not engage in anything that smacks of commerce; the parent companies of special-purpose banks under favorable state regulation are under no such constraints. This has long made these state charters a happy home for auto companies and manufacturers as formidable as General Electric. High-tech companies with far-flung commercial activities are now also clamoring for these same state charters. The OCC also has some ability to give out charters without the commercial-activity constraints otherwise applicable to insured depositories, creating another avenue for new-style banking (i.e., for financial-technology entities, or "fintechs")[9] with significant equality impact we will explore in Chapters 8 and 9.

In case you thought you understood the above, hold on. The US also has a "functional" financial-regulation framework. In many nations, any company that offers pretty much any type of financial service comes under a single regulator, more often than not the central bank. The functional-regulation approach preserves the US regulatory framework as it initially took shape in the 1930s before the barriers between banking and other financial services began to crumble in the 1980s. As a result, broker-dealers and asset managers are regulated by the Securities and Exchange Commission (SEC), generally under rules designed to promote investor protection, not safety and soundness or orderly resolution. Derivatives activities fall under the banking agencies, the SEC or the Commodity Futures Trading Commission (CFTC), an agency similar to the SEC in terms of its focus on investors and markets, not safety and soundness.

Although theoretically a "silo" system in which specific activities are under the jurisdiction of a specific regulator, functional regulation is both complex and often unclear because the same activity in terms of its economic result can often be provided in a bank or an SEC- or CFTC-regulated entity under totally different rules. The CFPB's rules apply to most financial companies in the same line of business, but only if they are big and generally not if the activity is considered to involve securities or insurance.

Insurance companies are also functionally regulated, with the barrier between banking, securities, and insurance activities thus even fuzzier. Insurance is regulated by insurance regulators located in individual states (there is no national insurance framework in the US), but parent companies and many insurance-company activities are outside this state framework and often also the reach of any other federal or state agency. Insurance regulation is premised on policy-holder protection, all to the good but not necessarily an approach that ensures an insurance company's safety-and-soundness through capital, resolution, or the other costly rules governing banks in the same or similar financial products.

For example, resolution standards – which are designed to ensure that companies in distress or failure do not harm innocent bystanders – apply to some insurance companies in each state, but few address an insurance company's operations in a parent holding company or in relation to non-insurance businesses within the same company. These can be significant, as was shown when a giant, global insurance company, AIG, failed during the 2008 financial crisis due largely to high-risk credit-default swap activities. Insurance-company activities across the country or around the world are also under uncertain consolidated regulation and resolution protocols.

No wonder many companies want the benefits of being a bank – FDIC insurance, payment-system access, Fed liquidity back-stops – without the restrictions on commercial activities or the cost of parent-company capital regulation. No wonder too that many nonbanks have decided to eschew these bank-derived benefits altogether, preferring instead joint ventures, partnerships, or other ways to work with banks while retaining all of the exemptions from costly bank rules. No matter how many bank-like activities are housed in a nonbank, virtually none is under safety-and-soundness regulation. Conversely, no matter what functional regulation applies, all nonbank activities in a banking organization still come under bank rules at the parent-company level. This at the least complicates being more than a traditional bank and, more often, adds so much cost to meeting the competition halfway that banking organizations do well only when their federal safety net or TBTF expectations in the marketplace are a deciding competitive advantage – that is, in a crisis, when it's too late.

As matters stand now, the same financial activities can be conducted in wholly unregulated entities that post-crisis parlance now dubs "shadow banks." To know who houses the same activity in what type of financial institution, follow the money – the less costly the rules, the more likely the activity will find its way there.

Four Fundamental Financial-Policy Flaws

The construct of US monetary and regulatory policy is at least a century old, with even the massive post-crisis reforms of the 2010 Dodd-Frank Act largely retaining all the complexities, overlapping jurisdictions, ambiguities, and escape hatches that made the great financial crisis in 2008 and then the COVID crash of 2020 all too possible and then so very costly. As we have seen, the US economy now is profoundly different than it was in 1913 when the Federal Reserve was established, in 1956 and 1970 when the Bank Holding Company Act redefined the relationship between banking and commerce, in 1999 when the Gramm-Leach-Bliley Act broke down barriers within the financial-services sector, and even in 2010 when Congress passed the Dodd-Frank Act. The US is far, far more unequal than it was even a decade ago. And, as we learned the very hard way in 2020, inequality and unequal financial policy concatenate with stress to create unprecedented damage not just to financial stability, but also prosperity.

The first fundamental flaw that created these ongoing crises is self-satisfaction. Federal banking agencies repeatedly congratulated themselves from 2010 until the crisis of 2020 on the putative success of post-2008 rules. A classic example of this is the Federal Reserve's comfortable assessment of US financial stability shortly before the coronavirus pandemic exposed all its underlying fragility.[10] This report, like so many others, pointed to how much safer banks, and especially the biggest banks, were in comparison to 2007. However, when a financial system isn't bank-centric, very safe banks are an ever-smaller part of an increasingly risky financial system dominated by the "shadow banks" described above.

The second fundamental flaw is the Fed's reliance on aggregate or average data to judge financial-policy impact. Until 2020, the Fed touted the "good place" characterizing the US economy,[11] with Chairman Powell at the start of the COVID crisis still suggesting all was well even as low-wage workers were already losing jobs at millions of shuttered businesses.[12] From 2008 to 2020 the Fed defended its extremely accommodative monetary policy on grounds that it advances employment and that employment is the best path to opportunity for low- and moderate-income households.

But what is employment for if not additional wage income? There's been precious little of that since 2010: taking discouraged and part-time workers into account, the unemployment rate fell from its crisis high of over 17 percent to 7.6 percent by the end of 2018[13] – about double what the Fed said unemployment was at the time. However, inflation-adjusted hourly wages for the median US worker averaged only 0.3 percent annual growth over roughly the same period. Household annual income looks as if it is finally going up after the Great Recession, but only if one doesn't look closely. Many more families are doing a bit better only because many more families now have more than one wage-earner and/or are working more hours.[14] In real terms, low-income workers did little better than they did before COVID did them in than they did four decades ago.[15] Finally, all of the Fed's data fail to account for the special misery of minority communities – as we saw in Chapter 3, African Americans and Hispanics were on the outside looking into the Fed's vaunted "good place."

The next chapters will show how other aggregate data such as growing net worth or rising house prices collapse when you disaggregate averages to see how the majority of Americans below average or median rates are faring. Given the sharp spikes in income and wealth held by fewer and fewer US households, judgments of average American well-being, prosperity, and opportunity are misleading at best and even deceptive once data for what's left of the middle class and the growing number of lower-income households are separated from gross totals.

The third error is all the complexity described above. This led to the failure of monetary and regulatory policy-makers to see how each of their own actions interact and whether sum total costs and benefits make any kind of sense in terms of shared growth, financial stability, and equality. Responding to a raft of unintended consequences, one of the few efforts to make sense of both monetary and regulatory policy came in 2015, when a high-level committee of global central bankers issued a report entitled "Regulatory Change and Monetary Policy."[16] The paper establishes that "financial regulation is evolving, as policymakers seek to strengthen the financial system in order to make it more robust and resilient. Changes in the regulatory environment are likely to have an impact on financial system structure and on the behavior of financial intermediaries that central banks will need to take into account in how they implement monetary policy." Translation: things changed and we're not sure why or what next to do. Since 2015, things have changed a lot more but no global or US body has sought to understand how the combination of unconventional monetary policy and post-crisis rules works in tandem not just for growth and financial stability, but also for equality.

The final analytical error is the one with which I started this chapter: decisions are determined by what policy-makers think financial institutions should do, not what they are in fact likely to do to keep their boards happy, their pay packets full, and their companies in business. Finance people don't care which policies move the money; they just follow it to make as much as they can as fast as they can. Economists decry this self-interest as much as they study it and politicians denounce it as they try to move the money to serve social policy or their own political advantage. Still, finance is largely inexorable. It makes what it can as it can, damaging or advantaging economic equality along the way without giving this consequence much thought.

The rest of this book is an effort to lead policy-makers to recognize these inexorable financial forces and then to contain and channel them for the equality that increases productivity, which in turns spurs prosperity that leads to political harmony. As we wend our way through the details of monetary and regulatory policy, we will see just how profoundly policy influences equality and how readily and even easily these effects can be corrected without even a change of US law. We will also see that controlling the money flows that fuel the inequality engine also gives us the power to prevent the repeated crashes resulting solely from prior financial-policy failures, failures that threw the inequality engine into turbo-drive. Many other equality solutions are controversial to the point of impossible or are changes to the fabric of core governmental infrastructure that take generations to show a beneficial equality result. Financial policy gives us the power to reach for the inequality engine's throttle and slow it down enough for all these other, more challenging solutions to be brought to bear. A slower inequality engine is an economic force far less likely to crash and far, far easier to put into reverse.

Chapter 6

How Monetary Policy Made Most of Us Poorer

The degree of inequality we see today is primarily the result of deep structural changes in our economy that have taken place over many years, including globalization, technological progress, demographic trends, and institutional change in the labor market and elsewhere. ... [T]he effects of monetary policy on inequality are almost certainly modest and transient.

– Ben Bernanke [*]

The Fed may feel all of this [its COVID rescue package] is essential to protect the financial system's plumbing and reduce systemic risk, but make no mistake that the Fed is protecting Wall Street first. The goal seems to be to lift asset prices ... and hope that the wealth effect filters down to the rest of the economy.

– Wall Street Journal Editorial Board, 4/9/20 [†]

---

[*] Ben S. Bernanke, "Monetary policy and inequality," Brookings Institution Blog, June 1, 2015, available at https://www.brookings.edu/blog/ben-bernanke/2015/06/01/monetary-policy-and-inequality/.

[†] Editorial Board, "The Fed's 'Main Street' Mistake," *Wall Street Journal* (April 9, 2020), available at https://www.wsj.com/articles/the-feds-main-street-mistake-11586474912.

What is this wealth effect and why might the Fed think it's good for all of us even though arch-capitalists like the *Wall Street Journal's* editorial board fervently disagree? Before the 2008 crisis and – despite that hard lesson – again in the run-up to the 2020 economic collapse, central bankers saw themselves as financial-market fixer-uppers, convinced that securing lucrative stock-and-bond trading would so profit financiers that wealth would trickle down to the rest of us. Economists call this the "wealth effect" and the Fed made sure that the wealthy indeed have happily felt the beneficial effect of its policies ever since Alan Greenspan adopted the wealth effect as a mantra in the early 2000s.[1]

Former Federal Reserve Board (FRB) Chair Ben Bernanke, the author of the unconventional monetary-policy theory he deployed as Fed chair during the 2008 great financial crisis, remains a stout defender of the way he marshalled the wealth effect, disavowing any collateral damage to economic equality. Mr. Bernanke's crisis colleague and successor, Janet Yellen, is no less unequivocal that post-crisis monetary policy did not contribute to economic inequality.[2] Federal Reserve Chair Jerome Powell stands by his predecessors, telling Congress in 2020 that, while it is important that inequality issues be addressed, "it's not really for the Fed to prescribe the measures to address them."[3]

Other central bankers do a better job than the US Federal Reserve at recognizing the economic inequality impact of monetary policy, but they share its distaste for taking actions that reduce or, better, prevent it. As the former head of the Bank of England noted, "All monetary policy has distributional effects, but it is rightly the role of elected governments to take measures to offset them if they so choose."[4] This august, imperial notion of central bankers that do good no matter demonstrably ill distributional effects might make sense if the wealth effect worked to achieve central banking's axiomatic employment and price-stability mandate. However, it didn't. From 2010 to 2020, the Fed made financial markets roar even as most Americans struggled in the midst of the weakest economic recovery in modern US history.

As it turns out, the Fed's wealth effect works for the wealthy, but not for the general prosperity or even for the vision of capitalism and free markets all Fed chairs espouse. As a longtime, legendary investor put it, "[F]inancial markets have come to expect the Fed to intervene in response to any sharp declines in equity prices.... With the federal government and the Fed firmly joined at the hip, the transformation of capitalism into statism is gaining momentum, perhaps irreversibly."[5] Or, as the *Financial Times* put it more succinctly, "US capitalism has been shattered."[6]

On April 9, US COVID-related deaths hit a then-record high, but US stock markets roared back from the depths reached early in the panic. The companies that rose the most were not those most likely to benefit from a faster return to normal. Instead, the big winners were the financial institutions rescued by the Fed's 2020 market interventions even though these firms were the same ones that, before the crisis, took the most risk thanks to all the Fed's pre-2020 freewheeling policy.[7] As the pandemic continued, broader markets also roared, with the S&P rising more in the second quarter of 2020 than it had in any quarter since 1998[8] even though, toward the end of the quarter, COVID was infecting record numbers of Americans and macroeconomic indicators ranged from pessimistic to cataclysmic.

At its June monetary-policy meeting,[9] the Fed's market-watchers put this anomalous behavior down to market confidence in everything ranging from a new coronavirus vaccine to a healthy renewal of risk-taking sentiment. As we'll see, virtually every other market observer attributed this irrepressible market recovery to all of the Fed's bailouts and continuing, ultra-low interest rates. Extensive research we'll explore here also shows unequivocally that the Fed's failure quickly to normalize its huge portfolio after the 2008 crisis ebbed and ultra-low rates made America far less equal and its financial markets considerably riskier at profit only to markets, not the broader economy.

It's not good enough to prove all this and then urge elected officials to counteract the Fed's wealth effect with some sort of redistributional imperative born of tax policy, new spending, or something else monetary policy-makers not only refuse to contemplate on their own, but also specifically to recommend to others. Given the confluence of unequal monetary policy, underperforming economies, high-risk finance, and growing public rage, a specific set of policy options is essential. I'll thus propose a newly conventional approach to monetary policy in which the wealth effect derives from freewheeling financial markets, not the largesse of central banks. In this unconventionally conventional construct, markets are regulated not to protect investors, but instead to protect the macroeconomy on which shared prosperity directly depends.

The Fed's Heavy Hand

It's no secret within the Fed that its policies do wonders for financial markets. The former president of the Federal Reserve Bank of New York, William Dudley, argued that large-scale asset purchases may not have boosted growth, but they nonetheless made it easier for the market to know what the Fed is up to. That is, no matter how little the Fed did for shared growth, Fed policy worked for the Fed in terms of signaling the market about its own next steps. This makes markets happy, but whether these next steps work as intended for everyone other than market-makers is apparently of little concern.

Focusing on markets – not households – is in fact a longstanding Fed preoccupation, with the Fed all too often setting policy according to the "Greenspan put." This is a bet that easing monetary policy to support markets increases prosperity. Even though it hasn't done so since at least the mid-1990s, Chair Powell was as ready to deploy the Greenspan put as his predecessors. When equity markets stumbled in December 2018, Mr. Powell was quick to reassure them that monetary policy would be gentle on their minds.[10] Despite long-delayed plans to "normalize" the Fed's huge portfolio, the Fed chair also said the portfolio would not drop much more than the market liked. And when the Fed guessed wrong about what the market wanted in October 2019, the Fed jumped right back in, bulking up its portfolio. For every 1 percent portfolio increase, the S&P equity-market index rose 0.9 percent between October and the end of 2019.[11]

Causation or correlation? Either way, the market was darn happy when the Fed opened its printing press, and markets reached new highs from October 2019 to March 2020, when the crash was catastrophic and surely worse than it would have been had the Fed not propped the market up each time a natural, disciplinary correction from worried investors might have stabilized the situation without still more central-bank billions.

If ever-upward financial markets led to shared prosperity, then this market-first framework might make sense. However, despite her brave face defending Fed policy against inequality accusations, Janet Yellen nonetheless conceded that she couldn't tell if post-crisis monetary policy actually worked because the recovery after 2010 was tortuously slow and fragile. A former president of another Federal Reserve Bank (Minneapolis) was blunt, saying that the Fed "had proven ineffective at achieving its macroeconomic objectives for well over a dozen years."[12] As we will see, the Fed after 2008 drove financial markets higher, making the wealthiest among us richer without ensuring any of the economic resilience or financial stability needed to withstand stress.

Why It's the Fed's Fault

Central banks, including the Fed, once relied on conventional policy setting interest rates up or down to guide employment, contain inflation, and thereby also comfort financial markets. When conventional policy failed to work after the 2008 crisis, the Fed was the first of the global central banks to craft an unconventional policy called quantitative easing (QE). This relies not only on huge asset purchases, but also on unprecedented, ultra-low interest rates. Unconventional policy has ruled ever since 2008 and the correlation between it, sharply increased inequality, and grave financial-market fragility is no coincidence.

Figure 6.1 shows that the Fed's huge balance sheet is unconventional and then some – before the crisis, it stood at around $800 billion; as of this writing, it is $7 trillion.[13] Lost in all these trillions is that the Fed initially thought the program would end as early as 2013 and be far smaller.[14] Even in 2019 before the COVID crisis, the portfolio was still huge, even though research shows that QE's impact changed dramatically over time, transforming QE from an effective crisis prophylactic into a long-term program resetting the balance of winners and losers in the US financial market.

The reason for QE's impact on equity prices is remarkably straightforward, albeit powerful. To understand it, follow the money.

Figure 6.1   Fed Balance Sheet Growth Since 2004

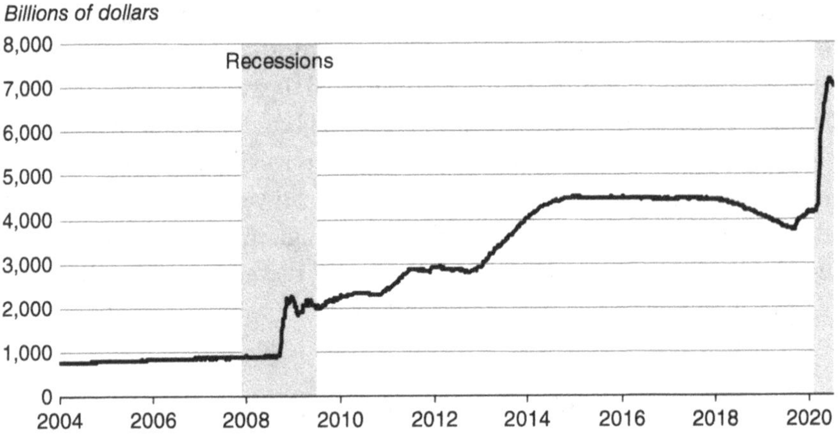

Billions of dollars

Source: Federal Reserve Bank of St. Louis, FRED Economic Data Series WALCL.

The whole point of quantitative easing is to take safe assets (e.g., US government bonds) out of the banking system, buying them from banks to give them the cash with which to make loans that then drive economic growth. But when safe assets disappear from the banking system into the Fed's enormous portfolio during periods of economic uncertainty and ultra-low rates, banks don't make loans. Banks of course are in the business of making loans, which is why conventional policy transmitted through banks under ordinary circumstances largely determined national interest rates. However, banks seek to avoid risk and, even if they're free-spirited, post-crisis capital rules combined with low rates to make lending both risky and unprofitable. Banks thus mostly put all the money they got from the Fed right back into the Fed, impeding rapid macroeconomic recovery and reshaping financial markets.

With QE, investors looking for a place to put their cash couldn't buy US government bonds or other safe assets at reasonable prices because the Fed and other central banks owned so many of them. With bank lending on hold and safe assets in short supply, demand spiked for other, riskier assets, sparking the yield-chasing bonanza that propelled stock markets higher and higher after 2010. Market risk accelerated because equity prices and those for high-risk ("junk") bonds became increasingly dissociated from the hard reality from which Fed market interventions spared them.[15] Financial markets also created complex "collateral-transformation" products that deployed ineligible assets to create financial-market liquidity.[16]

This complex financial engineering cracked in September 2019 when a critical part of the world's financial infrastructure – the "repo" market – collapsed, forcing a giant Fed rescue.[17] In March 2020, it blew wide open as investors searched desperately for safe assets as they fled collapsing financial markets, putting so much stress on the system that the Fed was forced in mid-March to stabilize markets with still more trillions of dollars of renewed asset purchases.[18] This intervention by then was necessary, but it still made markets only slightly safer, the Fed even bigger, and the dynamic of post-2020 financial markets still more inexorably in favor of giant finance and the wealthiest investors who profit thereby.

The link between Fed asset purchases and the market-price spikes that exacerbate economic inequality is apparent in an overarching survey of all of the research on the impact of the Fed QE tactic. The central bank for central banks, the Bank for International Settlements (BIS), found that the output (i.e., the amount an economy produces) and the employment impact of the Fed's portfolio faded over time to zero in terms of any contribution to macroeconomic growth.[19] This BIS paper in fact finds that QE's peak impact – that is, its impact across the years and all of its trillions – in the US had ten times more effect on stock prices than on maximum output. It thus concludes that unconventional monetary policy's output impact generally becomes insignificant over time, but the impact on higher stock prices is "persistently positive and statistically significant."

Another study of QE's impact[20] on the interest rates the Fed sought to lower through its unconventional policies also showed little persistent effect, reinforcing that the stock-price increases found by the BIS were not offset by greater US economic output. The disconnect between what the Fed did and who won thereby is also evident in a Fed staff paper.[21] It is models-based and thus far more hypothetical than the BIS's empirical evidence. Still, the models it uses find that monetary policy with no eye to averting inequality (i.e., what the Fed has done since 2010) increases the risk of "secular stagnation." As you might think, this isn't a good thing – secular stagnation means low growth and low infla-tion. Equality-blind monetary policy also leads to deflation, asset-price bubbles, and financial crises.[22] Fast forward to 2020.

Another Fed research paper[23] highlights financial-crisis risk. It empirically shows that lending as QE grew long in the tooth became increasingly risky, with a shift in bank lending to higher-risk, inequality-generating loans correlated with the last two of the Fed's three QE rounds. More risk-taking could have led to more lending to higher-risk, lower-income households for first-time homeownership or lending to start small businesses – key equality-generating engines as the FRB has acknowledged.[24] However, confidential loan data not available to other researchers showed that higher-risk taking came in the form of commercial real estate lending during the first QE round and commercial-and-industrial (i.e., established business) lending in the third. Since then, the Fed has repeatedly cited both types of lending as potential systemic risks – not that it did anything about them until, in 2020, it set up a raft of trillion-dollar bailouts for them to prevent the risks it foresaw but still failed to address.

How Ultra-Low Interest Rates Made America Still Less Equal and QE Still More Inequitable

Ever since 2008, global central banks, including the Federal Reserve, not only set rates at once-inconceivably low levels, but also kept rates at these ultra-low levels for over a decade until they dropped them still farther during the 2020 crisis. Ultra-low rates – most of them below zero in terms of real return after taking even minimal inflation into account – have become the new normal. Ordinarily, central banks raise rates when economic conditions improve. But, while the Fed throughout 2019 consistently told Congress and everyone else that the US economy was in a "good place,"[25] it kept rates far lower than its view of economic prosperity warranted. It did so due to fears not of the adverse impact economic cooling would have on lower-income households – most of which were already in the cold – but of the market consequences of even small rate rises. When the Fed lifted rates in 2018 just a bit, markets dropped, President Trump pummeled the central bank, and the Fed quickly changed course, ensuring still more inequality along with a year and a few months of steady market rises to the glittering precipice of the COVID crash in March 2020.

How low did the Fed go? Way, way down. Ultra-low rates hovered at or near the "zero lower bound" (ZLB) through the decade between 2010 and 2020 and now, if the Fed has its way, seem likely to stay at the ZLB bottom for another decade. This terminology was invented by economists' expectations that interest rates could no more be below zero than any mortal creature could lose so much weight as to weigh less than nothing. When nominal (not inflation-adjusted) interest rates are below the ZLB, banks essentially pay borrowers to take out a loan because negative rates erode the principal balance – that is, a $100 loan "costing" negative 1 percent requires only a $99 repayment. Conversely, depositors pay the bank to take their money – a $100 deposit "earning" negative 1 percent is worth only $99 after a year. This may seem like a fantastic eventuality, but it's been the case in Europe and Japan for over a decade. US interest rates before 2020 stayed above the nominal ZLB, but only by a little bit.

Thus, as we've seen, those putting money to work in the stock market did very, very well; those trying to save for a rainy day got wet. One study estimated a total loss across the US economy of $2.3 trillion in savings accounts and similar balances due to the very low interest rates from just 2008 through 2016.[26]

Some might say that negative savings returns don't matter to most US households because most US households don't try to save what they can. This isn't true. The "precautionary" savings balances of moderate-income households slightly increased after the 2008 crisis.[27] Millennials were particularly diligent savers despite their huge debt loads; approximately three out of four millennials are savers.[28]

The institutions designated to protect average households – pension funds and insurance companies – are also at great risk during periods of ultra-low rates. Historically, pension funds and insurance companies have invested only in the safest assets. These are, as noted, in scarce supply due to QE and comparable programs by central banks around the world.[29] As a result, companies that for decades have been secure backstops of family financial security are now yield-chasing – that is, trying to edge returns above the ZLB by taking lots of risk once thought wholly unacceptable for entities promising long-term financial security to those to whom they owe a "fiduciary duty" (an obligation to safeguard investors via extreme caution).

Some pension funds and insurance companies are not only yield-chasing, but also becoming underfunded, no longer holding the reserves needed to ensure their ability to honor obligations when pensioners retire or claims are made. Underfunded pension plans are so great a concern in the US that the agency established to protect pensioners from this risk, the Pension Benefit Guaranty Corporation, faces its own financial challenges.[30] Think about it – you pay in a small amount over decades in premiums to secure your children's future, but the insurance company or pension fund goes bust because its investments didn't pan out and all you invested then is lost.

All this lost wealth puts the equality engine in reverse because it is extremely unlikely that a decade or more of lost savings can be recouped as younger Americans seek to start a household, fund a child's education, and otherwise remain in or enter the middle class. All these lost savings also impoverish older Americans who are, as we have seen in Chapter 3, also distributed between a remarkably few households with ample retirement savings and everyone else. Average retirement savings before the COVID crisis stood at just $100,000,[31] and the median then was an even more distressing $50,000[32] – very little with which to finance years of post-retirement housing, medical care, and day-to-day life even with Social Security checks and, perhaps, some realized home equity.

Upper-income and wealthy Americans do lose ground with ultra-low rates, but nowhere near as much because their wealth doesn't come from savings accounts. Instead, it's housed in a raft of financial investments expressly structured to beat the cost of ultra-low interest rates.[33] These accounts are so important to banks that, when rates fall to the ZLB or even below it, banks often pay their largest customers above-market rates to hold on to these lucrative customers.[34]

Examining 14 advanced nations from 1993 to 2015, a Bank for International Settlements study found that banks shifted from deposit-taking and lending across the national economy to fee-based businesses (e.g., wealth management), trading stocks and bonds, and holding lots of funds in central-bank deposits, which, as we saw, make banks safer but don't boost employment or growth.[35] US banks didn't stop lending, but they shifted their lending to higher-risk assets – commercial real estate and big companies[36] – that created the financial-stability risks the Fed foresaw before 2020,[37] but did nothing to reduce.

The reason banks shifted from intermediation to products with no equality benefit is evident when you follow the money. The profit banks earn on ordinary loans under post-crisis capital rules during ultra-low interest rate regimes is just too low to satisfy investors. Banks thus change their business model, moving out of financial intermediation and transferring risk to what came quickly to be called "shadow banks." Ultra-low rates drove this financial transformation from regulated banks to the shadows, revving up high-risk lending for LMI households in the mortgage, auto, student, and personal lending markets and enormous debt burdens across the capital markets. At the beginning of 2020, one estimate placed world debt levels at $250 trillion – 320 percent of world GDP and about double the global liquidity funding all this risk.[38]

As with a huge Fed portfolio, heavy-handed interest rate policy thus has unintended but damaging inequality impact. It distorts markets, turns banks into wealth-management machines, revs up debt to unsustainable levels, and does nothing for broad economic growth but slow it down. This is not unique to the US. Another Bank for International Settlements comprehensive and empirical study of over a hundred global banks found that reductions in short-term rates are less effective as growth stimulants when interest rates are ultra-low, even after controlling for the changes in loan demand occurring after a financial crisis and differences among the banks surveyed.[39]

The High Cost of Low-Rate Debt

As we have seen, ultra-low rates make it impossible for low-, moderate-, and even middle-income households to save for the future, protect themselves with stable rainy-day funds, or put away money with enough of a return to fund near-term goals such as a home down payment, let alone longer-term objectives such as a secure retirement. Do they have a flipside that makes ultra-low rates a boon for these families by ensuring low-cost financing? The Fed has repeatedly argued that household debt levels are easily affordable, basing its assertion yet again on aggregate data about household debt levels compared to income,[40] a comforting approach that obscures a great deal of debt burden in a nation as unequal as the US. All but the wealthiest households had more debt as a percentage of assets in 2016 than they did in 1989.[41] Most of this debt was for mortgages and so perhaps most of it was offset at least to some degree by long-term benefits. Still, a lot of debt was just to sustain day-to-day consumption. Non-mortgage debt to nonfinancial nonresidential assets (automobiles, furniture, etc.) for all US households jumped from 38 percent in 1988 to over 100 percent as of the first quarter of 2018.[42] Given that households with so much debt in relation to their possessions are far more likely to be lower-income than those with financial assets, the magnitude of a risky debt bubble is instantly apparent.

All this debt may be low cost – and most of it is anything but – but households that have debt equal to or more than assets are floating their existence on debt, not income, putting them at the grave risk they in fact encountered in March 2020. A wave of bankruptcies resulting from debt – no matter its cost – imperils families for years, if not generations.

Worse, even if lower rates mean more affordable debt, it turns out that low interest rates often don't turn into low-cost loans for lower-income households. Mortgage refinancings (refis) are the most important way consumers benefit from lower rates because converting a high-cost home loan into a lower-rate one can save families the difference between comfort and still more credit-card or even payday credit to make ends meet each month. Did low rates allow low-and-moderate income (LMI) households at least to reduce their mortgage debt through refinancings? Again, these households were left behind. They continued to seek refis after the 2008 financial crisis ebbed to reduce their cost of financing a home, but subprime borrowers current on their loans regardless of loan-to-value (LTV) ratios were less likely than prime or super-prime borrowers to receive refi loans even though prime borrowers might or might not have been current on their mortgage payments.[43] Low rates were also little help to LMI households seeking a mortgage for their first home as an overwhelming majority of these would-be borrowers lacked the savings for the minimum down payment on a median-priced home and/or did not have enough income to qualify for a loan.[44] Low interest rates turn out to be a double-edged sword for lower-income families because they can neither accumulate meaningful savings nor qualify for low-cost loans.

A Federal Reserve Bank of New York paper[45] narrows this question to the US, also finding that lending drops as rates approach the zero lower bound because banks simply can't make money making ultra-low interest rate loans. This same study also finds that banks adjusted to persistent low rates by changing their asset/liability mix away from deposit-taking and longer-term lending to less costly funding sources and short-term, interest-bearing investments such as excess reserves held at the Federal Reserve. Following the money – not the Fed's models – we see again that the mix of monetary policy, regulatory requirements, and business-reality factors lead banks in an ultra-low rate environment to reduce lending, especially for longer-term, lower-cost loans critical to wealth accumulation.

The Low-Unemployment Myth

Ever since the Fed started QE and kicked interest rates to the floor in 2010, it has defended itself against assertions that it has a hand in increasing inequality on grounds that unemployment dropped to record lows and employment is good for lower-income households. This would be true if it weren't for the fact that more jobs didn't come with higher wages, that part-time and gig employment is often synonymous with underemployment, that many of these jobs were in families with at least two income earners struggling to make ends meet, and, in 2020, that the crisis partly wrought by a decade of unconventional policy led to the sharpest drop ever in US employment, starting first with the lowest-wage workers most vulnerable to missing just one paycheck.[46] From mid-March to mid-April 2020, the US lost 22 million jobs, more than the 20 million gained over the course of the entire decade before.[47]

Of course, all of COVID's cost isn't the Fed's fault, but that so many Americans enjoyed "full employment" in so tenuous a way is the Fed's fault first because its recovery was so anemic, second because the Fed was content with it, and third because the US central bank failed to understand how it made economic inequality so much worse. If solid wage growth was from the bottom up, then employment would be a sound measure of prosperity and a contributor to economic equality. However, it turns out that the way the Fed counts record low unemployment makes one of the fundamental mistakes highlighted in Chapter 5: the Fed looks only at top-line data, not at all the differences beneath it showing who is employed for what wages under what conditions.

The US "good place" was in fact far more inhospitable for low-wage workers than the Fed's sunny employment data suggested. Indeed, a study of wage increases from the Federal Reserve Bank of New York concludes that looking at aggregate wage growth obscures problems for lower-wage workers and assuming that the percentage of wage growth for low-income workers means increased prosperity misses the fact that percentage increases may be large but wages are still very, very small.[48] Further, the unemployment numbers on which the Fed relies often overlook the workers who left the labor force,[49] get by only on contract work,[50] and saw their wages stagnate or, worse, go downhill. Census data[51] show that US median household income before the 2020 crash rose largely because more households have multiple wage-earners. Two low-wage jobs may seem like more employment, but they in fact reflect the ever-greater struggle of lower-income Americans to make ends meet.

US underemployment (part-time or jobs for which an employee is overqualified) were the principal US wage generators before 2020. Studies going even more deeply into wage growth found nominal wage growth well below what "full" employment should create, especially for workers who are not college-educated white men.[52]

If the US economy was indeed the Fed's "good place" before the COVID crisis, then it should have been good for everyone. In fact, the "record unemployment" the Fed liked to tout along with the ultra-low-cost loans it often cited somehow managed to occur in an economy that also saw income inequality rocket up to records unseen in the decades since the Great Depression ebbed. Figure 6.2 tells this sorry tale.

Figure 6.2   Top 10% Income Share at its Highest Level in 100 Years

Source: "Income Inequality in the United States, 1913–1998" with Thomas Piketty, *Quarterly Journal of Economics*, 118(1), 2003, 1–39 (Longer updated version published in A.B. Atkinson and T. Piketty eds., Oxford University Press, 2007) (Tables and Figures Updated to 2018 in Excel format, October 2019).

The Anti-Wealth Effect

After 2010, US wealth inequality grew even though higher equity and house prices led the Fed to conclude that American prosperity had returned. This, it thought, was evident in the net-worth data buttressing the Fed's self-assessment,[53] but aggregate data are again misleading. Average net worth did indeed increase after 2010, but at a much greater rate for the highest earners compared to everybody else, as shown in Figure 6.3. Median net worth of the highest earners also grew at a pace significantly above that for the rest of the distribution, as also shown in Figure 6.3.

Worse, looking only at post-crisis data obscures the true extent of the damage the crisis caused and how muted the recovery has been: the median net worth in 2016 for each of the bottom four quintiles – all but the highest 20 percent of earners – was less than it was in 2001. That's 15 years of stagnation or worse for four in five Americans.

Figure 6.3   21st Century Wealth Growth

Year	Percentile of Income					
	Less than 20	20–39.9	40–59.9	60–79.9	80–89.9	90–100
Level (mean, thousands of 2016 dollars)						
2001	71.6	156.1	220.5	398.8	619.5	3,070.5
2010	129.1	141.4	220.0	324.9	627.0	3,254.4
2016	89.5	128.7	207.3	373.5	771.0	4,550.2
Change (percentage)						
2010–2016	–30.7	–9.0	–5.8	15.0	23.0	39.8
2001–2016	25.0	–17.6	–6.0	–6.3	24.5	48.2

Year	Percentile of Income					
	Less than 20	20–39.9	40–59.9	60–79.9	80–89.9	90–100
Level (median, thousands of 2016 dollars)						
2001	10.6	50.7	86.2	195.5	356.5	1,129.4
2010	6.8	28.3	72.8	142.1	316.8	1,320.0
2016	6.5	32.3	81.5	168.3	390.6	1,640.1
Change (percentage)						
2010–2016	–4.4	14.1	12	18.4	23.3	24.3
2001–2016	–38.8	–36.3	–5.5	–13.9	9.6	45.2

Source: FRB Survey of Consumer Finances (2016).

The reason for these sharp disparities in wealth results first from how rich the Fed made those who invested in the financial markets and then from the fact that almost everyone who invests in financial markets is well above average in terms of household wealth. Overall increases in investments, homes, and other asset values would boost prosperity evenly across the distributional curve if all households held more or less the same assets and all assets increased in value in the same way. That is, if every household had a portfolio held half in a savings account and half in the stock market and the returns on both asset classes were 5 percent, then all households would be 5 percent richer in a year. The rich would still be richer than lower-wealth households because their 5 percent is on a larger amount, but wealth-equality distribution would be unchanged.

Wealth inequality increased because LMI households and upper-bracket ones hold their wealth very differently, as can be seen from

Figure 6.4. The bottom 50 percent has very little net wealth, derived mostly from automobiles, not from other durable or financial assets that hold or gain value over time. The top 10 percent holds the bulk of its wealth in financial assets such as stock and business equity. Housing–asset prices have risen but reflect a smaller portion of total assets, with the top 10 percent far less leveraged than the rest of the wealth distribution. Here, the sum of assets is approximately equal to wealth (i.e., no net debt).

Figure 6.4   Trends in Who Has How Much of What When

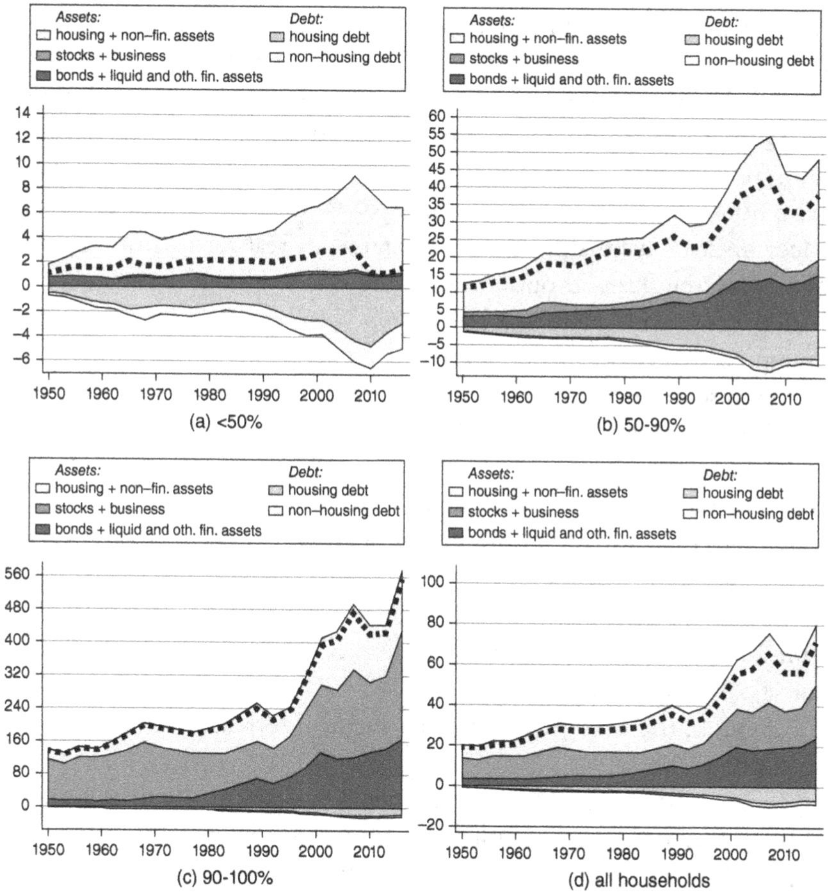

(a) <50%   *(b) 50-90%*   *(c) 90-100%*   *(d) all households*

Source: Moritz Kuhn, Moritz Schularick, and Ulrike I. Steins, *Income and Wealth Inequality in America, 1949–2016*, Federal Reserve Bank of Minneapolis, 34 (June 2018), available at https://www.minneapolisfed.org/institute/working-papers-institute/iwp9.pdf.

And the higher you climb through the top 10 percent to the orbit of the ultra-wealthy, the more financial assets account for the bulk of wealth accumulation. Although housing is the most commonly held household asset, families in the top 1 percent hold mostly private equity (i.e., shares in complex investment companies) and their own businesses; families in the bottom 25 percent own their cars, furniture, and the savings accounts they steadfastly maintain no matter their negative real return.[54] And, once you account for debt, these families own less than nothing – they have considerably more debt than assets.[55]

Sixty-seven percent of middle-class wealth is in home equity,[56] but only 9 percent of wealth for the richest 1 percent lives there. Importantly, house prices have grown sharply for higher-priced houses since about 2012, but remain depressed for lower-cost homes across the country, with many regions experiencing significant amounts of negative equity over a decade after the housing "bust."[57] Although there was sharp house-price appreciation in hot coastal markets, overall US house prices in 2016 were still down 10 percent in real terms from 2007.[58] Worse, households without homes of their own fell farther behind after 2008 because rents increased out of step with wage growth, leading to an unprecedented affordability crisis.[59]

Because of these asset and debt differences, middle-class wealth collapsed after 2008 and the share of the top 10 percent surged 6 percentage points in less than a decade.[60] This was the largest wealth inequality spike in post-war America. By the end of 2019, the top 1 percent of US households measured by wealth held more of it than those from the 90th percentage on down.[61]

Figure 6.3 (above) shows the wealth-equality chasm using Fed data from 2010 to 2016. The top 10 percent of American earners became almost 25 percent richer on their 2010 starting median net worth of $1.3 million; the bottom 20 percent's median decreased 4.4 percent on their initial $6,800.

In 2016, half of the US population had less real wealth than it did in 1971. Before the crisis, wealth-to-income ratios increased the most in the middle and bottom of the wealth distribution; after the great financial crisis, this ratio fell the most for these same households. Stunningly, the wealth of those below the 50 percent dividing line dropped by 52 percent from just 2007 to 2016.

Making Matters Still Worse

Although the Fed defers to fiscal policy when it disavows its own inequality impact, the Fed has played an outsized role in US fiscal policy ever since its portfolio ballooned up in 2008. The Fed has always been part of fiscal policy by virtue of its "remittances" – i.e., payments to Treasury based on the earnings it derives from the securities it holds in its portfolio. Even when that portfolio was what now seems small (the $800 billion the Fed held before 2008), these earnings were significant. With QE, they became huge. After COVID, the Fed essentially became a fiscal agent of the US government and, with that, it lost its august status as a politically independent central bank bent solely on moving interest rates around a bit and regulating banks for their own good.

After the Fed increased its portfolio starting in 2008, it quickly became the world's single largest holder of US Treasuries and of obligations issued by US agencies and the government-sponsored enterprises (GSEs).[62] This means that the Federal Reserve has also been the nation's largest provider of funds to the Treasury, remitting $54.9 billion in 2019.[63] Fed payments essentially subsidize the federal deficit because, if the Fed didn't hold these securities, then private investors would do so and the interest income would be theirs, not money recycled to and from the Treasury through the Fed. This interest-income carousel artificially supports government spending in the near term, but it has many distorting effects on US fiscal policy, most notably for understanding actual US fiscal policy based on real government revenues, not funds at the Fed essentially swiped from private investors.

The COVID crisis catapulted the Fed still deeper into US fiscal policy. The $6.4 trillion on the Fed's balance sheet as of April 16 didn't just appear; the Fed printed the money – or more accurately it increased the bank reserve ratios that serve as money.[64] The COVID-rescue laws then counted on the Fed to print at least another $4.5 trillion,[65] using the Fed not only as the lender of last resort – the long-honored role of central banks – but also as a market-maker and/or lender of middle and even first resort. With the Fed in the lead, Treasury could disavow accountability for an even bigger deficit and President Trump ahead of the election could tell anyone left hoping for a balanced US budget that all these trillions weren't his doing.

The Fed felt itself forced to step in because the US deficit had eroded public wealth even before the 2020 crisis. As we saw in Chapter 3, public wealth is all of the resources of the US government that each of us collectively owns – the parks, the aircraft carriers, and the resources that create great, peaceable, and financially secure nations. By printing money, the Fed seemingly preserves public wealth because the federal government's deficit isn't as big as it seems on usual Treasury accounts. As a result, domestic spending for benefits and entitlements can continue without the hard political decisions that put vulnerable households still more squarely in harm's way.

Modern monetary theory (MMT) suggests that deficits can rise and the Fed's dollar press can churn on without dire consequences as long as interest rates stay ultra-low.[66] Maybe, but the scale of combined Treasury and Fed spending now is so enormous and the economy still so weak that this will prove dangerous even if one discounts the harm to LMI households done every day by ultra-low interest rates. As the supply of dollars grows, global investors will demand more in return for absorbing a huge supply of Treasury obligations as other nations recover their fiscal footing.

Early warning signs abound. During the seemingly benign market conditions of September 2020, the repo-market crisis mentioned earlier struck markets not only due to post-crisis financial policy, but also to sharp spikes in Treasury-obligation issuance that overwhelmed the market. This sharply increased Treasury's cost of funding and disrupted Fed efforts to set interest rates. This same phenomenon hit with still more force in March 2020, when investors dumped Treasury and GSE securities, forcing the Fed to increase its balance sheet by $2 trillion in just three weeks to restore at least a bit of order to global markets.

The Fed can't keep doing this inevitably because even its printing press has limits. Simply put, when the deficit is huge and Treasuries flood the global economy, markets are already struggling safely to follow the money. A huge Fed may seem to compensate for this, but as we have seen, its portfolio depresses output. Thus, the Fed's own huge portfolio threatens public wealth even if MMT is right and markets infinitely tolerate a huge, albeit low-cost, US deficit. As we have seen, the Fed's portfolio combined with ultra-low rates to drive equity prices higher without spurring sustained, shared growth. The bigger the portfolio and the lower the rates, the greater the odds of exactly the high-flying markets we saw before the COVID crash of March 2020.

The 2008 great financial crisis cost global taxpayers $3.5 trillion;[67] the cost of the COVID crash – not all of which is of course the Fed's fault – has yet to be measured. When the Fed pulls about $10 trillion out of the US economy in 2020, public wealth – such as it was – is raided to pay the cost of that catastrophe. Even without the added inequality effect of a huge Fed portfolio, lost public wealth exacerbates inequality and starts the whole high-risk cycle all over again.

The day of reckoning may be delayed due to MMT, but it may still come and, when it does, the consequences will, as always, hit the most vulnerable with the greatest force. Sharp cuts in public spending will erode US public wealth even more, favoring the wealthy and leaving the US with still less with which to honor promised entitlement and public-benefit spending.

A Bigger Fed, Lower Rates, an Extreme Financial Crisis

Tinkering with the fundamental structure of financial markets through unconventional policy is a dangerous game. As we have seen, it made America less equal and, as demonstrated in Chapter 4, nations in which the majority of the population is mired in debt – no matter how low rates may be – are nations prone to devastating financial crises.

Inequality over time and in many nations is the most effective predicter of financial crises. However, none of these nations had the unique US witch's brew: a highly indebted population in which the central bank also levered up financial markets by virtue of a huge portfolio stripping the market of low-risk assets and starving it also of the reasonable rate of return impossible to achieve when interest rates bounce along the zero lower bound.

All of this came crashing down in March 2020. I've said it several times before, but it bears repeating here: the Fed cannot be held accountable for the COVID-19 pandemic, nor can it be blamed for the policy missteps that made it still worse. However, the economic consequences of the COVID crisis would have been far less disastrous if Fed policy had been far more equitable and thus considerably more effective starting as soon as the 2008 crisis turned into the 2010 financial-market reboot.

Only epidemiologists can stop pandemics, but all of the economists at the Federal Reserve could and should have anticipated the devastating impact of the US central bank's anti-equality actions from 2010 to 2020 and the profound financial-system weakness they created. Their bosses in the corner offices should also have noticed that year in, year out, Fed policies missed the mark even as inequality accelerated. Knowing this, they could and should have done more than assign inequality responsibility to others and instead taken it on themselves. It's not good enough simply to say that monetary policy is anti-equality; it's essential then to review why this is and redesign policy as quickly as possible to take one fuel source out of the inequality engine as quickly as possible.

We have seen here how Fed policy exacerbated economic inequality by dint of market rescues, moral hazard, a huge portfolio, and ultra-low interest rates buoyed by misleading economic analysis. None of these mistakes was inevitable or unavoidable − a raft of empirical research demonstrates that much of this was also predictable. In the next chapter, we'll go from understanding why this didn't have to happen to new policies to be sure it doesn't happen ever again.

Chapter 7

How to Make Monetary Policy Make Us More Equal

Mr. Hoover was an engineer. He knew that water trickles down....
But he didn't know that money trickles up.

— Will Rogers[*]

American capitalism has entered a new and dangerous phase, one in which the Federal Reserve has assumed the role as a financial backstop and lender of last resort to every major corporation, along with the banks and investors that provide them with capital. ... As a result, Wall Street and the corporate sector have now achieved that state of financial nirvana in which private investors earn outsize rewards during good times, while in bad, outsize risks are socialized through government rescues.

— Steven Pearlstein[†]

[*] Will Rogers, "And Here's How It All Happened," *St. Petersburg Times* (November 26, 1932; printed November 27, 1932); reprinted in "Will Rogers on 'trickle up' economics," WiredPen Blog (January 30, 2015), available at https://wiredpen.com/2015/01/30/will-rogers-trickle-economics/.
[†] Steven Pearlstein, "Socialism for investors, capitalism for everyone else," *Washington Post* (April 30, 2020), available at https://www.washingtonpost.com/business/2020/04/30/socialism-investors-capitalism-everyone-else/.

Although Will Rogers was talking about the early 1930s, he is right on point for our own times. The cowboy-sage of the Great Depression highlighted that Herbert Hoover, the US president in 1929, believed that protecting Wall Street would save Main Street. In 2020, the Congress, the Trump administration, and the Fed again believed that trickle-down policies would do the same. Trying hard to prove the point, the Fed even opened something it called the Main Street Facility, an ironic tribute to Herbert Hoover given that it was a giant open window backing loans over $250,000 to companies with as much as five billion in annual revenue – in short, not your local barbershop.[1] With this and its other COVID-crisis facilities, the Fed protected big borrowers, often from themselves, even as households and small businesses who had been prudent before the crisis got nothing directly from the US central bank. Socialism for some, capitalism red in tooth and claw for the rest.

The Fed's inability to tell Main Street from Park Avenue predates the COVID crisis. As we have seen, the Fed's huge portfolio and ultra-low interest rates quelled the worst of the 2008 great financial crisis but the Fed didn't stop there. It kept its spigots open for another decade. Frightened that markets would drop a bit were the Fed to stop propping them up, the US central bank kept its portfolio at unprecedented size and sunk rates ever lower even though, as we have also seen, its policies did far more for wealthy investors than anyone else. The years that followed 2008 came to be called the Great Recession because economic growth was not just inequitable, but also negligible. One can sum up the decade from 2010 after the first financial crisis ebbed until 2020, when the next one roared in, as ten years in which the Fed helped to make millions of Americans worse off, doomed younger households to lower expectations than those of their parents, returned economic conditions for African Americans to those before the Civil Rights Era began in the 1960s, and propelled the few and the fortunate into still greater plenty. The Fed didn't mean to do all this, but it did.

This we know all too well from prior chapters. However, inequality isn't just bad for all the reasons we also know. It turns out that all this inequality – ignored by the Fed in its monetary-policy and financial-stability models – also leads to monetary-policy misfires that exacerbate inequality that makes monetary policy still more ineffectual, and – after this feedback loop ricochets for a while – blows up the economy and financial system with devastating impact on the most vulnerable households.

As late as the fall of 2007, Ben Bernanke was assuring Congress that there would be no housing crisis.[2] The Fed also missed the structural impact of declining labor-force participation and productivity on output, assuming instead that high-tech workers and innovation would ensure robust growth. Puzzled by why inflation did not increase as time-worn models predicted after 2008, Janet Yellen looked not to the way the US population borrowed or saved, but instead to possible explanations as tenuous as falling mobile-phone bills.[3]

In January 2020, the minutes of the Federal Open Market Committee (FOMC) record that the FOMC "expected economic growth to continue at a moderate pace, supported by accommodative monetary and financial conditions."[4] The panel that makes US monetary policy also said that employment was "solid"[5] and household debt levels were "fairly low,"[6] even though commercial real estate valuations were "elevated"[7] and leveraged loan markets were characterized by high levels of corporate indebtedness and weak underwriting standards.[8] Less than seven weeks before the Fed poured trillions into the financial system, the FOMC found it to be "resilient."[9]

Had the Fed better understood the US before COVID, the US economy and financial system would have been more resilient when the pandemic struck and far better prepared to buffer the pandemic's secondary impact on the financial market. All the trillions the Fed poured into financial markets might then have been used for average Americans and small businesses, leading to upward monetary policy that would have buffered a good deal of COVID's widespread economic destruction for the millions of hard-working families and essential small businesses on which the national economy depends. But, because aggregate employment seems robust, the Fed thought the US was prosperous. Because some households could afford record debt levels, the Fed thought households were financially resilient. Because banks were highly capitalized and met their liquidity rules, the Fed thought the entire US financial system was only a bit riskier than might be nice.[10]

Not only was the Fed wrong, but it also misunderstood what US law tells it to do right. The Fed's mission as dictated in law is to promote maximum employment across the population, seek price stability without looking only at markets, and – wholly ignored for years – ensure moderate interest rates. A fourth mandate stipulates also that the Fed secure financial stability. As this chapter shows, it flunked all these requirements up to 2020, revving markets up to levels that helped to make the pandemic's macroeconomic cost into a financial-market disaster.

Here, we will travel along the Fed's negative feedback loop to show how it reverberates to such ill effect. We will also make it clear that the Fed has ample authority to disconnect this loop and then show how to make monetary policy more effective by also making it more equal. The simple fixes to monetary policy in this chapter will help to make Fed actions less destructive to both equality and prosperity. However, the Fed must also change the overall construct of monetary policy to reverse its inequality impact, but this requires changes paralleling those for financial regulation and even the definition of money to which we will turn next. Here, I spell out surprisingly easy fixes to enhance equitable monetary policy; at the close of this book, these changes are wrapped together with additional, more complex ones in a multifaceted action plan easily achievable under current law.

The Aggregate-Data Error

The first and perhaps easiest thing the Fed can fix is how it counts. Just as Will Rogers' Great Depression wisdom shows the fallacy of trickle-down economic policy, another major player of the time – Frances Perkins – annihilated aggregate data. Before Ms. Perkins became FDR's Labor Secretary and thus the nation's first female Cabinet officer, she was a high-ranking official in New York State. During the Hoover years, she watched his trickle-down policy evaporate, concluding:

> If one family has $100,000 in surplus, it will still buy only one toaster. But if 100,000 families have one dollar in surplus, among them many thousands will buy toasters. ... Insufficient buying power, not insufficient capital, was aggravating the Depression.[11]

The honorary lecture delivered to the American Economic Association in 2015 by Amir Sufi put this another way.[12] Although it's a mouthful, Professor Sufi rightly describes reliance on aggregate data as the "standard representative agent dynamic-stochastic-general equilibrium model that is the workhorse for monetary policy formulation and analysis." He then goes on to quote another scholar who says more directly and also correctly, "During the crisis, the dominant class of models either had nothing useful to say about the policy questions that needed answers, or provided answers sharply at variance with both common sense and empirical evidence."[13]

Leaving his colleagues to contemplate the intricacies of the representative agent dynamic-stochastic-general equilibrium model, Professor Sufi concludes, "Monetary easing over the past 7 years has been fighting an uphill battle of trying to induce households with the lowest consumption sensitivity to boost spending."[14] That is, the Fed keeps expecting measures based on "representative agents" of actual nationwide consumption to make the economy move, but actual US consumption varies enormously based on how equal the consuming population is or isn't.

Put another way, the Fed thought the wealthy would respond to lower interest rates by buying lots of toasters, but US household consumption instead relies on low-, moderate-, and middle-income households already spending all their income thanks to large amounts of debt that is unresponsive to interest-rate signals. The last thing most of these families can afford is a new toaster that shows up in a still bigger credit-card bill, so most families make do as best they can. And, as Frances Perkins said, even the wealthiest households which can buy lots of toasters, usually don't want more than just one super-deluxe appliance.

Case in point: when Jeff Bezos's Beverly Hills estate set him back $165 million in 2020,[15] the median house price then was $265,900.[16] His one home thus gobbled up the equivalent of more than 620 American home purchases. Once, these homes were a fundamental engine of US economic growth due to the employment benefits of home construction and renovation combined with purchases of new furniture, garden equipment, and the like. When all this economic activity is instead concentrated in the hands of one man who already has more than anyone could dream of, all that's likely to be purchased is a replacement floating island for the on-estate water park.

Monetary policy has failed in part because the Fed failed to understand America as it bought, saved, and borrowed, not as old, representative-agent models predicted. Since 2008, the Fed has shoveled money to the richest Americans because it believes that the wealth effect created by high-flying markets combined with low-cost funding induces marginal propensity to consume (MPC). However, consumption in recent years has shifted from the top tiers of the economy to the bottom, with lower- and moderate-income households powering spending not to buy employment-promoting housing and durable goods, but instead to make day-to-day ends meet.

Worse, consumption isn't based on wages or savings, but on still more debt. The bottom 60 percent of US income earners accounted for most of the rise in spending from 2016 to 2018 despite their declining wealth – a break with the Fed's assumptions based on prior data, in which the top 40 percent of households did most of the spending.[17] Under stress, this trend is still more pronounced – when COVID hit in March 2020, the top earning quarter of US households were responsible for 50 percent of the sudden and sharp drop in consumer spending.[18] In contrast, low-income spending was down only 30 percent at the worst of the crisis and only 5 percent after government assistance for them kicked in. These percentages are striking, but they understate the economic impact of the sharp difference between high-versus-low income spending. Since rich people spend a lot more and support critical employment engines for low-income workers (e.g., restaurants and travel), loss of their spending has profound adverse macroeconomic effects wholly overlooked by the Fed's continuing adherence to old-school MPC assumptions.

Further, not only did most of the spending increases – i.e., the hard evidence of MPC – come from lower-income households, but this spending also depended not on wages and other income sources, but on debt. All of the Fed's monetary-policy thinking is premised on the view that ultra-low rates spur economic growth, but most low-cost debt isn't available to lower-income households and most middle-income households are already over their head in debt.

Table 7.1 shows that the middle class essentially doubled its debt-to-net-worth ratio between 1983 and 2016.[19] At the same time, the middle-class ratio of debt to income also rose sharply, as the table also shows. In contrast, the top 1 percent saw both of these ratios drop

Table 7.1   Where Households Keep Their Wealth 1983 vs. 2016

Composition of Household Wealth by Wealth Class, 1983 and 2016 (Percent of gross assets)					
Component	Top One Percent		Next 19 Percent		Middle 3 Quintiles	
	1983	2016	1983	2016	1983	2016
Principal residence	8.1	7.6	29.1	25.6	61.6	61.9
Liquid assets (bank deposits, money market funds, and cash surrender value of life insurance)	8.5	4.6	21.4	7.7	21.4	8.5
Pension accounts	0.9	6.0	2.0	22.4	1.2	16.6
Corporate stock, financial securities, mutual funds, and personal trusts	29.5	31.4	13.0	18.6	3.1	3.9
Unincorporated business equity other real estate	52.0	49.0	32.8	24.5	11.4	7.9
Miscellaneous assets	1.0	1.4	1.6	1.2	1.3	1.2
Total assets	100.0	100.0	100.0	100.0	100.0	100.0
Memo:						
Debt/net worth ratio	5.9	2.4	10.9	10.1	37.4	58.9
Debt/income ratio	86.8	35.0	72.8	88.9	66.9	120.4

Note: Author's computations from the 1983 and 2016 SCF.
Source: Edward N. Wolff, "Household Wealth Trends in the United States, 1962 to 2016: Has Middle Class Wealth Recovered?" *NBER Working Paper 24085*, 50 (November 2017), available at http://www.nber.org/papers/w24085.

by about half, as seen in the table. All of these figures show clearly that the Fed is pushing on a string trying to get the middle class to borrow when interest rates drop and funds from the Fed flow into the banking system. Worse still, even if its signals succeed in getting households with consumption capacity to consume, this debt-fueled consumption threatened the financial resilience of most families along with overall financial-market stability.

We saw this very clearly in the COVID crisis, but the Fed should have known better from a warning tremor in 2018. The federal government shutdown then deprived many federal workers of two paychecks, leaving them in arrears as soon as the first paycheck failed to arrive. At the time, this stunned economists – after all, the average full-time federal salary in 2018 was \$85,556,[20] making average-salaried workers denizens of the second highest US income quintile and many doing far better than that. Even so, 62 percent of furloughed employees reported[21] that they experienced significant financial hardship evidenced in struggles to pay rent, meet mortgage obligations, or make even minimum credit-card payments.

A sweeping survey of global literature on post-crisis policy confirms that monetary-policy effectiveness depends on understanding households. Once US households were well understood through representative-agent data because they were relatively equal. Now, as I have shown, they for sure are not. If income and wealth were more evenly distributed, then a broad middle class with an ability to consume and capacity to borrow safely would determine credit demand and send the Fed's rate signals effectively through the economy. Without a broad, financially secure middle class, Fed signals fizzle out.

The Fed's Real Mandate

The second fix for the Fed is a good look at the lawbook. Not only should the Fed have done better, it also could have done better. Questioned often about inequality by members of Congress and the public, Fed leadership always says that the central bank's hands are tied by law from doing more than hoping for the best.[22] Its congressional mandate permits, so the Fed says, only limited efforts to ensure employment and price stability. However, the Fed has fallen short on its mandate as it understands it as well as on the actual mandate as articulated in federal law.

Specifically, the Employment Act of 1946 reinforced by changes to the Federal Reserve Act in 1977[23] states, "The Board of Governors of the Federal Reserve System and the Federal Open Market Committee shall maintain long run growth of the monetary and credit aggregates commensurate with the economy's long run potential to increase production, so as to promote effectively the goals of maximum employment, stable prices, and moderate long-term interest rates." In short, the Fed has a triple mandate, not the dual one it cites, and the employment and price-stability planks are also set in law to mean employment and price stability for everyone, not just those the Fed chooses to count.

Analyses from the Federal Reserve Banks of Richmond,[24] St Louis,[25] and Kansas City[26] provide useful historical context for the statutory requirements that define what the Fed must do. Dating back to 1946, Congress declared:

> [I]t is the continuing policy and responsibility of the federal government to use all practicable means consistent with its needs and obligations and other essential considerations of national policy with the assistance and cooperation of industry, agriculture, labor, and state and local governments, to coordinate and utilize all its plans, functions, and resources for the purpose of creating and maintaining, in a manner calculated to foster and promote free competitive enterprise and the general welfare, conditions under which there will be afforded useful employment, for those able, willing, and seeking work, and to promote maximum employment, production, and purchasing power.[27]

The Full Employment and Balanced Growth Act – more widely known as the Humphrey-Hawkins Act of 1978[28] – also told the US central bank to ensure maximum employment and went on to demand "genuine full employment" and "real income."

Unsurprisingly given the Fed's focus on markets, these 1977 and 1978 laws were only expressly reflected in regular FOMC statements after September 2010. Each of the Reserve Bank studies noted above ponders the question of why the Fed waited so long to add maximum employment to its long-standing public prioritization of fighting inflation, but it may well have been due to the depth of the 2008 crisis, not to mention the acute political pressure on the central bank then to show that it was doing more than propping up big banks.

Although maximum employment and price stability are now a Fed mantra, moderate interest rates – another and equally binding statutory injunction – are still missing. In 2007, a Fed governor explained the complete disregard of this third mandate on grounds that neither maximum employment nor price stability is possible without moderate long-term interest rates.[29] That might well have been true before 2008. However, all the data demonstrate now that interest rates that are anything but "moderate" undermine "genuine" maximum employment, and subdue inflation to the point at which living returns suitable for meaningful wealth accumulation are out of reach.

Judged by its three statutory mandates, the Federal Reserve failed on every count from 2008 to 2020, with the period between 2008 and 2010 providing a breather due to the depth of that crisis not applicable thereafter nor an explanation of why, if the Fed met its mandate up to 2020, the economy fell apart so dramatically and destructively. Up to the COVID crisis, employment was anything but maximum because wages for low-, moderate-, and middle-class households were insufficient to make ends meet, many people worked part-time or several jobs, many families needed multiple wage earners, and more than a few Americans simply dropped out of the workforce in total frustration. After 2010, the Fed failed consistently to meet the 2 percent inflation threshold it considers price stability, flunking this criterion so decisively that even the Fed acknowledges that its post-crisis policy needed redesign.[30] And, of course, interest rates hovering at the zero lower bound or below it after taking even a small amount of inflation into account aren't "moderate."

The Fourth Mandate

The Fed has also failed its fourth mandate: ensuring financial stability and, if you doubt this, check out what happened in 2020. The Fed's express statutory authority defines its mandate as only maximum employment, price stability, and moderate interest rates. However, the Fed also has an array of other statutory duties, many derived from the Dodd-Frank Act,[31] also to ensure financial stability. As a result, the central bank often cites financial stability as part of its statutory charge.[32] As with the rest of its mandate, Fed adherence to this one is more evident in the wish than the deed.

The Fed seeks to execute its financial-stability mandate in two ways. The first is via all the additional powers detailed in Chapter 5. In general, this authority governs not just the holding companies that own insured depository institutions (mostly banks), but gives the Fed power also over the payment system, key parts of the US financial infrastructure, and – under certain circumstances – systemic nonbanks. The next chapter will address how all of these rules not only didn't make the

US financial system safe or sound enough to withstand stress before 2008 and again before 2020, but also how they combine with anti-equality monetary policy in destructive ways.

Suffice it here to say that monetary policy is the responsibility of one side of the Fed, regulatory standards come under another, and gigantic payment-system operations are still in another division. None of these fiefdoms talks much to the others and each is staffed by very different people (economists versus lawyers versus technologists), but all report up to only seven politically appointed people on the Fed's Board of Governors with varying professional backgrounds and expertise placed in a fractious relationship with the president and Congress. Even more confusingly, the twelve Reserve Banks within the Fed System are public-private entities with close ties to local business communities and a most uneasy relationship with the Board of Governors and its staff.

These decision-making silos compound with political pressure to create contradictions among all of the Fed's critical responsibilities, contradictions with unintended but nonetheless destructive equality consequences. Significant organizational restructuring would take a change of law, but organizational improvement is well within reach. Thus, the third easy fix for the Fed is to connect its views of financial stability with the reality resulting from monetary policy and the risks embedded in the payment system.

The Fed's Giant Faucet

The fourth fix is bigger: it requires the Fed to recognize all the problems detailed so far and reorient its financial-stability efforts from trickle-down to ground-up constructs.

The Fed's financial-stability powers also govern emergency liquidity. This was once accomplished solely through use of the "discount window," the liquidity window created for the banking system in concert with the establishment of the Federal Reserve System in 1913. The discount window provides banks with liquidity in two circumstances: the seasonal ones cited in the 1913 Act to smooth the flow of funds for banks that at the time often struggled to finance farmers in the spring without payment until the fall. The discount window over time also became an established emergency liquidity backstop in crises ranging from the savings-and-loan debacle of the 1980s to COVID.

The law intends the discount window to be a last resort – indeed, the Fed's function under this mandate is usually described as being the "lender of last resort" cited above. This fundamental principle comes straight from Walter Bagehot, the founder of modern central banking, stipulating then as now that central banks are to provide liquidity support but only to banks and then only to those banks that are very likely to pay it back.[33] Until the 1930s, operating the discount window was the Fed's principal task, with its mandate only broadened starting in the 1930s and then refined to address macroeconomic activity under the three mandates discussed above.

It was only in 2008 that the Fed used additional emergency-liquidity authority housed in Section 13(3) of the Federal Reserve Act.[34] In 2008, the Fed cobbled together rescues for a huge insurance company (AIG) under these powers and also created an array of windows to support the largest companies and most complex funding products in the US financial system. So appalled was Congress with this ratification of moral hazard that, in the 2010 Dodd-Frank Act, Congress thought it sharply rolled 13(3) back.[35] Restated in the 2020 COVID rescue law,[36] US law now allows the Fed to provide emergency-liquidity support only in a "broadly based" way, only in "unusual and exigent circumstances," at penalty rates, and only with the approval of the Secretary of the Treasury.

Despite the express language in 13(3) and the emphasis given to it in the 2020 restatement, the Fed's COVID windows came very close to the law's restrictions and may well have gone beyond them. For example, the Fed didn't just provide funding to lenders facing short-term liquidity strain in order to ensure ongoing credit capacity in the crisis. For the very first time it established a facility in which the Fed through a complex legal workaround actually directly made loans to large companies. Although the first version of this facility tried to limit access only to reasonably sound entities,[37] the Fed quickly relented and opened it to borrowers the market called "junk."[38] One observer noted at the time, "To put it bluntly, the Fed isn't allowed to do any of this."[39]

Each of the Fed's announcements for these facilities trumpeted their benefits for "households and business," but households and small businesses were ravaged by the end of April. Nevertheless, the S&P 500 index rose 12.7 percent in April, its best monthly performance since

1987.[40] No wonder. As these market rescues piled up, the Fed not only saved the market, but also became the market. When the crash came in March 2020, insured banks, savings associations, and credit unions had $20.2 trillion in assets.[41] Not only did the Fed in early April directly hold $6.6 trillion, but the indirect obligations and assets it planned to buy totaled another $4.5 trillion – virtually half the banking system in its entirety. Looked at another way, the Fed's portfolio was about half of US total economic output before the crash.[42] Following the money yet again, it's clear that trillions on offer from the Fed with only a few strings attached brought out big money looking for more from the US central bank. Although the facilities were meant only for entities *in extremis*, almost anyone could apply and pretty much everyone did. Many evaluated the funding on offer not in terms of whether it could be repaid, but whether a sufficient return could be achieved – one investor set its minimum at 40 percent.[43] Others were eager to borrow from the corporate-lending windows, but only if the Fed waived limits on their own executive compensation and on stock buybacks.[44] As it turned out, even awesomely profitable companies such as Apple – the largest in the US by market capitalization in June 2020 – saw their stock prices rise thanks principally to the Fed and the direct impact of its corporate-bond backstops.[45] Was Apple in "exigent" circumstances? At the time the Fed bolstered huge companies, it sat on one of the largest piles of corporate cash in US history.

It might have been wise for the Fed to skirt the law if its intervention supported shared prosperity. But, as a former Deputy Treasury Secretary and Fed governor put it, the Fed's huge backstops led to a "major transfer of wealth to holders of junk bonds and other risky asset classes"[46] From whom is this wealth taken? Two major investors who ought to know said that the Fed facilities will result in "an acceleration of two economywide transfers of wealth: from the middle class to the affluent and from the cautious to the reckless."[47]

Like so much else, this didn't have to happen. The Fed in March 2020 had ample authority to provide assistance from the ground up, providing credit to households and small businesses. In fact, I called for this at the time, laying out how a "Family Financial Facility" would work.[48] Suffice it here to say that the Family Financial Facility never came to pass. Markets roared; low- and moderate-income households whimpered.

Possible Solutions

Although the magnitude of Fed actions in 2020 is off the charts, those after 2008 came under critical scrutiny from all sides of the political spectrum. Few of these proposals had equality considerations at their heart because this book is the first to show how critical this is. Still, all are useful guides to how to proceed – or how not to.

Progressives prioritize economic equality, but none of their proposals acknowledges the inequality effects all too demonstrable from the Fed's own efforts at ultra-accommodative intervention. Before and throughout 2020, progressive Democrats and activists such as the "Fed Up" coalition[49] called for a huge portfolio and very, very low interest rates. The progressive option was based on beliefs that these will stimulate so much growth and employment that low- and moderate-income households would finally realize meaningful wage growth. However, all of the evidence suggests strongly that an even larger portfolio will make wealthy Americans even richer without generating any more lending for social-welfare gains or any more growth than the negligible results attributable to both QE and ultra-low rates. The Fed's post–COVID crisis efforts were also so huge that anything more would not only make financial markets still more bulletproof, but also spark acute risk of deflation. In deflation, prices drop because demand is so weak for goods and services that companies reduce their cost. This might seem to be good for lower-income households struggling to manage day-to-day consumption, but low prices also mean low or even no wages. For those without wealth, wages are of course essential.

Even without deflation, ultra-ultra-low rates will also put lower-income and younger households still farther behind when it comes to accumulating the nest eggs essential for family security through homeownership, educational opportunity, and secure retirement. Conversely, ultra-ultra-low rates also hurt older Americans. The pension crisis has its origins partly in the shortages of public wealth that lead employers, especially governmental ones, to underfund their pension plans. But even underfunded pensions have a hope of paying claims when interest rates are enough above the rate of inflation to ensure a meaningful return on investment. When they aren't – and they haven't been in at least a decade – secure retirements also go up in smoke.

Former Treasury Secretary Lawrence Summers took a more nuanced, but still strongly progressive, view of post-crisis Fed policy. Based on the construct of secular stagnation discussed in Chapter 6 – the idea that Fed policy was miring the US in ultra-low rates and slow growth – Mr. Summers urged the Fed to rethink its entire policy construct.[50] Considering why the Fed was so unwilling to change its fundamental construct no matter its deeply disappointing results, Mr. Summers concluded that it was because the Fed had "an excessive commitment to existing models and modes of thought."[51] Going on, he noted that it "usually takes disaster to shatter orthodoxy." Here, he was wrong – even in COVID's tornado, the Fed kept working from its 2008 playbook.

Is there a more equality-effective solution on the conservative side of the monetary-policy battlefield? "Hawks" such as former Treasury Undersecretary John Taylor[52] and former Fed Governor Kevin Warsh[53] take the flipside of the progressive proposal, urging the Fed to bring its portfolio back to pre-2008 minimums and to raise rates far more quickly. While progressives focus on the Fed's employment mandate, conservatives seek to ensure price stability. Inflation is the equality flipside of deflation. Inflation frightens those with wealth because the dollar you have today buys less tomorrow. Progressives like inflation, at least up to a point, because demand for goods stokes jobs for those who provide them, good times seem to be rolling, and these "hot" economies generate growth, at least until they fizzle. However, for investors looking to secure wealth today for yachts tomorrow, inflation may price them out of the market.

Given that nothing the Fed did seemed to work, other and more radical solutions were being widely discussed before the COVID crisis washed the blackboard clean. Building on a 2003 paper from Ben Bernanke while he was still a Fed governor, the UK's top financial regulator in 2013 posed this question: "How Do We Get Out of This Mess?"[54] In it, Adair Turner took up an idea to which Ben Bernanke returned in 2016 when no longer chairman: "helicopter money."[55] With this in the back of the toolkit, helicopter money is supposed to rain down in bushels so big that every corner of the financial markets gets dollars, even though, as it turned out in 2020, most Americans never felt a drop.

As Mr. Bernanke was quick to make clear, helicopter money flung about by central banks was first posited by Milton Friedman, who developed the idea based in part on the fact that the Federal Reserve essentially printed money to fund US expenditures during the Second World War. As we saw in the last chapter, printing money creates a shadow deficit in which public spending is accomplished without the pain of public taxation. Helicopter money – also known as overt money finance – thus crosses the political divide, with socialists such as Bernie Sanders also espousing it[56] to fund desired spending without controversial tax hikes. The 2019 progressive "Green New Deal" was also a program many believed might best be funded by the Fed,[57] and global central banks around the world worked on ways to get directly into green finance until 2020 diverted their attention.[58] Debates over helicopter money were made academic in 2020 when the Fed on its own authority and then as also directed by Congress printed money with the abandon Milton Friedman admired during the Second World War.

But, even if helicopter money is somehow better than QE, one first needs to ask several fundamental governance questions. First, would it work in the absence of a crisis as sweeping as World War II? Indeed, did it really work then given the sharp and sudden recession that gripped the US in 1946 until accommodative fiscal policy kicked in? And, even if helicopter money works, do we want unelected officials taking over a core constitutional duty – taxation – from members of Congress and the president?

Secure in the impregnable self-confidence that increasingly distinguishes central bankers, overt-money advocates such as Messrs. Bernanke and Turner are quick to add that helicopter money should only be dropped when a central bank – not its parent government – thinks best. Is this really better? Central banks are still the government, albeit government more remote from voters than elected officials. Their vaunted independence is intended to shield monetary policy from political influence. However, when monetary policy is used to determine winners and losers not across the economy as a whole – touchy enough – but instead by asset classes or even individual companies, political accountability is indispensable.

If helicopter money lands on financial markets – as the Fed believes it should – economic inequality will get still worse. If Congress directs the

Fed to fund progressive projects so it doesn't have to make controversial taxation demands, equality could get better for a while, but public wealth will shrink in the wake of the still larger deficit comprised of shortfalls on the federal government's own books and printed money substituting for tax revenues at the Fed. As we have seen, strong though the US dollar may be, it is not invincible.

Despite an enormous amount of central-bank, academic, and political commentary, only one authoritative approach to monetary policy taking inequality into account was proposed before the COVID crisis blew everything back to the drawingboard. It came from the Federal Reserve Bank of St. Louis in 2019,[59] proposing an "optimal" monetary policy based on a complex model with several uncertain assumptions, no conclusion about whether it would work in concert with a still-huge Fed portfolio, and nothing more than a theoretical hypothesis. But not only was the Federal Reserve Bank of St. Louis trying, but it also understood − as no one at the Fed then seemed to − that aggregate data don't represent America as it is. Complex and uncertain though its thinking is − and the paper readily acknowledges it's just a starting point for debate − its new approach relies on "heterogeneous data" − what Professor Sufi demanded and the facts support − not the representative-agent assumptions still powering Fed decision-making.

Slowing the Inequality Engine

In this chapter, I've laid out several straightforward and fast-acting equality improvements: better data that see America as it is to which the Fed actually pays heed; adherence to its four-pronged mandate as Congress directs, not as the Fed prefers; reorganization to ensure that equality figures in all key decisions; and recognition that financial stability depends on shared prosperity, not high-flying financial markets. This may well seem too little too late, and in some ways it is. But we need to start somewhere and each of these actions is straightforward and, one would think, noncontroversial.

More must come, of course. It's tempting to demand that the Fed immediately and dramatically reverse course. However, the Fed's control over the engine of inequality is so strong that simply destroying it risks sending the economy off a cliff. Each of the steps in this chapter ensures that the Fed reverses course institutionally so that monetary policy can do the same – first slowly and, over time, decisively.

Better analytics aren't the usual call of rabble-rousing reformers, but they will ensure the Fed knows what it's doing as well as give those of us without thousands of economists on our own staffs the data by which to judge both US financial policy and the extent of our economic inequality. Congress has already stipulated equality as the Fed's first and overarching mandate. Knowing this and then holding the central bank accountable will make a still more meaningful difference. Finally, monetary policy that puts the macroeconomy, not markets, first will powerfully reduce inequality by simultaneously slowing the now-inevitable rise in wealth inequality and at the same time giving low- and moderate-income workers a far better shot at the higher wages and remunerative savings essential for economic security.

This chapter shows how to pump the brakes. The next describe other accelerants in the engine and then lay out the way to put the brake down hard.

Chapter 8

Reckoning with Regulation

The recent financial crisis might have provided the occasion to develop a new economy, more attentive to ethical principles, and a new regulation of financial activities that would neutralize predatory and speculative tendencies and acknowledge the value of the actual economy. Although there have been many positive efforts at various levels which should be recognized and appreciated, there does not seem to be any inclination to rethink the obsolete criteria that continue to govern the world. On the contrary, the response seems at times like a return to the heights of myopic egoism, limited by an inadequate framework that, excluding the common good, also excludes from its horizons the concern to create and spread wealth, and to eliminate the inequality so pronounced today.

– The Vatican*

---

* Francis, "Oeconomicae et pecuniariae quaestiones" [Considerations for an ethical discernment regarding some aspects of the present economic-financial system], Vatican (May 17, 2018), sec. 5, available at http://press.vatican.va/content/salastampa/en/bollettino/pubblico/2018/05/17/180517a.html.

Myopic egotists? I shall leave it to the Pope to judge the souls of financial regulators. Although many I know are dedicated public servants, all the evidence in earlier chapters does lead one to conclude that, if not egotists, then some of those in charge are at least myopic. Unconcerned with the impact of financial policy on economic equality, US regulators concluded that the US financial system was resilient because all of the post-crisis rules made banks safer even as the post-crisis financial system increasingly dispensed with banks. As this chapter will demonstrate, this bank-centric policy not only exacerbated monetary policy's anti-equality impact, but also enabled "shadow banks" that came to dominate key consumer-finance markets and encouraged incursions into finance by giant technology companies. In 2020, the financial crash was worse than it had to be because so much of the US financial system was outside the reach of safety-and-soundness rules and so many households had more debt at higher cost than would have been the case if consumer-protection and prudential rules had been evenly applied across competing firms.

Tempting though it might be to trust theological edicts, we need instead to follow the money as it courses through financial regulation. Had US agencies done so, they would have seen as early as 2011 that asymmetric rules applicable only to banks were likely to reshape American finance in high-risk ways.[1] Had they then been on watch, they would have seen irrefutable signs of structural realignment and growing risk as early as 2014.[2] By 2020, unchecked risk exacerbated COVID's carnage because the US had a lowest-common-denominator financial system driven down by ultra-low rates and resulting high-risk yield chasing combined with high-cost prudential standards leading and even compelling banks to abandon traditional financial intermediation. Following the money as private firms must, banks became enablers of nonbank lenders, which could not raise funds as cheaply as banks but were empowered by the absence of regulation to make far more money than banks in the businesses banks once called their own.

If regulated banks disappeared because they no longer served what the Vatican calls the "common good," then that might not be fine for equality, but it would at least be the industry's just desserts. But when policy compels regulated banks to reconstruct their operations to support unregulated companies offering increasingly inequitable and risky products, then financial policy requires not just forgiveness, but also reform.

In this chapter, we will see how US finance went so wrong, why most American households were left behind even as they took on far more debt than most could afford, and how this toxic combination made the 2020 crisis far worse than it had to be. We will also see that equitable finance requires even-handed regulation – that is, the same financial services can and should come under the same rules so that profit is not earned solely by the ability to take the most risk at the greatest expense to vulnerable households and to the financial stability on which shared prosperity depends.

US law already demands equitable monetary policy, as we have seen. It turns out that it also gives US regulators the tools they need to craft financial rules for the common good. Using these powers, the fragility born of high-risk finance for lower-income families can be quickly remedied.

Consumer Finance Before the Crash

As we will see, consumer finance before 2020 was inequitably regulated, damaging to economic equality, and – worst of all – dangerous to lenders, borrowers, and the nation as a whole. By the first quarter of 2020, US households held $14.3 trillion in debt.[3] This was close to an all-time record after taking inflation into account, but it didn't worry the Federal Reserve. Its quarterly survey concluded that Americans could handle all this debt no matter the 14.7 percent unemployment rate at the time the study was released[4] because, so the Fed said, Americans had ample lines of credit.

However, this was yet another mistaken Fed conclusion resulting from reliance on aggregate data. Although by March 31, 2020, Americans had more than $3 trillion in lines of credit through their credit cards, those for upper-income households averaged $14,000, while the average for middle-class households was around $5,000 and for lower-income ones it was just $1,900.[5] Home equity lines of credit were held only by 3 percent of lower-income households, but upper-income families had credit backstops 11 times those of lower-income households.[6]

With the imperturbability that central bankers think behooves them, the Fed's analysis of American financial resilience as COVID struck concluded that debt-ridden households would do fine by taking on still more debt. This might have saved creditors from a reckoning, but it only put households with high debt burdens and low wages at increased risk; another Fed report found that, before COVID hit, 28 percent of US households either couldn't pay monthly bills or would fail to do so after just a $400 unexpected expense.[7]

All this debt resulted from a collision between economic inequality miring all but the wealthy in a day-to-day struggle to make ends meet and the transformation of the US financial system wrought by post-crisis monetary and regulatory policy. It doesn't take a meta-analysis of hundreds of studies to know that, where there is large demand and small supply, prices go up and product terms and conditions favor the provider, not the customer. With banks effectively barred from traditional consumer finance, money flooded into unregulated and sometimes even predatory consumer finance.[8]

This did not go unnoticed, but high-flying consumer lenders defended their offerings on grounds that they enhanced "financial inclusion." A seemingly innocuous – indeed, even indisputable – objective, any product that reached households not previously served by regulated banks received inclusion accolades. This echoed those the decade before for subprime mortgages, which lenders dignified with claims that high-risk loans "democratized" credit.[9] However, as we will see, much consumer finance outside the reach of safety-and-soundness and even of consumer-protection regulation is inclusive only in that it puts more struggling households at still greater financial risk. Products outside the reach of the rules may have seemed less costly to vulnerable consumers and thus indeed inclusive, but these low costs often came with complex terms and conditions that conveyed greater risk that less-educated households or those for whom English is not a first language were hard-pressed to discern. And even truly low-cost debt is still debt that must be repaid, at best reducing the odds of long-term wealth accumulation and at worst exposing households to the same debt shocks that set so many back so far in the 2008 crisis and showed again with formidable destructive power in March 2020.

The Fed comforted itself not only by all the credit lines that seemingly prevented default, but also because it thought that all this debt wasn't burdensome because most of it – aggregate data strikes again – was held by borrowers with high credit scores. Right before the COVID crash, the median credit score on newly originated mortgages was 773,[10] a level once reserved for very low risk borrowers on the widely adopted scoring scale running from 300 to 850.[11] Even so, when COVID hit, the government promptly allowed all borrowers with government loans to defer mortgage payments because so many of them were unlikely to be able to honor their obligations.

Are Debtors Just Deadbeats?

One remedy to all this debt might be to tell lower-income households to be less profligate, but it turns out that much of this debt was accrued in hopes of gaining economic opportunity, increasing wages, and making ends meet. Student loans were the nation's leading non-mortgage consumer debt, totaling $1.54 trillion as of the first quarter of 2020.[12] Before the 2020 cataclysm, millennials with student debt on average had student debt over 100 percent of their income, and lower-income student borrowers had student debt exceeding 372 percent of income.[13] Heading into an unprecedented threat to their economic survival, Americans in early 2020 also racked up $1.35 trillion in auto loans,[14] 22 percent of this in subprime, high-cost loans often for low-quality used cars.[15] These got Americans to and from work, but at a cost often so high as to threaten repayment even without a personal or broader economic downturn.

As we have seen, the "record" employment in which the Fed took such pride left low-, moderate-, and even middle-income workers behind. As a result, lower-income borrowers also relied on short-term, high-cost loans generally known as "payday" products. With 80 percent of payday loans carried over from one pay period to the next, these borrowers were literally robbing Peter (themselves) to pay Paul.[16]

Middle-class households may not have been desperate enough to get payday loans, but many still lived paycheck to paycheck due to wage stagnation and the high cost of consumption and debt. Even before COVID, middle-class households were in what they often call survival mode.[17]

Average household income for those with a high-school diploma grew 15 percent from 2008 to 2018, but overall consumption costs grew 20 percent over this period.[18] Key middle-class goods were up even more: house prices rose 26 percent, medical costs rose 33 percent, and college cost 45 percent more over just this same decade.[19]

Although debt growth has been highest for lower-income households, middle-class Americans have seen sharp increases in the growth of their debt-to-income ratios since 2010.[20] While debt held by those between the 50th and 90th income percentiles was mostly composed of loans on their homes, this debt is inaccessible for handling short-term or unexpected financial needs. Wealthy households can sell a bit of stock to raise cash, but taking a cash-out refinance loan is, as we have seen, challenging for all but the most affluent,[21] and home-equity lines of credit are hard to get without advance notice and, under stress, impossible to find.[22]

As a result, to handle household expenses, middle-class families increasingly used online installment loans – higher-cost debt offered at rates as high as 150 percent.[23] More affluent borrowers with maxed-out credit cards also turned to unsecured personal loans, a business that grew "like a weed" after 2015 largely powered by online nonbank finance companies.[24] Average balances on these loans were $16,250 in 2019,[25] with most borrowers in the "near-prime" category, indicating that they had previously had credit problems.

Are Banks to Blame?

Over this same period of time, US banks made fewer loans when measured in real, inflation-adjusted terms, demonstrating that banks changed their business model in the wake of post-crisis rules while risks ran unchecked.

Figure 8.1 shows the drop in inflation-adjusted bank lending once raw data – i.e., total annual dollar amounts of loans – are adjusted for underlying private-sector GDP. Using FDIC data, the chart breaks out loans by all FDIC-insured institutions as a percentage of private-sector GDP. It shows that pre-COVID loan levels are well below what they were between 2005 and 2010 – i.e., before the post-crisis rules kicked in. GDP is indeed not a good indicator of equitable growth, but it's also a

Figure 8.1   Bank Lending Remains Below Pre-Crisis Levels

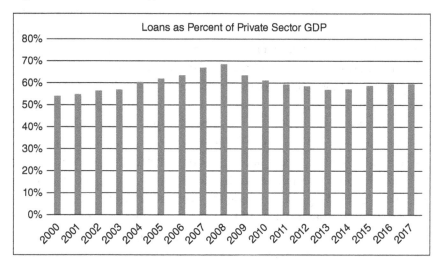

Source: Data from FDIC Quarterly Banking Profile & Bureau of Economic Analysis, National Data, Gross-Domestic Product.

standard one and here works well to assess whether lending in aggregate terms kept up with the size of the private sector. Lending by banks is for economic activity by households and private-sector institutions, while government-spurred GDP comes courtesy of the US taxpayer. While the goods (e.g., aircraft carriers) on which it is spent may spur growth, this is not a market that relies on private lending. Judging lending by total GDP is thus misleading.

Another way to look at this question shows that, had lending proceeded at its usual rate between 2000 and 2008 after the sharp break in the financial crisis, loans in 2017 would have been more than $12 trillion,[26] instead of $9.7 trillion[27] – a 19 percent difference. Extrapolating this methodology to 2019 shows that on-trend lending would have been about $13 trillion at year-end, but actual bank lending was only $10.5 trillion[28] – again, 19 percent less.

Where did all the loans go? Data[29] show that in the decade after 2008 there was a virtually perfect swap on bank balance sheets between lending and the excess reserves banks held at the Fed. Starting in 2019, banks began to turn excess reserves into Treasury investments due to market factors such as the deluge of new US government securities needed to fund the Trump tax cuts and changes in the Fed's balance sheet. However, lending remained suppressed – banks played the market instead of making equality-focused loans. Where loans were made, they often went to large corporations, not households or small businesses – commercial-and-industrial lending in 2019 was 21 percent of total bank loans.[30] Before COVID, loans also went to the wealthy – wealth- and asset-management businesses catering to high-net-worth households were a bright spot in big-bank earnings as the business adjusted to all the new rules.[31] Indeed, big banks increasingly focused only on big money because of the big profits it engenders; for example, banking for the wealthy is about twice as profitable at JPMorgan as banking for everyone else.[32]

In 2014, 22 percent of Wells Fargo's loans with disclosed credit scores were to high-risk consumers and low-risk consumers were 15 percent of the bank's consumer loans; at year-end 2019, the high-risk exposure was halved while that for the lowest-risk consumers – most often higher-wealth ones – more than tripled.[33] Another bank said of its business at the end of 2019 that it is focused on "prime and super-prime" consumers.[34] The COVID crisis exacerbated all this inequality, with "banking for billionaires" proving a very bright spot even at the worst of the crisis.[35]

The Businesses Banks Left Behind

In March 2020, bank regulators realized the harm done to vulnerable households by denying banks the ability to offer responsible small-dollar loans,[36] but by then it was too late and, even then, the capital costs of making these loans remained prohibitive. The banking agencies rushed to "neutralize" capital costs for loans to money-market funds and other giant entities,[37] but they cut no break for lower-income households that could have traded in a bit of high-cost debt for more advantageous offerings from the regulated sector.

No equality-essential sector shows the transition from regulated to unregulated finance as clearly as residential mortgages. Punishing banks for the excesses before 2008, post-crisis rules imposed numerous capital and other safety-and-soundness restrictions even as government agencies increased what was known as "put-back risk" – that is, the risk that a mortgage originator would be forced to take back loans that violated the express strictures of a secondary-market agency's underwriting standards. These changes combined with post-crisis rules to make it unprofitable for banks to originate or service lower-balance mortgages.

Nonbanks had little to fear because they were exempt from capital rules and had little at risk if loans were put back to them in large volumes but their ability to make money going forward. Without capital or other assets, many nonbanks had few reserves with which to buffer the cost of dud loans and most liked it that way because of all the market share they gained with lower-cost offerings. In 2009, banks originated 90 percent and serviced 94 percent of US residential mortgages; by 2019, this was down to 49 percent and 53 percent.[38] This might sound like a healthy share, but the business was transformed by post-crisis rules. Banks generally originated and serviced loans for themselves – keeping the highest-dollar amount, "jumbo" loans that could not be sold to the government. But where the government was most important and least demanding – loans for Ginnie Mae – nonbanks reigned. In 2013, they had less than 40 percent of this sector; by 2019, it was 85 percent.[39]

By the end of 2019, the US Financial Stability Oversight Council (FSOC) came to fear that unregulated nonbanks would pose systemic risk,[40] and so they did in March 2020. Without capital and liquidity reserves, the nonbank mortgage servicers on which the $11 trillion[41] US residential-mortgage system increasingly depended were so desperate that they begged for a federal emergency rescue facility.[42]

Other Precursors of the Crash That Came

As the decade drew to a close before the COVID cataclysm, US retail finance became an increasingly high-risk sector in which nonbanks came to replace banks for all but the safest financial services regulators allowed.

At the same time, the landscape changed in wholesale finance – i.e., that for high-wealth households, other financial institutions, and large corporations – and again banks did not sit idly by as their rules realigned strategic realities. Instead of directly taking risk, banks used their vast networks to identify it, package it, and then pass it along for a sizeable fee.

A case in point is leveraged loans – loans considerably bigger than a company's annual corporate earnings are likely to support. Given the risks involved, federal banking agencies discouraged their charges from making leveraged loans starting in 2013.[43] Although these rules were relaxed after the Trump administration took over,[44] the market had changed and banks were still enablers, not direct risk-takers. Right before the COVID crash, leveraged lending stood at a record $1.2 trillion, most of it made by nonbank "private lenders."

The Fed worried anew about all these loans in the last financial-stability report released before the crash,[45] noting also that banks often organized these loans and enabled high-risk lending without running afoul of post-crisis rules. But, just as consumer loans facilitated by banks created systemic risk even if banks didn't end up holding the loans, so it was that leveraged lending enabled by banks proved risky even though banks weren't at immediate risk. By March 2020, the Fed was bailing out this sector because, while banks were safe, everyone else in it was at grave risk. Along with the Fed, many leveraged lenders knew the risk they took, but few stopped because most expected ongoing profitability thanks yet again to the Fed's sure and certain market support. This they got to the tune of a $750 billion open Fed window[46] reaffirming not only that safe banks don't mean safe markets but also that unsafe markets have a very important friend at the Fed.

Leveraged lending was not the only high-risk sector in which banks played a peripheral – if profitable – role after 2008. Many other forms of higher-risk lending – e.g., for commercial real estate and lower-quality corporate debt – also moved outside the banking system into money market and other investment funds. Loans often started on bank balance sheets but didn't stay there long, moving quickly into the portfolios of higher-income households and institutional investors such as pension funds and insurance companies (the latter also becoming a major lending force in their own right at great concern to global regulators powerless to stop it).[47]

Trillions thus moved out of banks into the investment market without the capital or liquidity needed for resilience under stress. The Fed in 2013 pressed for tough rules in this sector, but investment funds beat this back with a far less stringent standard from the Securities and Exchange

Commission.[48] Risks thus ran rampant until 2020, when the Fed was so frightened by all the systemic risk outside the banking sector that another liquidity facility – this one unlimited – opened for the investment-fund sector.[49]

Even before COVID, cracks were evident in the Fed's bank-centric construct of financial stability and the Fed's willingness to bail out high-risk markets was on full display. Before 2008, very large banks were the mainstays of the repurchase – i.e., the "repo" market – in which much of the world's wholesale financial-market infrastructure once ran. However, the cost of post-crisis rules led some large banks to abandon key segments of this sector[50] and others to cut way back. As banks pulled out, nonbanks became far larger repo-market forces,[51] reducing resilience without risk – at least to them – because the Fed rescued the repo market in September 2019 and every week thereafter until July 2020 even though the Fed kept hoping markets would somehow stabilize. Perched on this precipice in March 2020, risks in the repo and related markets became so acute that the Fed provided still more support, adding almost $2 trillion to its portfolio in just three weeks.

Capitalism and Capital Regulation

One might well ask why banks did not make responsible, competitive consumer loans before 2020, precluding higher-risk lenders from offering high-cost, unsustainable debt and saving their business model. One might also ask why banks stepped back from core wholesale financial markets that came to depend on nonbanks no matter the peril and lost profitability. If there's a market, there ought to have been a way. But there wasn't.

A critical tenet of post-2008 financial regulation – capital standards – made banks much safer than nonbanks, but also drove up the cost of making loans or even just holding risk-free securities to uncompetitive levels that opened the way for higher-risk finance by nonbanks. In 2020, this higher-risk finance exposed not just households to crippling debt burdens, but also the financial system to a round of Fed rescues and taxpayer bailouts that made 2008 look cheap. Although banks also came under stress, they served as critical financial-market and macroeconomic stabilizers at the height of the crisis. From mid-March through early April, US banks absorbed $761 billion in deposits that flooded in from investors fleeing high-risk holdings[52] and made $539 billion in new loans.[53] Banks were also the focal point of critical rescues such as the Paycheck Protection Program for small businesses. These too could have gone better, but they would not have gone at all had banks lacked the resilience and operational capacity to act as the federal government's financial infrastructure in the midst of this unprecedented storm.

Banks would likely have been no more resilient than nonbanks were it not for all the regulatory reforms mandated after 2008. The most important and costly set bank regulatory-capital requirements, doing this the most for the very biggest banks. As one might infer from the entire construct of capitalism, "capital" lies at the heart of a business enterprise. Capital comes from the hard cash that buys you "equity" in a company – that is, your ownership stake. Capital substitutes for debt; if you didn't invest in the company, then its management would need to raise cash from depositors, lenders, or other funding sources to support operations. Deposits are a critical funding source for banks, but they are ultimately your money – that is, a liability on the bank's balance sheet. Capital is the cash investors put up to own shares in a bank that back the loans and other assets on the other side of the ledger.

Debt and capital are indistinguishable as funding sources, but very, very different in terms of safety and soundness. The more capital a company has in terms of shareholder interests, the more diluted its ownership structure – that is, lots of investors must share rewards versus tightly owned companies in which just a few founders or lucky investors own the lot. Because investors are at first risk when a company fails, equity capital as a funding source is almost always more expensive than debt, especially when the debt comes from FDIC-insured deposits that encourage people to give banks their money at low cost thanks to a full-faith-and-credit taxpayer guarantee. Debt is also cheaper than equity because a borrowing company can deduct its interest payments against earnings because the interest paid to lenders is considered an ordinary business expense. There have been many calls to reform the debt preference to encourage greater reliance on equity investment,[54] but none has ever been enacted in the US.

All solvent businesses have at least some capital, but regulated companies have to have a lot of capital because law and rule demand it. Capital works like this:

> A company with $100 of risk and $20 of shareholder equity backing it is leveraged 5:1; a company with $1 against $100 is of course a 100:1 bet that nothing goes wrong. For as long as things go well, the 100:1 shareholder is a very happy shareholder because his or her investment earns a proportionately higher return compared to the shareholder in the lower risk 5:1 company. When investors think a big bet can't go bad – i.e., when there's "moral hazard" – they are far more likely to go for the highly leveraged firm than the conservative one.

In the wake of the 2008 crisis, US regulators understandably believed that lots of capital would forestall lots of risk. They thus compensated for lax pre-crisis rules with a dizzying array of regulatory-capital standards – 39 separate ones when the full framework was finally put in place in 2018.[55] Although market demands for capital backstops just look to see who has how much money backing how much risk, bank capital requirements are nuanced under all these rules in an effort to set standards based on how much risk a particular loan is likely to present, how much risk a bank's assets as a whole are likely to present without specific regard to each asset's risk (the leverage ratio), and how each of these standards is likely to fare under varying stress scenarios. We will see in Chapter 10 that these rules misjudge the risks presented by LMI borrowers; first, it's critical to understand how capital regulation works and thus how it defines the respective roles of banks versus nonbanks in the same line of business taking the same risks.

Although US banks recognized the need for capital repair after the costly learning experience of the 2008 crisis, they complained bitterly about the cost of these capital rules and the impact they had on the ability of banks to hold their own against aggressive nonbanks immune from comparable or even often any capital requirements. By 2020, Congress and the Trump administration began to dismantle it. Its appointees at the Federal Reserve, Office of the Comptroller of the Currency (OCC), and FDIC recrafted big-bank rules into a set of "tailored" capital rules[56] that then factored into a combined capital and stress-test regulation to create an extraordinarily complex construct called a "stress capital buffer."[57] This was finalized on March 4, 2020; by March 23, the agencies were dismantling it to ensure that banks could support troubled financial institutions and the Fed's facilities bailing them out.

Even though Trump appointees loosened post-crisis rules, they joined their Obama-era colleagues in dismissing the adverse impact of capital rules on economic inequality – indeed, I can find no statement from any senior official even contemplating this concern, let alone attempting to address it. However, the moment stress struck, the agencies apparently had an epiphany about the impact of capital rules on bank lending. Capital "neutralization" waived key rules for any exposure suddenly deemed essential. Global regulators joined the US on this seesaw – first, there were tough, inequitable, and asymmetric capital rules undermining family and financial system resilience. Then, in a crisis, there was a rush to "neutralize" these rules and, where they remained, encourage banks to use and indeed go through buffers initially built to ensure that banks had sufficient capital to withstand stress.

Despite these changes, banks remained acutely aware of the need to conserve capital against looming risks even as they came under intense investor pressure to continue to pay dividends. As a result, banks sharply cut back lending for all but their largest and wealthiest customers and others backed by all the new Fed and Treasury facilities. Many banks immediately stopped making mortgages other than for the government-guaranteed backed secondary markets or for high-wealth customers[58] and credit card lines were pulled back on most consumer cards[59] while prime cards added new benefits to substitute for the travel-and-leisure ones wealthy customers no longer craved under COVID's lockdown.[60]

This boom–bust construct is called *procyclicality*. It means that financial institutions make more loans at low rates related to risk (i.e., the risk premium) at the height of the business cycle – a boom – and then so rapidly retrench to repair their balance sheets that they cannot support credit creation in a recession, prolonging economic hardship and often making it even worse. Bank capital rules exacerbate procyclicality because regulatory risk-based capital models vary based on loss experience, meaning that banks that have experienced large losses in a downturn have to hold high amounts of capital on loans that might well be less risky as the economy begins to recover; conversely, loans at the height of a boom look low-risk until they aren't, when the bank takes big losses that make recovery even more difficult. Risk premiums also go upside down – too low in the boom, they should instead be low during a recovery but are often very high not because of actual risk, but instead because losses during a crash lead banks to set rates as high as possible to restore profitability as quickly as they can. Higher capital heading into a downturn not only ensures ongoing credit availability, but also gives banks the wherewithal to price new loans at the affordable rates essential to recovery.

The 2008 crisis taught bank regulators a hard lesson about procyclicality and they thus built a "countercyclical capital buffer" (CCyB) into post-crisis rules. The Fed finalized the US version of the CCyB, but never deployed it and thus gave banks no comfort zone under acute stress. Even worse, the US CCyB applied only to the very largest banks, meaning that all but eight banks were not subject to any kind of countercyclical cushion and nonbanks across the land were at still more risk.

A Capital Cure

What if bank regulators understood procyclicality in more than theory and retargeted capital rules before economic inequality put so many families and so much of the US financial system in harm's way? We'll never know, but we do know that research well ahead of 2020 made it clear that the post-2008 capital construct was structurally flawed and, in many ways, an accident waiting to happen.

In 2017, one influential study concluded that it was very difficult to tell which of all the post-crisis capital requirements set the "optimal" level or is in practice likely to be an individual company's binding constraint.[61] Researchers at the Bank for International Settlements also looked at a raft of studies on post-crisis regulation.[62] They reached high-level conclusions suggesting that more bank capital had minimal impact on credit supply and some adverse impact on cost, but data across many countries and over time were, they also said, inconclusive. Nothing in this sweeping database went on to see what actually happened to economic equality or other policy-critical factors. However, another meta-analysis of academic research up to 2016 on post-crisis capital regulation found that "there are opportunity costs in terms of reduced lending and economic activity as bank capital requirements rise."[63] This global survey also found that each additional percentage point of regulatory capital forces banks to reduce lending by 1.4 to 3.5 percent over time.

Industry research may be self-interested, but it confirmed these high-level conclusions for the financial products most essential to economic equality. One key study plotted the differences in lending by large and small banks and found that residential mortgage, credit card, and small-business lending is sharply lower at large banks, likely due to the different and more binding rules applied by the stress tests and other aspects of big-bank capital rules.[64] Because the large banks in this study accounted for about 70 percent of US loans made by banks, the difference between the largest banks under the toughest rules and small banks not only tells us a lot about regulatory impact, but also the effect on the loans most critical to LMI households. It's worth noting that big-bank stress tests failed to constrain record-breaking high-risk corporate lending,[65] even as banks were pushed out of critical consumer finance, ceding territory to unregulated nonbanks and all the risks – none stressed by the Fed's models – created for vulnerable households and the financial system.

Going with the Flow

Sweeping though they are, the capital rules were not the only standards that constrained US banks in the wake of the great financial crisis. Almost matching the capital requirements for their strategic and inequality impact were rules designed to ensure that banks always have funds on hand with which to honor their obligations. These liquidity rules may seem even more technical and irrelevant to economic equality than the capital standards, but in concert with them and post-crisis monetary policy, they redefined the ability of large banks to take the deposits and make the loans that accelerate income growth and wealth accumulation.

As a thorough report on liquidity regulation by global regulators made clear,[66] the liquidity rules encourage banks to hold unsecured (i.e., riskier) assets that alter the types of loans banks are likely to make as well as increasing their risk. Thus, while the liquidity rules in theory favor household deposits over other funding sources, in practice the rules reduce interest rates on household transaction accounts and reduce bank willingness to make long-term, low-cost loans to higher-risk consumers and small businesses.

In addition, the rules create strong incentives for banks to alter their balance sheets to favor holding excess reserves over making consumer loans. The nation's largest bank, JPMorgan, in fact did just that.[67] The asymmetric rules governing nonbanks versus bank liquidity rules also created incentives for banks to provide nonbanks with large lines of credit, with these exposures actually doubling from 2013 to 2019.[68] As of early 2019, lines of credit to nonbanks totaled over $1.4 trillion, an amount a Fed study at the time said could pose systemic risk if all were drawn down at the same time.[69] This they were in 2020 and so it was. Banks handled the stress, but the Fed still had to create billion-dollar backstop facilities to make sure the markets held.

And just as the capital rules spawned shadow banks, so too did the liquidity rules beget "shadow liabilities." Examples are non-deposit, short-term liabilities such as money market investments, commercial paper, and repos. Obscure though many of these shadow liabilities are to most of us, they aren't insignificant – many of the Fed's multi-trillion-dollar rescue facilities were expressly aimed at bailing them out in 2020 to avoid a financial-system meltdown. Shadow liabilities exacerbate the procyclicality built into post-crisis capital regulation.[70] Much research has focused on the ability of the very largest US banks to engage in activities like repurchase agreements that support market liquidity, anticipating the repo-market crash that so stunned the Fed in September 2019. However, this work also predicted that cash-equivalent instruments such as money-market funds (MMFs) would respond to bank rules by becoming major alternatives to traditional bank deposits. Investments gathered for MMFs and mutual funds do not offer protection against loss of principal, despite the fixed net-asset values (NAVs) associated with many funds. These funds may also not support transaction and payment processing in an equivalent fashion to bank deposits, creating barriers to investor liquidity and market function. To the extent they intermediate funds provided by their investors – i.e., by holding these investments in funds comprised largely of corporate loans – they also contributed to acute pre-COVID risk buildups that, as we have seen, forced the Fed to bail them out with hundreds of billions of dollars.

Death without Destruction

The third major plank of post-2008 reform is a set of rules demanding that banks lay in enough capital and liquidity ahead of time to ensure that, under acute stress, failure comes only at cost to shareholders and, if necessary, to risk-taking debt holders, not also to insured depositors, taxpayers, the financial system, or even the economy writ large. Although the Dodd-Frank Act devoted an entire title to creating an orderly liquidation authority (OLA) to ensure that banks and even systemic nonbanks could be resolved without moral hazard,[71] the US by 2020 had only a partial OLA rulebook and no clear indication that the FDIC – charged by law with implementing OLA – had a plan ready to go for systemic-scale financial risk. Although banks were required to write complex resolution plans to limit the odds of bailout, Trump administration rules rolled some of these back[72] and nonbanks have never been forced to reckon with their own demise.

I wrote as early as 2012 that the best way to ensure sound finance without unequal result is to ensure that large financial institutions and – more importantly – their investors take risks only with sure and certain knowledge that wanton risk-taking leads to institutional failure and personal financial loss.[73] We'll never know if finance after 2008 could have been made strong enough to withstand the COVID crash because only banks were prepared for failure. However, the odds are high that removing moral hazard would have had salutary benefit for the financial system because banks held firm even as nonbanks across the spectrum of shadow asset and liability portfolios sought and generally received trillion-dollar Fed rescues.

In 2020, those betting on moral hazard were right – investors really could put trillions into high-flying nonbanks that put vulnerable households at risk without loss to themselves. Going forward, they should know this is a wrongheaded bet and, if they still expect Fed rescue, then they should be proved still more wrong. In the last chapter, I described how Fed facilities can and should support vulnerable households and truly small businesses under acute stress none could have seen coming; later on, I'll lay out how to do so in detail. Here, suffice it to say that equality-enhancing financial regulation must be paired with household-focused monetary policy so that rescues go only to the unprotected, not to the lenders that put them at so much risk.

The Consumer-Protection Quagmire

In the wake of the 2008 subprime-mortgage debacle, the Dodd-Frank Act also created the federal Bureau of Consumer Financial Protection (CFPB).[74] It sets standards in many, but not all, areas of consumer finance, but directly governs only financial institutions with assets over $10 billion. Somehow, Congress thought it made sense to exempt smaller (but still quite large) consumer-finance firms on grounds of undue burden even though – as the debt numbers above make painfully clear – small lenders outside the scope of appropriate regulation can do a lot of harm to a lot of people. Further, the law left much nonbank regulation – or the lack of it – to the states and, conversely, retained much in prior law regarding the authority of the OCC, FRB, and FDIC to write rules and examine banks for compliance with consumer-protection rules if it could be said that any of them affected bank safety and soundness.

With this authority, the banking agencies after 2010 used their consumer-protection power not to safeguard consumers falling through the CFPB's cracks, but to bar banks from serving LMI households. With the subprime crisis lodged in their minds, bank regulators thought that all LMI households were by definition high-risk households. It was for this reason that the OCC barred national banks from making small-dollar, short-term loans,[75] creating a vacuum in which far less scrupulous, state-regulated payday lenders offered vulnerable household loans with interest rates averaging almost 400 percent and as high as 667 percent judged on an annual basis.

As we've seen, the safety and soundness rules governing US financial institutions are asymmetric – that is, critical capital, liquidity, and resolution rules only cover banks even though nonbanks are major players across the entire retail and wholesale financial market. But if prudential rules are asymmetric, then those for consumer protection are downright askew. Although CFPB rules often appear to apply equally to banks and nonbanks, in practice they don't because in reality there is no established supervisory mechanism for many nonbank financial companies and almost all of them fall under state – not federal – rules that permit far greater latitude than federal standards. The CFPB can and indeed does impose fines on wayward nonbanks, but its enforcement regime during the Trump administration was forgiving and, in any case, its reach is very limited. As we have seen, nonbanks took over much of US mortgage finance in part due to their regulatory-capital advantage, but another reason for this transformation lay in consumer-protection regulation. Although this nominally applied in the same way to large bank and nonbank mortgage originators, nonbanks discounted consumer-protection worries even as banks changed their business model to focus far more on large loans to wealthy consumers on which attention to detail could be cost-effectively provided.

The case of just one rule illustrates how directly – if unintentionally – the post-crisis rulebook has changed consumer finance. The Dodd-Frank Act includes "the Durbin Amendment."[76] Aimed at protecting consumers from high debit card fees, it limits the fees banks may charge on the "interchanges" associated with debit cards. Together with a 2009 law limiting credit card fees,[77] large banks saw significant drops in non-interest income (i.e., fees as this law came into effect). Consumers may or may not have saved some money on these transactions, but reduced fee income hits banks very hard.[78]

Showing again the power of financial reality over regulatory theory, banks continued to handle debit card and credit card transactions at reduced return, but sharply curtailed free checking accounts for low-balance customers to make up the difference. A Federal Reserve study in fact found that only about half the free accounts expected at banks were offered due to cutbacks directly attributable to the Durbin Amendment; even when free checking accounts were still available, minimum balances to get them went up at least 50 percent.[79] Wealthier households usually have more than enough money to worry about checking account fees. It's lower-income households with lower balances that pay these costs, which combine with ultra-low interest rates to make it even harder to earn a real return on hard-earned savings.

Another quixotic consequence is found in a Fed study of debt-collection constraints.[80] These are meant to protect vulnerable households from unscrupulous debt collectors, but it turns out that nonbank lenders continue to make loans to high-risk borrowers even when it may be harder to repair delinquencies or collect after a consumer stops paying back the loan. Even more intriguingly, these debt-collection practices appear to put vulnerable households at risk of even worse financial results because they are able to take out all the debt on offer from high-risk, often nonbank lenders with less fear of ever having to pay it back – i.e., the borrower has moral hazard because more debt does not mean more repayment. This of course works only for a limited amount of time, after which the Fed study found growth in the number of households with unsustainable debt.

An Unreadable Rulebook Thrown Only at Banks

Although longer than I would like, the discussion above of post-crisis regulation is extremely abridged. Many of the rules I've mentioned go on for hundreds of pages and the responses required of banks often go on for thousands and, for resolution plans, even tens of thousands. The only certain conclusions one can reach about all of these post-2008 rules is first that they were so complex that no one ever knew if they worked, second that they didn't work given the disaster of 2020, and third that all of these rules were written by and for regulators, not with an eye to how regulated institutions really work nor how their customers were then put at risk.

Although the US banking agencies stoutly resisted calls from Congress to judge the sum total impact of all of these rules,[81] an assessment of all of the post-crisis US rules demonstrated that this complexity created mispricing risk because regulatory models – not markets or a firm's acumen – set prices.[82] This means that complex rules on their own and taken together forced so much attention to detail that big-picture risks were often neglected.

Complexity also exacerbated arbitrage opportunities through "regulatory loopholes."[83] These ambiguities create competitive advantage derived solely from finding small details omitted from or mistaken in the body of the rules.

Rules as huge as all of those discussed above and fraught with contradictions within and among them were ripe for loophole-finding lawyers and the financial institutions that profit thereby. No one is evading the rules if these loopholes genuinely exist; the problem with a rule-driven financial system is that, when it does not comport with financial-market and profit reality, regulated companies will find a way both to comply and to thrive while unregulated companies will take over the markets left behind.

Even if the post-2008 framework has been right in terms of its models, data, and risk reduction, was it right in terms of structural and equality implications? The data I've provided on an indebted nation unable to withstand even a week or two of stress show empirically that post-2008 rules had profoundly unequal – if wholly unintended – consequences. There is no body of research to inform us on this critical question because post-crisis assessments were model-based and models mostly do not reflect the real-world effect of unequal economies and bank behavior in the face of short-term business and regulatory pressures. A 2019 global-study creating a repository of research on post-crisis rules highlights this problem, concluding that there was simply too little supervisory data to judge whether capital rules made banks safer without doing equality damage given the unknown interplay between post-crisis rules and other market factors.[84]

The Bleak Outlook and a Better Future

Despite the lack of studies, the sharp rise in economic inequality leading to 2020 and the devastation this did under COVID's attack demonstrate clearly that the sum total impact of all of the rules described above, the asymmetric way in which they were applied, and the incentives that dictate financial-industry behavior created an unequal and highly vulnerable financial system. As we have seen, household debt right before COVID struck was at near-record levels and huge volumes of high-risk leveraged and higher-risk corporate loans flooded the financial system.

The cost of all these rules also led banks to abandon smaller and rural markets to serve the wealthiest citizens in the nation's biggest cities. As the *Wall Street Journal* observed, "Big banks have boosted profits in recent years by focusing on the largest US cities, which are densely populated and more affluent [than exurban or rural areas]."[85] This same article notes that more than one-third of rural counties now have no locally owned bank, largely due to the disappearance of over 11,000 small community banks – those with $1 billion or less in assets.[86] A Fed study[87] looking at these "banking deserts" found that banks offered preferential services to vulnerable households compared to digital-delivery (i.e., fintech) options. Small businesses were also hard hit since the Fed survey found that they prefer dealing with a physical branch rather than their phone. Epitomizing the high-risk credit problem from nonbank options, this study also found that small businesses with weaker credit used online nonbank lenders even though borrowers complained about deceptive and costly credit terms.

All of the rules described above would have changed the bank business model after they came into full effect around 2015, but the intersection of costly, asymmetric regulation combined with ultra-low rates to transform the industry. All lenders make money from the fees earned by selling loans on to the government or other purchasers and from the difference between their cost of funds and the rates they are able to charge on deposits, with profits resulting when this margin is wide enough to absorb additional business costs. This margin factors into the critical "return on asset" calculation that determines which loans are profitable and which are not. When a company is regulated, its costs include not just those due to its funding and operations – similar to those incurred by nonbanks – but also the cost of all of the rules described above. These are of course asymmetric costs, which mean that banks have to charge a higher rate of interest on loans to obtain returns sufficient to satisfy demanding investors. When rates were high, banks could make these margins work at least in some sectors for some borrowers. With ultra-low rates, high capital costs, and the operational burden associated with all the obligations of regulated firms, margins are too thin on equality-essential finance and banks leave the field wide open for unregulated providers who, as we have seen, flooded consumers with debt few could afford under even a bit of stress, let alone what befell them when the pandemic struck in 2020.

In the next chapter, we will see that the basic business of banking isn't the only one fleeing to nonbanks due to the confluence of new rules and anti-equality monetary policy. The very nature of money is being redefined, along with the basic business of banking. This transformation is profound and will prove irreversible if not quickly challenged by a new construct of like-kind rules for like-kind financial companies backed by new incentives for equality-essential finance. As we will see, nothing is stopping US policy-makers from creating a new regulatory construct that enhances safety, equality, and competitive equity. All it takes to change is the will to act.

Chapter 9

Remaking Money

"Papa! What's money?" ...

Mr. Dombey was in a difficulty. He would have liked to give him some explanation involving the terms circulating medium, currency, depreciation of currency, paper, bullion, rates of exchange, value of precious metals in the market, and so forth; but looking down at the little chair, and seeing what a long way down it was, he answered: "Gold, and silver, and copper. Guineas, shillings, halfpence. You know what they are?"

"Oh yes, I know what they are!" said Paul. "I don't mean that, Papa. I mean what's money after all?... I mean, Papa, what can it do?" returned Paul, folding his arms....

Mr. Dombey drew his chair back to its former place, and patted him on the head. "You'll know better by-and-by, my man," he said. "Money, Paul, can do anything."

— *Charles Dickens, Dombey and Son**

---

* Charles Dickens, *Dombey and Son* (New York: John Wiley, 1848), 103–104.

Mr. Dombey was a proud, wealthy merchant ultimately undone not because he misunderstood money's power, but because he failed to see that money's true worth is found only when money is shared. He is not the only one to make this costly mistake. The Fed's longstanding preference for saving markets, not households and small businesses, ensured that those who had money got still more from 2010 to 2020. And, as we have seen, financial policy after COVID made this still more true even as America grew still more unequal and angry. We thus know that financial policy has been an engine of economic inequality, but what we don't know yet is what powers the engine. In this chapter, we turn to what money is, what it is becoming in the wake of the digital revolution, and how money that moves only through one part of the inequality engine makes the engine run even faster in the wrong direction.

When money was goats and chickens, we all knew what it was and whether we had any. Now, our money is essentially a conceit of collective agreement – that is, we all agree first that dollars are money and then that the numbers in our account statements show how many dollars we have obtained from whom. Because money doesn't wiggle anymore, it is easier for those with the power to set the terms of economic exchange also to define the money that executes it. Governments and central banks mandated to act on the behalf of all the people once had the power to define money in everyone's interest; increasingly, that's less and less true. In fact, central banks fear that they may soon lose their grip on the money we each choose to trust because new money is coming fast from powerful nations such as China and companies such as Facebook, which, backed by billions of customers, could easily challenge the current collective construct. As a result, central banks including the Federal Reserve are considering countering other mighty economic forces with a new form of money all their own. If the Fed is as blind to inequality in its new money design as it has been in the construct of financial policy, the inequality engine may not just speed up, but also run over a lot of innocent pedestrians.

Tempting though it is to trust the Fed more than Facebook, a simple takeover of new money from giant technology companies by central banks will not reverse the inequality engine unless the fuel goes to the right part of the engine and then the engine is safely steered toward shared prosperity. This chapter takes on the critical question of the meaning of money in our high-tech era and what it must be made to be to enhance economic equality instead of accelerating already dangerous and destructive policy trends.

What Money Is and Will Be

According to economists,[1] money comes in inside and outside varieties and in tokens and account-based forms. This taxonomy may seem academic and so it is. However, understanding it guides us through not just the concept of money, but also how it fuels in the inequality engine.

Inside money circulates in private systems in which those who agree to save in the money or to engage in commerce do so only with each other. Inside money can be points in a video game awarded for performance or points on your credit card traded in for a free hotel room. You cannot offer your video game winnings or credit card points in exchange for anything outside the inside system unless or until they are converted into outside money (i.e., cash).

Outside money can be feely exchanged with anyone anytime for what you want from anyone. These days, outside money is generally "fiat currency" – that is coins and cash deemed the coin of the realm for the payment of taxes, settlement of debt, honoring of employment agreements, or transactions across borders.

Inside or outside money can be tokens – money instruments you can exchange inside a network like a video game or a digital currency construct like bitcoin in which no one knows who you are but everyone accepts what you've got. Or money can be account-based, relying not only on what you have – whether it be credit card miles, dollar bills, or data signifying dollars – but also requiring you prove you are you and that the person asking for your money does the same.

Only very simple money systems are just one of these types of money – i.e., nothing more than a gold bar or even a few nice shells you give or take to exchange on the street with someone you don't know for something you want. You may think that token-based money went out with the barter system, but bitcoins and other forms of new money are exchanged online as tokens much as shells once were.

The difference now is that bitcoin holders also hope to exchange them eventually for outside money – i.e., for dollars – and then they want to place these dollars in bank accounts where they are safe and sound. Some digital currencies are also bartered tokens through which stocks, bonds, or other giant financial transactions move with greater speed and efficiency thanks to the new digital-ledger technology (DLT), often called blockchain. However, there's a reason some forms of digital and token money are called cryptocurrency. In these monetary systems, the power of DLT is harnessed for anonymous, speculative investment often outside the reach of tax authorities or for trading in drugs, guns, or even people.

Only account-based money fuels financial intermediation and thus economic growth. It was thus an early step in the development of money, coming even before outside, fiat-based currency came to be. Account-based money is as old as the totally non-digital ledgers kept by goldsmiths representing how much gold you had with them. Goldsmiths issued "scrip" you could show in another town to acquire a new horse even as the hometown goldsmith used your gold on deposit also to fund the local cobbler until the goldsmith in the neighboring town asked him to send over your gold in exchange for the horse. When money moved from inside exchanges of tokens to account-based money, money's economic power grew exponentially because the account-holder could use one person's money to fund another person's business in a far more certain form of exchange that was also considerably easier to transport when it came time to settle accounts. When money moved from inside systems in which only a few people agreed on what money was to outside systems in which a national government established money via fiat currency, an entire nation's commerce could grow through account-based finance.

No matter all this intermediation – the process that turns one person's deposit into another person's loan – sound account-based money is still readily retrievable when depositors want their money unless or until every depositor wants all of his or her money back all at once – i.e., when there is a "run" on the bank. The fundamental rationale of bank regulation is thus to ensure that money in a bank account, even if it's inside money – i.e., numbers, not dollar bills – comes back to you as money readily on hand when you want it. In the era before FDIC insurance and broader bank regulation, depositors seeking their money back in a bank run were often just given scrip – that is, an IOU from the bank promising outside money – cash, coins, gold, whatever – when times improved. This risk has disappeared in regulated banking, but has proved to be a real concern in some cryptocurrencies and could come to be a significant worry in the new-money systems to which we will shortly turn.

The "public-good" proposition of central banking is in fact premised not only on stable macroeconomic policy, but also on a central bank's ability to direct the flow of money for macroeconomic growth, financial-market stability, and economic equality. Central banks do this most essentially by ensuring public trust in fiat currency such as dollars that are the only money accepted for official purposes such as paying taxes. In recent years, central banks believe that they have better secured this public good by also regulating banks as well as running the rails – i.e., the payment system – on which money travels to ensure that payors and payees are certain that a dollar into the payment system or deposited at a bank is a dollar they are likely to get back.

The Great Unequalizer

The form money takes is critical to who gains the most from the value of having it. As we will see, digital-currency advocates often tout the "inclusion" benefits of their new money constructs, central banks have come to believe that digital money is the next form currency must quickly take, and even progressives hoping for greater equality think a "digital dollar" will renew economic justice. However, as is often the case, the lives of LMI Americans do not comport with the concepts developed by wealthier Americans. It turns out that lower-income people rely far more on cash than wealthier Americans glued to their phones may realize.

Although nations such as Sweden are going completely cashless, cash such as the US dollar remains the most reliable store of value and medium of exchange. This is especially true in the US. Although at least 22 percent of the population is unbanked or underbanked,[2] banks and cash dispensaries are everywhere. For most Americans, banking is "frictionless" – that is, omnipresent. While there are large hot spots often called "banking deserts " due in part to post-crisis rules,[3] the US still has 5,256 banks[4] with 77,647 branches[5] across the nation, supplemented by 5,469 credit unions,[6] and 470,000 ATMs also dispense cash without most of us having to take even a few extra steps to get some physical dollar. Lower-income households without the means to use an ATM also rely on check-cashing shops. While costly, these too are everywhere in LMI communities.[7]

Reflecting this, cash-like instruments are also widely used in LMI communities. Because of barriers to bank access and the cost of low-balance transaction accounts and their slow speed, many employers of large groups of LMI workers use prepaid cards instead of paychecks or direct deposits into an employee's bank account. Retailers with the clout of Walmart also offer "money cards" with much of the functionality of bank accounts and, in some cases, even with terms better than those on offer from most banks.[8] Payment cards have the advantage of being readily presentable at an ATM for instant cash that can then be used to pay the rent and other bills. However, like cash, a prepaid card that is not also an account-based card is token money. Once lost, it's gone forever. An LMI family deprived of its wages through loss or theft of a card is thus in a very difficult position. As a New York Fed official has observed,[9] the entire framework of consumer rights and remedies applied to bank payment has yet to apply not just to digital money, but also even to many electronic forms of money derived from consumer bank accounts housed outside regulated banks.

It is thus unsurprising to find that low-income households prefer cash to all the other money instruments on offer. Households with incomes below $25,000 prefer cash over other payment instruments by very large margins,[10] meaning that these households used the dollar in its original token form and largely do so in the outside-money system because they are likely to be unbanked or use accounts only in very limited ways (i.e., to withdraw cash upon receipt of a payment).[11] In 2018, 29 percent of households with incomes of less than $30,000 used cash for some or most of their transactions; only 7 percent of households with incomes over $75,000 did the same. Cash is so important to LMI households that several states and cities bar merchants from refusing to accept it, with federal legislation also proposed to mandate this nationwide.[12]

Cash also has important value in the increasingly strange economic times in which we live. Interestingly, cash use took a sudden and dramatic spike up for general usage in the course of the COVID crisis.[13] It will take time to understand this phenomenon and dissect its equality impact, but it demonstrates the innate appeal of cash in times of stress across populations as a whole, whether they are banked or not. Cash use has also risen sharply in nations such as Japan and Germany with persistently negative interest rates.[14,15] As we have seen, with rates below zero, money in a bank account loses value; cash in a safe or even under the mattress at least holds its own.

Turning Money into Data

Due to the nature of the US banking system along with embedded US inequality, digital currency is only now emerging in the US. It is, though, already a fixture in other major economies. Indeed, the market capitalization of these new-currency powerhouses has sometimes surpassed that of the world's largest financial institutions.[16] Alibaba in China combines the retailing power of Amazon with a vast network of deposit, payment, investment, and asset-management services all conducted in its own digital currency. At the beginning of 2020, Alibaba was the seventh largest public company in the world, with a market capitalization exceeding $600 billion.[17] Despite its huge scale, Alibaba's currency may or may not be money, but the Chinese central bank isn't waiting to find out. It has preempted private digital currency with one all its own to create a state-sponsored digital currency that functions just like Chinese fiat currency but is even more closely controlled by the Chinese government. This, it believes, is good not just for enhanced monetary-policy control, but also for an even larger state surveillance system across the length and breadth of the nation. And so it might be on both counts – only the Chinese government will again create currency and the Chinese government will know who has how much of it and where it is spent for what purpose.

Another form of new money is known as "stablecoin." Facebook's Libra is the most prominent of the private versions of global stablecoin initiatives.[18] In Libra, Facebook's currency company sets up a construct in which its coin – the Libra – transcends older inside products such as bitcoin because the stablecoin is valued in comparison to a basket of outside money – i.e., various global currencies including the dollar. In theory, this new coin is stable because it can be exchanged for a like-kind amount of outside money at any point in time. In reality, this is far from clear, nor are the conflicts of interest between Facebook as the new global central bank and Facebook as the gigantic social-media company either clear or without sweeping risk.

Global central banks are so concerned by the concept of a private form of outside, account-based global money that they are not only seeking stiff new governance restrictions, but also contemplating a global stablecoin all their own. This would work in concert with central bank digital currencies for national markets such as the one China has developed and the Fed version we will assess later on. One reason central banks are considering a global stablecoin of their own, not of Facebook's devising, is that, under Donald Trump, faith in the US dollar as a reliable store of value dwindled to the point at which other nations no longer trust the dollar as the global standby – i.e., the "reserve currency" – by which the majority of cross-border trade and financial transactions is valued.[19] The UK and other nations now contemplate a global stablecoin that would not only take over from Libra, but also reduce the role of the dollar and thus the need to rely on the United States.

As scholars have observed, "The advent of these new monies could reshape the nature of currency competition, the architecture of the international monetary system, and the role of government-issued public money."[20] That's a lot, but only a prelude to the critical question of what digital money and the changes it wreaks then do to economic equality, which is determined by who gets how much money how. Academic and central-bank analysis of new forms of money so far focus exclusively on central-bank implications,[21] bank or digital-currency profitability,[22] or implications for the theory of money.[23] Inferences of equality impact may be drawn from this work, but none has dealt directly with Facebook's assertion that Libra will enhance financial inclusion[24] or similar claims by other new-money creators.[25] As we shall see, it is far more likely that unregulated new currency will pose grave threats to equality, compounding those already posed by the activities of Facebook, Amazon, and other "Big Tech" companies.

These tech platforms have of course already redesigned how we communicate, purchase goods and services, and even make political and personal decisions. If they control not just what we do, but also how we pay for it, their power and profits will grow, but risks to financial privacy, security, and even stability could also sharply increase with resulting, adverse impact on equality. The critical question in the transition from old, outside, and account-based money to new, digital forms of inside and token money is thus whether new money is as good as old money and for whom its good is done.

What Makes Money Good Money

First, money is good money if it is a store of value when it can be securely put away for later use, whether this is in a coin purse, safe, bank account, or digital ledger with a giant tech company. Stores of value are readily understood by others and freely accepted over time for the accomplishment of many different personal, social, and business objectives. The value of money may well change due to inflation or deflation, but good money retains its nominal value because a coin you had years ago is still worth something years later. Labor, trade, and commerce based on barter, not money, does not establish stores of value because the goods received in return are often perishable, of interest only to a few traders, or otherwise of uncertain long-term value. Moving from the way-back to the far-out, cryptocurrencies such as bitcoin are not yet sound stores of value because their value changes in both nominal and real terms so frequently that they are often a vehicle for speculation or illicit commerce. There are at least 5,000 variations on cryptocurrencies.[26] In 2018, all this new money had an estimated value of $800 billion;[27] in 2019, it was only $222 billion.[28] The daily exchange rate of the US dollar fluctuated a bit over this time, but not so anyone who wasn't a foreign-exchange trader would notice.

These wide variations in the value of digital currency weren't supposed to happen. Bitcoin's initial design was meant to ensure constant value due to built-in limits on how many bitcoins could be in circulation at any given time. This is akin to the original construct of the gold standard in which an ounce of gold was assumed to have a constant value and thus ensure stability for any currency system backed by gold. In fact, gold supply varied tremendously, with huge stores of gold discoveries in the 17th and 19th centuries uprooting established monetary systems and even contributing to the economic chaos of the Great Depression and its aftermath.[29] Bitcoin value varies first on whether someone comes up with a new cryptography adherents prefer – a choice not possible within the boundaries of the US or most nations when it comes to fiat currency. Secondly, cryptocurrency supply varies not due to new discoveries, but in reaction to sudden disappearances due to theft, embezzlement, and the other risks to which a complex token system with no supervision or internal controls is heir.[30] Each of our own pockets can be picked, but the Fed is, at least so far, immutable.

The second criterion for good money is that it is also a sound medium of exchange. Judging this is remarkably simple. Money is good money for this purpose if many people who do not otherwise know each other readily accept each other's money in return for labor, goods, and services. This occurs because many people expect that the money on offer will be readily honored at face value the next time they want to buy, borrow, or invest.

A store of value – i.e., an antique chair – may be something for which you can exchange a sofa, but it isn't money because it has no readily comparable value assuring that once I get the chair, I can do something more than sit on it. Take this simple example and extend it to virtual currency and it's clear not only why money must be a reliable store of value but also why this alone doesn't make money good money. Good money must also be valuable because you can readily use your money to conduct your economic life not just in the nanosecond given to you on a digital ledger, but also when you buy groceries or save for a new house or a child's education. The antique chair or bitcoin may be effective inside money for at least some transactions, but it cannot be readily or reliably converted into outside money such as dollars that are then good for transactions with anyone with whom you want to buy or sell something or for whom you choose to work in return for compensation you hope will be good for something in years to come.

Crafting a Good Digital Dollar

Most new-money initiatives paralleled the transformation of global commerce from 2010 to 2020. At the start of that decade, commerce was largely conducted in physical transactions – if you wanted paper towels, you went to the store. Before COVID, commerce was already transformed into far more digital form – we of course bought far more online and spent hours a day using digital media also for communicating with others, deciding what to buy and where to go, and even choosing for whom to vote. In 2020 when COVID forced social distancing on an incredible scale, many more aspects of our daily lives were suddenly conducted remotely – i.e., digitally.

The transformation from physical to digital commerce also redefined the money we use – many of us started in 2010 with a wallet from which cash was used every day for the bulk of small-value transactions and paper checks or plastic cards linked to our bank accounts handled the rest. Now, the wealthier we are, the less we use cash or these other payment instruments because only the data they represent is needed to buy the world now easily on offer across the Internet and in more and more physical places of commerce. In essence, we have gone in just ten years from a system dependent on outside money – i.e., dollars and other official currencies – conducted in an account-based, bank-centric financial system into a decentralized, digital network of money flows inside and outside bank accounts powered by Big Tech companies epitomized in the US by Amazon, Facebook, Google, Apple, and Microsoft. By 2020, money was as likely to be in the cloud as in your bank.

Digital currencies reflect not just our newly digital lives, but also the asymmetries in the financial rules that, as we have seen, now empower nonbanks to run rings around regulated banking organizations. New money has also often been developed largely because it is outside the reach of costly regulation. This makes digital money not just cooler than old money and also considerably faster and cheaper, but also dangerous to vulnerable consumers. In private, unregulated currencies, there are none of the protections accompanying money in the bank – i.e., deposit insurance, rules, reserves, and all the rest. Most fiat-currency payments do most of their traveling under government control that ensures that a nominal dollar out is a nominal dollar back in each and every minute of each and every day. Government control of the payment system and its reliance on banks with large reserves also means that payments enjoy "finality" – that is, there is little reason to fear that your money will go missing without remedy and reimbursement when we deposit paychecks, pay bills, or send money to Mom in Mexico.

Some of the protections afforded by rules may be matched if new money is backed by old stores of value such as gold or baskets of currencies, but these constructs are complex and prone to conflicts of interest. A better option is to demand that the companies crafting the new currency and providing payment services outside the reach of bank regulation hold high-quality, liquid assets in reserves equal to the payments they process. Officials at the International Monetary Fund have proposed that tech companies engaging in digital-currency activities with access to the payment system would have to post holdings of high-quality securities or cash equal to the amount of their currency liabilities. This takes the idea of stablecoin and makes it truly stable because the new-money provider can't use the reserves or fudge their value. While it's an expensive proposition, it would make new money if not altogether good, then at least a lot better, especially if a regulator or central bank has the power to ensure and enforce not just these reserve requirements, but also other consumer and financial-market protections.

Given the speed with which digital currencies are advancing, resolving their equality challenge is urgent. Money that isn't money when it comes to getting it back is money that poses an array of risks. Central bankers are attuned to those that worry them such as sudden liquidity outflows from new money into old, fiat instruments when money-holders suddenly fear that a new-money provider may not be able to handle its obligations or overall market conditions grow worrisome.[31] This is risky given the all-too-clear link between liquidity strains, financial crises, and still worse economic inequality.

However, less noticed and equally worrisome is the fact that money that isn't a reliable store of value threatens low- and moderate-income savers even if a new-money provider never grows large enough to threaten national finance, let alone that across the globe as some fear might be the case with Libra.[32] The reason for this is simple: those without much suffer a lot when even just a little is lost.

How Money Moves

Sound payment systems are thus as essential as sound money to economic equality. Even if your money is always good money, waiting for it or losing some along the way can be the difference between comfort and a day without dinner for low- and moderate-income households. Money's functionality as a medium of exchange is thus a critical foundation of economic equality because income lost in transit is income that can never generate wealth. Any digital currency seeking to be money must thus not only be a reliable store of value and medium of exchange in person-to-person transactions, but also travel quickly, reliably, inexpensively, and with certainty throughout the entire payment-system infrastructure that is each economy's backbone.

Because of money's mission-critical macroeconomic role, payment systems around the world have become public utilities regulated, managed, and even owned by central banks in virtually every nation. In the US, the Federal Reserve regulates, operates, and even owns much of the national payment systems to ensure that a dollar in is a dollar out. There is one major private payment system (The Clearing House), but it's not just run by regulated banks under their own safety-and-soundness regulation, but also tightly regulated on its own by the FRB to ensure that payments through this private system are as certain as those funneled through the Fed.

This bank-centric system is, well, bank-centric – freezing out non-banks and the giant tech companies forced to enter and exit the payment system with costly tolls at each end. There is thus a strong effort under way to open payment systems to these tech-platform companies. Redefining payments in this new digital era to accommodate new electronic-commerce companies along with new digital currencies may well make money move faster, but it is far from clear that it will also move with at least as much certainty or without new threats to personal privacy and competitive equity.

Tech companies with both our data and our money are still more formidably empowered arbiters of our daily lives. Case in point: knowing how much money we have could empower Amazon or Google to alter prices to maximize profitability by targeting searches to higher-cost products or even marking up prices secure that certain consumers can afford them. Conversely, LMI consumers might find themselves frozen out of mass retailing unless they allow the tech company to handle their payments because the products they purchase are low-margin, low-profit offerings. We pick a physical store based on its affordability and attractiveness and then select the merchandise we want from an uncensored set of choices based on what we need and think we can afford, not on what our banker might advise and, if our banker also owned the store, what he or she would pick for us without allowing us to see other choices. The conflicts of interest are in fact the reason why banks since at least 1956 have been barred from commercial enterprise.

We know that big data already give giant tech platforms enormous power to select what we read, think we know, with whom we associate, and what we buy as they target information, product selections, and so much more to our every known like or dislike. The terms of discourse, commerce, and even our love lives can only change still more in favor of tech-platform companies once they are empowered by still more data not only about what we like, but also what we can afford.

And even if digital-money providers promise never to peek, are they trustworthy enough to ensure payment certainty? We take certainty for granted now only because payment "finality" is now a fact of life within the bank-dominated payment system. But it hasn't always been true that payments sent were payments received. One reason central banks control payment systems is to ensure this finality since, without it, individual consumers and companies can suffer unexpected loss and the financial system can become unglued. Money lost in the payment stream is dangerous to the financial system and, even in small amounts, toxic to low- and moderate-income households.

Payments on nonbank and digital systems have few of the protections US consumers enjoy by law and rule with direct bank providers. These include the reserves banks must post with the Fed to execute transactions on the payment system and the capital and liquidity mandated by all the rules (see Chapter 8) protecting not just banks, but also us. Nonbank payment systems transactions outside bank-offered instruments are also exempt from critical safeguards such as the $50 loss limits that protect consumers from all but minor risk and usually none at all when paper checks and credit or debit cards are lost, stolen, hacked, or otherwise used in unauthorized and often very, very expensive ways. We trust tech companies with our funds now because tech companies are embedded in the bank-centric system well enough so that the risks they take are often borne by banks – that is, if a transaction you execute at an online or even a physical retailer goes astray or amiss, the bank makes you whole even if system weaknesses are the merchant's – not the bank's – fault.

A system without banks would require that nonbanks are as resilient and that consumers have as many rights and safeguards – a costly proposition sure to be fought each step of the way.

The Central-Bank Solution

Facebook's audacious Libra launch in mid-2019 jumpstarted longstanding discussions among and within central banks about the need to preempt Big Tech with central bank digital currency (CBDC) while central banks still had a chance to control their payment systems. Nothing, many thought, would supplant these high-risk newcomers and at the same time modernize payment systems to speed monetary-policy transmission, secure ongoing reliance on fiat currency's resilience as a store of value, and also create a new payment system that is fast, safe, secure, and certain.

There are many reasons many people favor CBDC, not the least of which is that central bankers like the idea of increased centrality and many in the citizenry prefer central bankers to big bankers and Big Tech. First, no one is more ubiquitous than a central bank, nor is certainty better assured then when it's backed by the full faith and credit of the US Treasury even if the money being moved isn't a dollar. CBDC advocates think their digital dollars would fuel the entire transactional system across an entire national economy and, it is thought, also seamlessly integrate with the global payment system to ensure fast and secure cross-border transactions. Although their power is waning, central banks still exercise direct and indirect control over much of the payment system; CBDC might well translate these benefits to digital currency along with ensuring that new money is as sound a store of value and resilient a medium of exchange as the old money now moving through the payment system.

Central bankers aren't the only ones who think so. Progressives in Switzerland pioneered the idea of "people's money" then picked up by progressive Democrats advocating a "Fed account" open to everyone that would bypass both banks and Big Tech.[33] Just as Libra jolted central-bank CBDC thinking, so COVID catapulted progressive proposals for what they now call a "digital dollar." Championed by Congressional Democrats in concert with other COVID legislative-relief packages in 2020, the digital dollar would empower the Federal Reserve to become the be-all and end-all of US currency creation, payment-system operation, and even financial intermediation.[34]

CBDC has such great appeal because government agencies do more than follow the money; they also follow their mandates. However, governments are also awesomely powerful. Without accountability and transparency, CBDC could prove a powerful tool for control, not change. Government agencies are notoriously slow – see above for how this has made the US payment system so anachronistic that Big Tech is running rings around it. Governments are also inherently bureaucratic; that is, institutions first favor their own interests and only then think about everyone else's. And, as we saw in our assessment of the Fed's mandate in Chapter 7, mission statements enacted in law mean little if powerful central banks read the law their own way. CBDC is a good idea given all the other fast-flying forms of digital money coming from unregulated providers on untested payment-system rails. However, CBDC not only requires careful build-out to be sure it doesn't result in still more central-bank power along with still less economic equality. CBDC on its own also doesn't answer the fundamental question of whether payments should remain bank-centric or succumb to Big Tech's awesome presence and allow them a large role as well. In the next chapter, I lay out how best to design CBDC to construct a sound, pro-equality payment system moving newly digital money equitably across the US economy. To do so, we also need a new, pro-equality regulatory system that puts tech companies and nonbanks on an equal footing with banks to enhance innovation without sacrificing inclusion. It can be done under current law and now we'll see how.

Chapter 10

Rules to Equitably Live By

If you want to change the way your banking system is regulated, if you want to learn the mistakes of what's gone wrong, then you have to change your government.

— George Osborne*

Must we overturn government as we know it to regain economic equality? We saw in Chapter 4 that inequality threatens the very fabric of our government even as many Americans think their government threatens their equality. And, even if one thinks government as a whole still functions well, one might easily conclude from the analysis in Chapters 8 and 9 of post-crisis financial rules that regulation has run amuck and must be

---

* Former UK Chancellor of the Exchequer George Osborne, Interview with the *Financial Times* (July 19, 2009), available at https://www.ft.com/content/f199e7c8-7447-11de-8ad5-00144feabdc0.

tightly curtailed. Conversely, one might conclude that companies that follow money can never be held to higher purpose and thus must be nationalized so that better forces govern finance. Either way, one might despair of constructive reform without wholesale regime change.

However, as we have seen time after time, blunt-force deregulation is dangerous to systemic stability and economic equality. Government control may well do no better and could well be still worse. We have already seen that well-intentioned Fed control of the financial system only makes inequality worse. What if so much economic power or still more were granted to a less well-meaning government agency? We could allow capitalism to rule or overtake it with socialist solutions; many of each are certainly on the table.

There is, though, a middle and more practical course. It does four things: applies like-kind rules to like-kind activities; reduces unnecessary barriers to financial services for underserved or at-risk households; creates special-purpose, regulated charters focused solely on equality finance under rules ensuring that regulatory rewards are obtained only upon providing high-value equality services; and designs a new payment system that includes digital currency crafted with equality objectives kept firmly in mind.

Each of these four equality strategies is summarized on Table 10.1. They are optimal, not complete, because all of them are guided by the dictated underpinning analysis throughout this book: equality-enhancing solutions must be politically plausible if they are to be anything more than rhetorically satisfying.

These standards are within the reach of political consensus and achievable without changes in law, let alone government. They are, though, radical in their own way. At their core, these solutions overturn a fundamental assumption that has long governed the Federal Reserve and the other US financial regulators: inequality and even endemic racism are awful, but still someone else's problem to solve. This view is so embedded that FRB Chairman Powell even laid it out before a skeptical Senate Banking Committee in June 2020.[1]

This chapter counters with regulatory tools he and the other federal agencies can easily pick up to reduce both inequality and racism. In the next chapter, a course of immediate action is also laid out for Fed

Table 10.1 Equality-Essential Regulation

Tool	Action	Impact
System-Wide Standards	Barriers to taxpayer-backed benefits Like-kind CRA coverage Enforceable barriers to discrimination Resolution planning	• Safer financial system • Safer payment system • Profit based on competitiveness, not regulatory arbitrage • Enhanced consumer protection • Increased community lending investment • Increased equity as well as equality • Increased community development • Increased reliance on regulated, sound providers • Market discipline • End moral hazard
Refined Regulation	Revised-risk based capital rules Internal securitization Increased credit for equality finance Forbearance	• Lower barriers to equality finance • Increased credit availability • Rapid innovation • Increased low-balance lending • Increased resilience
Postal Banking	Authorize post offices to serve as government-benefit utilities	• Fewer banking deserts • Enhanced benefit delivery
Equality Banks	Authorize new special-purpose charters	• Fewer banking deserts • Effective regulation • Enhanced innovation • Mobilization of private capital • Market discipline
Faster Payments	Accelerate Fed faster payments Token-based CBDC	• Less short-term, high-cost debt • Enhanced certainty • Safe integration with ecommerce • Fewer un- and under-banked households • Continued private-sector lending

monetary policy. Combined with these rule changes, it will overturn a decade of Fed actions and inactions that have made a few Americans ever richer, the rest of us frightened of our economic future, and all too many very, very angry.

Why Not Just Deregulate?

Wholesale deregulation would certainly be popular to a phalanx of powerful financial-industry lobbying groups. However, industry-focused deregulation without equality-enhancing recalibration would repeat all too many previous incidents in which policy-makers rushed to reduce what was described as unnecessary "regulatory burden" on grounds that it increases "American competitiveness." These ended in disastrous financial-market and even macroeconomic crashes.

We know this going back to the 1920s, when Congress roared into a regulatory rewrite dissolving many of the rules on finance demanded by Theodore Roosevelt and his progressive allies. We learned this again in the 1980s when the savings-and-loan crisis – then the biggest financial crash since the Great Depression – was fired up by regulatory relaxations such as a memorable plan allowing regulators to issue "net-worth certificates" that masqueraded as capital in the name of increased homeownership.[2] We learned the dangers of carefree deregulation the hard way all over again in 2008. Even as finance trembled in 2007 ahead of the great financial crisis, the Bush administration's Treasury Department issued a "blueprint" replete with regulatory rollbacks that made big banks, securities firms, and private-equity companies very, very happy.[3] There wasn't time enough to roll back all these rules before the 2008 financial cataclysm eviscerated the industry.

In 2010, Congress reversed course, directing a tough increase in safety-and-soundness regulation and, as we have seen, this made banking safer but most of us still poorer. Even so, bank regulators in the Trump administration were busily deconstructing the 2010 rulebook when, in 2020, crisis struck yet again.

The risks of light-touch regulation were all too evident in 2020 not because banks were fragile – they largely weren't thanks to what was left of the post-2010 rules – but because the rules applied asymmetrically.

This opened the way for nonbanks to take many of the risks banks were forced to eschew. Highly leveraged hedge funds, investment funds that took over from bank lending, and private-debt markets were just a few of the high-risk sectors that would have crumbled in 2020 had the Fed not backstopped or – less charitably – bailed them out with all of its giant market-rescue facilities.[4] Nonbank mortgage servicers didn't fail, but they certainly faltered to such an extent that they lobbied hard for their own Fed rescue backstop.[5] They ultimately didn't need salvation because another regulator – the Federal Housing Finance Agency – changed its rules to send them a lifeline,[6] but their near-death experience was largely due to their exemption from the kind of capital and liquidity rules that kept bank mortgage servicers humming.

Economic resilience, financial stability, and household strength under stress require that the lenders on which consumers and small businesses depend carry on not just at the best of times, but also when borrowers need them most. In the mid-2010s, online "marketplace" lending outside regulated banking took off to the point at which the Treasury Department in 2016 issued a report worrying that the fast-growing sector might create systemic risk under stress due to its lack of stable, deposit-based funding.[7] In 2020, the sector was still too small to pose systemic risk, but many borrowers who had come to rely on it suddenly found themselves without a go-to creditor.[8] Nonbank "fintech" lenders performed well in 2020 in terms of delivering federally backed small business loans, but they largely did so thanks to "rent-a-bank" arrangements in which insured deposits funded loans outside the reach of bank-capital and other safety-and-soundness safeguards.[9]

Although the Fed in 2020 loosened bank stress tests to ensure lending capacity across the business cycle,[10] this regulatory rollback had barely taken effect when the pandemic hit. As a result, banks had more than enough capital to turn deposit inflows (that is, the money rushing out of investment funds) into an unprecedented surge of loans resulting from federal government and Fed rescue programs along with demands from companies to draw down outstanding credit lines for added funding in the midst of the crisis. Had banks not been able to make these loans, the federal government would either have had to do so directly or a financial collapse would have followed COVID's macroeconomic apocalypse in very short order.

Of course, banks are far from sinless – cross-marketing within bank products put vulnerable consumers at risk at one large bank[11] and their mortgage, credit card, and customer service records are still far from sterling. But, unlike nonbanks, banks can and often are punished for their misdeeds – maybe not enough, but at least to a considerable extent not matched for many nonbanks because many nonbanks are able to pick the state regulator that views them most kindly. Consumers must thus win redress largely through litigation, a tremendous challenge due not just to the cost of taking a big lender to court, but also to the mandatory arbitration clauses included as boilerplate consumer-agreement language that often bar redress via less expensive class-action litigation.

Finally, insured depositories have another unique obligation to low-, moderate-, and middle-income families and to small businesses in their neighborhoods. Congress in 1977 enacted the Community Reinvestment Act,[12] a mandate that banks make loans, invest in community development, and otherwise do their best for economic equality in the communities from which they draw deposits. No such standard applies to nonbanks offering like-kind services even if their funding derives directly or indirectly from FDIC-insured deposits or they rely on government-sponsored enterprises (GSEs) and federal agencies in key product lines.

Learning to Love Like-Kind Rules

Clearly, we need to ensure that any entity offering an equality- or stability-essential financial service is under effective equality-enhancing and stability-protecting regulation or – better still – knows along with its customers and investors that any big risks will not be rewarded with big bailouts if bets go bad. We could of course simply identify those financial services and products that are critical to financial stability and equality and then regulate them all under a new, single umbrella for safety and soundness, consumer protection, and resolvability. This would level the proverbial playing field, enhancing financial stability as well as economic equality. However, as I've said throughout this book, equality solutions must not just be potent – they must also be practical.

Leveling the financial-regulatory playing field requires a complete rewrite of US financial-services law, action that would be stoutly and effectively resisted by battalions of well-paid lobbyists. A politically plausible approach to reducing many of the regulatory hills and raising up the valleys instead uses the body of current law to the greatest extent possible to allow access to taxpayer-backed benefits only to companies that are directly or indirectly bound by the rules established to protect taxpayers and the nation more generally.

Doing so would ensure that taxpayer-backed seals such as those that come with FDIC deposit insurance also come with the rules applied to banks to protect both the FDIC and bank depositors.

Similarly, entities expecting Fed support (e.g., the hedge funds active in critical financial-infrastructure markets) should ensure that they back their bets with bank-like capital and liquidity reserves. The rules for banks and nonbanks accessing taxpayer-backed benefits such as the payment system need not be identical, but they must nonetheless be like-kind in terms of critical factors such as safety and soundness, resilience under stress, and consumer protection. If they're not, then the US will become a still more deregulated financial system and risks such as those the Fed was forced to confront in 2020 will be even more difficult to contain the next time around.

How to define the list of activities that require like-kind rules? The Dodd-Frank Act gives US regulators powerful tools with which to do so even if Congress cannot bring itself to act.

The Dodd-Frank Act established a Financial Stability Oversight Council (FSOC) under the Department of the Treasury. It is comprised of major regulators with the power to designate risky, giant nonbanks and then subject them to rules similar to those demanded of large, systemic banks.[13] However, the Obama administration did very little of this designating and what designating it did was then undone by the Trump administration.[14] But systemic designation wouldn't have solved for unequal, high-risk finance even if the Obama administration had persevered and the Trump administration hadn't touched its handiwork. Firm-by-firm designation is an arduous process that would surely have left large swaths of inequality and systemic risk untouched due to the administrative, political, and statutory obstacles to systemic designation. And, even if designations proceeded apace, systemic nonbanks would have come under the Fed, which has no experience with nonbanks and which has, as we've seen, little inclination to do much about inequality other than gather a bit of data and make a speech or two.

A better approach to equality-focused financial regulation with a keen eye on risk is to be found in another section of the Dodd-Frank Act authorizing this same Treasury council to designate activities and practices "if the Council determines that the conduct, scope, nature, size, scale, concentration, or interconnectedness of such activity or practice could create or increase the risk of significant liquidity, credit, or other problems spreading among bank holding companies and nonbank financial companies, financial markets of the United States, or low-income, minority, or underserved communities."[15]

Under President Trump, the FSOC rightly changed its focus from designating firms to looking at activities.[16] In this new construct, the FSOC can and should identify equality- and stability-essential financial activities and practices and – more important than naming names – also the best ways via new rules that ensure that new money follows irresistible injunctions to do well by also doing good. These new rules can and should dictate standards such as new capital, liquidity, and consumer-protection standards applicable across products and providers regardless of the charter under which a financial institution chooses to operate.

And, there's another way to level the playing field even more potent than activity-and-practice designation if those who adopt it are understood in the market to mean it: an FSOC edict mandating sure and certain failure for firms that take undue risk. Now, financial institutions can count year-in and year-out on Fed market protections and, when these fail, on direct transfers of trillions of taxpayer dollars. The federal government should never be a speculative investor picking winners and losers as it provides the equivalent of bankruptcy financing without the restructuring demanded when private-sector lenders throw lifelines to failing firms instead of shutting them down. As we saw in Chapter 8, the Dodd-Frank Act lays out a way to close even the biggest financial institutions without taxpayer protection, but only large banks are in fact forced to prepare for doing so. Big banks are likely no longer to be too big to fail, but the rest of the financial system still enjoys the luxury of this status and the moral hazard it fosters.

The Specifics of Symmetric Regulation

So far, we've seen how to ensure that systemic institutions and activities are symmetrically regulated. This isn't enough – too many companies could still take undue risk or threaten vulnerable consumers. An effective symmetric regulatory construct must thus go deeper, expanding the restrictions on the parties with which banks may do business not just to ensure effective compliance as done under applicable third-party "vendor" rules,[17] but also to demand that companies that rely on regulated banks for access to consumers or businesses adhere also to bank-like safety-and-soundness and consumer-protection standards across their operations.

This will be controversial, but also doable under current law. For example, if a nonbank lender uses a bank to gain federal preemption of state usury ceilings or relies on indirect FDIC-backed funding, the loans it makes should be backed by the same amount of capital a bank would have to post under the same consumer-protection standards. Adherence to the Community Reinvestment Act should also be a cost of doing business with an insured depository, increasing the number of low-income communities that are supported in return for the deposits they send into the banking system.

Further, if a nonbank payment provider pushes money into and out of bank accounts, then the protections for the funds being transmitted should be the same as those demanded of banks when they handle account-holder payments – after all, the transaction is seamless to the customer and much of the benefit to the nonbank derives from consumer faith in the rules governing only the bank. If a nonbank loses your money, it matters just as much to you as if the bank does, but you know that, if the bank loses your money, you have remedies and the bank is required and able to make good on them. If it can't, then the FDIC steps in to make you whole. If a nonbank loses your money, the same safeguards should apply, with nonbanks brought under rules by way of limits to accessing regulated banking organizations.

Symmetric regulation also requires symmetric access to Fed facilities and other taxpayer-backed benefits. The law has long afforded regulated banks unique Fed privileges: rights to hold interest-bearing funds at the Fed, access to the payment system, and use under stress of the "discount window," a Fed lending facility providing funding in return for collateral. Over time, the Fed has dropped the bank-only nature of many of these benefits in a vain effort to make monetary-policy transmission more effective or, as we saw yet again in 2020, to salvage key nonbank sectors in the financial market under stress. Just as forward guidance tells the market what it needs ahead of a structural, equality-enhancing redesign of monetary policy, so equality-enhancing rules should follow a new set of regulatory policies announced well enough ahead of time and implemented following public comment. Forewarned is forearmed – nonbanks unwilling to meet bank-like standards to enjoy bank-like privileges at the Fed would get ample warning and either find alternative arrangements or realize the value of taxpayer backstops and pay up to retain them or live and die by their own hand. Disclosures mandated by new Fed rules would ensure that consumers and investors know the difference.

However, the Fed isn't the only government agency with a big bet on financial companies that should be protected by like-kind prudential buffers. Fannie Mae, Freddie Mac, and the Federal Home Loan Banks – collectively, the GSEs – have $6.3 trillion of assets deployed to support mortgage finance and market liquidity.[18] The taxpayer bet on finance gets even bigger when government agencies such as Ginnie Mae and its $2.2 trillion of guarantees enter into the taxpayer-benefit equation.[19] Both banks and nonbanks make ample use of these taxpayer-backed entities, but only banks pay for it with capital and liquidity backing up the taxpayer's bet.

Raising Up the Regulatory Playing Field

Of course, opposition to new rules restricting both access to banks and to Fed benefits will be fiercely opposed. This is inevitable – no one likes to change, especially when change comes with a big price tag. As a result, the second pillar of equality-enhancing financial regulation goes beyond symmetry to ensure that rules are not just like-kind, but also equality-enhancing. That is, the rules governing banks that now inhibit equality-enhancing financial services should be reviewed and, in many cases, rewritten.

Case in point: the regulatory-capital charges for consumer loans to borrowers with seemingly high-risk profiles due to low credit scores or other traditional risk indicators. Many sources of alternative data are increasingly available that identify safe borrowers within the overall group of low-income borrowers,[20] and capital rules should recognize these enhanced analytics instead of relying on old methodologies such as credit scores or loan-to-value ratios.

Although some borrowers may have lower incomes than cautious debt-to-income ratios countenance or traditional risk indicators tolerate, "subprime" borrowers are often borrowers very dedicated to repaying their loans in full both as a matter of honor and out of fear of being frozen out of future financing. During the 2020 crisis, subprime borrowers for auto loans, credit cards, and other personal loans were stronger at COVID's outset than pricing, risk-based capital, and underwriting anticipated.[21] This was, one executive posited, because subprime borrowers in this sector are aware of the risk nonpayment poses to future credit availability.[22] As we have seen, debt is the new lifeline for all too many lower-income households, making the consequences of default far graver than for households that have another car to drive when the convertible is towed away.

For all the talk about how "subprime mortgages" caused the 2008 crisis, it turns out that prime borrowers who used their mortgages – often without telling their lenders – for second homes, investment properties, and even speculation were far riskier.[23] Unlike lower-income borrowers, these debtors could lose one home because they had at least one other. Even so, rules and GSE underwriting failed to distinguish high-risk prime borrowers and, instead, punished lower-income ones. Like banks, they continue to do so,[24] and this now makes even more of an inequality difference – Fannie and Freddie alone now control nearly half of the US residential-mortgage market.[25]

So, a first fix to raise up equality financing without heightening risk is to realign risk-based capital to target risk where it really lives instead of just assuming that it's always to be found on the other side of town. The second is to eliminate regulatory barriers to small-balance lending.

It is a truth undeniable that it is more profitable to make big loans than small loans and that big loans are most safely made to higher-income borrowers. This is, though, not because high-wealth borrowers are necessarily lower-risk borrowers. As we have seen, they often aren't. Rather, it's because the cost of selling, making, closing, and servicing loans is essentially fixed regardless of loan size. As a result, the cost of making small loans is disproportionately higher and their profit is concomitantly lower.

However, affordable small-balance loans are an essential financial product for low- and moderate-income households and the communities in which they live. One reason lower-income neighborhoods in cities such as Detroit were ravaged after 2008 is not only that African Americans were targeted by predatory lending before the great financial crisis,[26] but also that the homes they owned were often inexpensive and became even more so after the great financial crisis turned into the never-ending Great Recession that mired African American and Hispanic households long after white families resumed ordinary economic life. Homeowners in Black neighborhoods often couldn't refinance their mortgages to save their homes because this downward home-price spiral reduced the already low value of their homes and no lender was willing to take the trouble to process their applications. It was also essentially impossible to sell homes because purchasers couldn't get small-balance mortgages, turning once-stable neighborhoods into "Mad Max" landscapes of abandoned and looted homes used for criminal purposes.[27]

As we have seen in Chapter 5, lenders are profit maximizers – indeed, all private financial institutions, no matter how socially conscious they are, must still ensure survival via profitability. As a result, finance for lower-income households must not just set favorable risk-based capital rules for lower-risk, lower-income borrowers, but also alter the profit equation for the low-balance loans most lower-income households are qualified to obtain. One option might be to allow what I'll call "internal securitization" – i.e., permitting a bank to make lots of little loans that are then packaged into a single instrument held on balance sheet with a favorable risk weighting reflecting its diversified risk profile. Artificial intelligence could actually be of great equality benefit here by serving as a cost-effective way to compare large numbers of small loans and craft them into a coherent package accomplishing bank profit objectives.

This way, a lot of little loans go into one way-big loan, with the cost of origination reduced by capital advantages combined with more efficient credit underwriting and loan administration. Even better, the GSEs and Ginnie Mae can and should be required to purchase these internal loan packages and then blend them into larger loan pools to achieve still more efficiency and, thus, lower pricing.

We also now know that being tough on borrowers struggling to make payments at times of overarching macroeconomic stress undermines not just individual households, but also the communities in which they live. In the 2008 crisis, many policy-makers, including top ones in the Obama administration, believed it better to take quick action to foreclose on borrowers behind on their mortgage payments. Longstanding experience in ordinary times teaches – correctly in such cases – that action sooner is better than later because losses only grow the longer it takes to foreclose. However, crises affect borrowers for no fault of their own for whom disciplinary action does no good. In the 2008 debacle, California led the nation in protecting both homeowners and neighborhoods. A study of that time demonstrated that delaying foreclosure and forcing lenders to maintain vacant properties on which foreclosure could not be averted salvaged $300 billion in household wealth in the areas of the state hardest hit by house-price declines.[28]

There's a lot more that regulators can do to encourage community lending and investment. For example, they can and should expand the definition of eligible "public-welfare" investments and, for good measure, give them a capital break as long as holdings stay within a limit – say 5 percent – of capital. The same can easily be done for community-focused lending: give banks a list of equality-enhancing loans and the terms on which they may be extended and then give banks a risk-based break for portfolios within size limits – 10 percent of capital, for example. Banking regulators give banks lots of breaks in the capital rules for financial exposures that have nothing to do with economic equality; for example, big banks get a break on capital related to complex derivatives exposures as long as these remain below 15 percent of a key capital metric.[29] Surely the same latitude is warranted for lower-risk activities that are also equality-enhancing.

Building a New, Equality-Focused Banking System

Although it is not just essential but also possible to bring like-kind providers under like-kind, equality-enhancing rules, it will not be easy. Some rules will remain because some low-, moderate-, and middle-income loans are indeed risky. It's also often cost-intensive to provide financial services to new entrants into the US economy due to a combination of essential protections against money laundering and the complexity of advising vulnerable, disabled, or non-English-speaking customers. Older Americans increasingly have urgent need for financial services to safeguard what little they have, but doing so also poses complex delivery and consumer-protection challenges. Institutional, if often unintended, barriers to serving people and communities of color will also take time to break down.

Further, innovative new products need to be introduced with cautious new safety-and-soundness buffers as well as with expensive safeguards for consumer privacy and protection, anti-discrimination, and conflicts of interest along with guardrails reflecting technological complexity. These will also prove controversial and take time to construct for multifaceted financial institutions, significantly slowing or even frustrating equality-enhancing financial innovation.

It's also very expensive to maintain retail-product delivery channels with the personnel presence and contact essential for consumers with lower educational levels for whom product disclosures may be confusing, as well as for consumers for whom English is not a first language, for older consumers who are uncomfortable with digital delivery, and for the disabled for whom digital delivery is all too often simply inaccessible. And, as we have seen, new business models founded on the efficacy of artificial intelligence also come with the opacity that may obscure discrimination whether by intent or only by accidental effect.[30]

There are at least three ways to conquer these cost barriers to equality-enhancing finance: open post offices as banking facilities, create new "Equality Bank" charters, and bring forth a "digital dollar" from the private sector or, more equitably, the Fed. None of these options is mutually exclusive and each has promise, promise that can be fulfilled if this new US banking construct is built with care.

Banking While Mailing

The United States Postal Service (USPS) was a mainstay of US banking until 1967.[31] Those hoping to revive it via legislation[32] or other means view the post office as a branch network that would transverse rural and inner-city areas increasingly becoming banking deserts.[33] Given their omnipresence, this is tempting; given the Postal Service's huge unfunded liabilities and debt – $161 billion at last count[34] – and uncertain operational capacity, this is considerably less certain.

The best near-term use of post offices – which after all are an arm of the US government – would be to serve the government's needs in getting payments out to American households. This has two benefits.

First, Postal Service participation in government-benefit delivery would increase speed and certainty. The Treasury sought to use bank accounts and IRS tax records to distribute the individual and per-child benefits allotted by the COVID-relief CARES Act.[35] Millions of households eligible for these urgently needed benefits failed to get them because they didn't have bank accounts, hadn't filed federal taxes online, or were otherwise invisible even though eligible.[36] Child-related benefits were particularly problematic due to dubious records about who had how many children and which children lived where. At the same time, dead people received at least $1.4 billion in government benefits.[37]

An alternative delivery system in which live, eligible individuals elect to show up in the post office, present needed identification, and receive payments from the federal government in cash or to a bank account would have worked far better. Had state unemployment insurance – also plagued by enormous snafus[38] – also been distributed via post offices, funds would similarly have moved faster and thus been of greater use at so sore a time of need.

Second, the fact that the USPS is handling only government payments obviates broader concerns about a government-dominated financial system. The role of government as payment overseer – and the risks to privacy and even civil liberties thereof – is in my opinion critical, but generally omitted from those advocating for a more omnipresent postal bank.[39]

It's one thing to choose to provide your identity to cash a government check at the post office and allow the government officials there to see personal facts of your life, starting with the fact that you are receiving government benefits and the amounts thereof. It's another to have the government know all about your salary, your children, and many other facts of life while handling your financial transactions. Banks know much of this or could if they looked, but they are barred by law from disclosing it to most third parties and, in any case, banks aren't the government and thus really don't care to whom you made a political contribution. The government, or at least some within it, might view these transactions very differently.

Establishing Equality Banks

An Equality Bank at its simplest is just what the name implies: a bank focused on equality. The nation is dotted with banks including the words "commerce," "business," "home," and "savings" in their names. These words are increasingly an homage to long-ago missions or even charter-defining law rather than current activities, but they are testament to the fact that the US has a long history of chartering banks to achieve an economic mission. What could be a more urgent mission now than economic equality?

Equality Banks can be chartered at least two ways: via new laws establishing what are often called "public banks" or by chartering various forms of private institutions with a mission to enhance economic equality subject to a stiff enforcement regime that ensures they actually do so.

The US has a long history of public financial institutions that, no matter the lofty ambitions with which they are chartered, quickly devolve into profit-making machines with little real regard to mission. Public banking in the United States has its roots in the land banks of the colonial era, chartered by colonial governments to finance mortgages and other loans through the issuance of promissory notes. These banks died out by 1740, but the young United States tried this again starting with a public bank in Vermont in 1805. By 1812, this bank closed due to counterfeiting and a host of other scandals, charting a path for public banks across the US ever since. The lone standout as a public success is the Bank of North Dakota, which was founded in 1919 and lives on, albeit largely only as a secondary lender allied with small banks across this huge, rural state. Community development financial institutions

(CDFIs) backed by the US Treasury Department have been generally successful, but are limited by funding shortages and other challenges.

Fannie Mae and Freddie Mac are hybrid public-private enterprises engaging in a core banking service: buying mortgages and packaging them for sale into the secondary market. Founded in 1938 and 1989 respectively,[40] these GSEs are federally chartered institutions owned to this day by private shareholders. Before 2008, they touted the American dream of homeownership to defend their privileges, not to mention high-flying executive pay. In 2008, they spectacularly failed, examples of public service diverted for private gain, two examples that cost the US taxpayer $191 billion.[41]

There are also wholly private charters with an equality mission, credit unions most important among these. Credit unions enjoy a generous federal tax break to achieve the mission first set for them in the 1930s:[42] support savings and offer credit to those ill-served by banks or other traditional financial institutions. Many small credit unions still serve this mission, but the largest ones have grown to rival regional banks and now focus at least as much on high-cost lending as community service.[43] They, like the checkered history of public banks and GSEs, illustrate the importance not only of setting lofty chartering goals, but also rigorously enforcing them. Even without shareholders to appease, private companies have management teams that, if freed of mission constraints, will focus on what's good for them, not necessarily anyone else.

Instead, special-purpose Equality Banks should be chartered under rigorous terms in which regulatory benefits are provided in exchange not just for community service, but also on condition of acceptance of stringent supervision, measurable and transparent performance goals, and nasty penalties effectively imposed if mission objectives fade into private gold. Federal banking agencies should each determine what type of charter in their portfolio is best adapted to advance economic equality and which regulatory modifications are essential to achieving and measuring success on specific goals for specific target markets. Qualifying equality banks should then get breaks from selected, mission-critical costly prudential rules, but never, ever from those governing consumer protection and the fair provision of financial services.

Federal and state law already provides several charter options well-crafted for equality banking. These include "bankers' banks" that help member banks meet needs none can handle on its own. Current law[44] gives the Fed wide latitude to exempt bankers' banks from applicable rules, with prohibitions on receiving FDIC insurance and on directly serving consumers, additional safety-latches on what could quickly prove a powerful equality-oriented charter for banks of all sizes and new entrants dedicated to equality-essential finance. The Office of the Comptroller of the Currency (OCC) has also authorized a "special-purpose" charter, so far doing so only for private financial technology ventures.[45] The special-purpose charter construct serves as a model for a special-purpose national Equality Bank. Again, FDIC insurance is not involved and the OCC can set whatever restrictions it thinks necessary to ensure that special-purpose banks are actually fit for equality purpose.

Another appealing option comes in the form of the "public benefit corporation" (PBC) charters authorized by thirty-five states and the District of Columbia.[46] These PBCs could hold bank charters and thus enjoy FDIC insurance and serve consumers, but these charters also include restrictions such as a fiduciary duty to consider missions other than profit. Tax and governance breaks further these public-service goals and, if removed, also punish those who go astray. These state benefits can be matched with regulatory ones under, again, strict requirements that these companies indeed provide measurable, meaningful public benefit.

New Money for a New Mission

As we have seen, economic equality is directly obstructed and even set back by slow payments. Speeding them up outside the reach of safety-and-soundness and payment-certainty requirements would certainly move money faster, but many households could lose their life savings along the way. It is for this reason that the Fed should quickly put the pedal down to bring its own faster-payment system, FedNow, to market as well as partner constructively with private-sector payment services able now or in the immediate future to ensure sound and real-time retail payments.

It is also for this reason that the FDIC has rightly taken extra care when nonbank payment companies are allowed to establish the nontraditional banking charters generally known as industrial banks that offer access to the payment system without a full banking license and the Federal Reserve holding-company supervision for the parent firm that goes with them. These tech-based banks must hold more than double the minimum capital required of small banks, a requirement designed to stand in for parent-company regulation and the lack of established regulatory performance through the business cycle and under operational stress.

The complex interaction between special-purpose banks and profit-maximizing, unregulated parent companies make these special-purpose charters extremely controversial. Some of this stems from the desire of banks to block powerful competitors, but banks have a point: privileged charters have competitive advantages born not of skill, but of regulatory loopholes. Large retailers such as Walmart or e-commerce companies such as Japan's Rakuten operate under asymmetric regulation, allowing what many believe to be inappropriate use of consumer personal information and a dangerous opportunity to tie product sales to the cost, construct, and availability of financial services. If Amazon, Google, or other Big Tech companies win the right to access the payment system via these charters, risks would rise exponentially. Nonbank access to the payment system should come with bank-like or better privacy protections and bank-like safety standards such as high reserve requirements as proxies for capital and liquidity standards to ensure payment certainty.

The second step to equality-enhancing payment systems is to modernize the money that moves through it. Many digital-currency proposals reflect the fact that traditional payment systems will remain slow as long as they operate on old-school platforms without the efficiency possible through the use of digital-ledger technology (DLT or blockchain) and other fast-moving technology developments. It is possible – albeit not yet proven – that DLT would permit funds to move across the nation and indeed around the world as fast as sending a text message. As we have seen, this prospect combined with distrust of traditional banks led progressive Democrats, including senior ones in the US Congress, to propose "FedAccounts" that would bypass banks and all the costs that go with doing business with them and establish a new, supreme government-based, government-backed, and government-controlled banking system for individuals, households, small businesses, and – in some proposals – everyone else.

Despite all the equality benefits of no-cost banking at a no-risk central bank accelerated by instantaneous DLT, this uber-dollar poses numerous equality challenges. These include the continuing preference for cash evident at low- and moderate-income households, the dangers of handing over so much personal information to the government, and the fact that a central-bank deposit-taker would need the power also to make loans to prevent short-circuiting the essential macroeconomic and equality engine fueled by the process of turning deposits into loans.

To ensure economic growth, the Fed would have also to become the nation's lender – a threat to innovation as well as to borrowers whose tastes don't suit the government – or somehow figure out how to enlist banks to act as its agents. This destroys regulated financial intermediation as it has been known for centuries and is thus worth careful consideration. FedAccounts offered solely through the Fed create a nationalized banking system that will only suit you if the government of the day does as well.

Thus, the way to speed payments is not to allow private companies to redesign the dollar or to allow the Federal Reserve to take over both the banking and payment systems via an ill-designed central-bank digital currency (CBDC). Instead, the answer lies in an equality-focused CBDC design that speeds payment and financial-system innovation without the heavy hand of government control.

As detailed in Chapter 9, money comes in both "token" and "account-based" forms, with tokens now dollar bills and US coinage. Most private and CBDC proposals prefer an "account-based" system in which the currency provider or transmitter controls transactions that always remain digitally within the system without the need for physical, token currency. This is efficient – assuming these systems are as iron-clad as proponents espouse – but they exclude not just households who prefer cash, but also lower-income, rural, and disabled Americans for whom digital access remains limited, expensive, and often wholly inaccessible. To be equal, CBDC must ensure much as banks do now that funds in and out of the account-based system can be converted into tokens – i.e., cash – on demand.

Over time, digital tokens might come to replace cash much as prepaid and debit cards now sometimes replace bank accounts and small-dollar cash transactions. However, "over time" is not yet now.

To bring forth a new CBDC, private providers should work with the Fed to create a new system in which a token-based form of digital money moves through established, regulated banks and money transmitters along with, as it evolves, new, blockchain-based infrastructure within and without the central bank. As sketched out in one proposal,[47] this CBDC system would parallel and thus complement regulated providers, ensuring that they – not the Fed – continue to have the deposit wherewithal with which to make loans. At the same time, this system would be far better adapted for electronic commerce and ready and able to take on benefit payments across the country under both ordinary and high-stress circumstances.

Under this construct, reserves held at the central bank combined with tough rules will ensure payment-system certainty and stability as well as the ability of deposit-holders to get their money back in hard currency, i.e., token, or account-based form when and how desired. Banks would still likely be the depository of choice since only banks would carry the FDIC insurance necessary for household financial security, but an array of options that interact seamlessly with household wage payments and government benefits would also reduce the cost of day-to-day transactions, especially for those unwilling or unable to open bank accounts.

In short, this digital-dollar system combines the benefits of regulated banking, deposit-insurance protection, and payment-system certainty with those proffered by electronic commerce. It would work even better if nonbank e-commerce providers such as the Big Tech companies are allowed access to the new system on the same tough terms described above for payment-system access. Big Tech would also need to ensure compliance with a new body of law and rules protecting transaction integrity and consumer privacy.

This all enhances equality by virtue of its speed and inclusiveness, ending the roadblocks and risks all too evident when the Treasury and states couldn't figure out how to send urgently needed payments to the millions of Americans eligible for them at the start of the 2020 pandemic. It would be considerably more inclusive than the current banking system not just because of efficiency and speed, but also because of ease of access by anyone with or without electronic devices or the broadband capacity needed to enable real-time payments. And, importantly, it would avoid top-down takeover of the national economic financial system by the Fed. For all its virtues, such omnipotence in the hands of one, ultimately political central bank is a very, very bad idea.

Chapter 11

Financial Policy for an Equitable Future

Life is both complex and intense, and the tremendous changes wrought by the extraordinary industrial development of the last half century are felt in every fiber of our social and political being. ... The conditions which have told for our marvelous material well-being, which have developed to a very high degree our energy, self-reliance, and individual initiative, have also brought the care and anxiety inseparable from the accumulation of great wealth in industrial centers. Upon the success of our experiment much depends, not only as regards our own welfare, but as regards the welfare of mankind. ... There is no good reason why we should fear the future, but there is every reason why we should face it seriously, neither hiding from ourselves the gravity of the problems before us nor fearing to approach these problems with the unbending, unflinching purpose to solve them aright.

— *Theodore Roosevelt**

---

* President Theodore Roosevelt, "Inaugural Address of Theodore Roosevelt" (speech, Washington, DC, March 4, 1905), published by Yale Law School Lillian Goldman Law Library, available at https://avalon.law.yale.edu/20th_century/troos.asp.

How then to approach inequitable financial policy to solve it aright? It has been the purpose of this book to show American economic inequality as the chasm it has so quickly become, marshaling convincing data to lay clear the depth of the divide between the few whose wealth grew ever greater after 2010 and the many with scant resources not only to secure daily comforts before COVID, but also to shield themselves from the pandemic's ferocious effects. I have also shown that, while monetary and regulatory policy is not inequality's only cause, it is a powerful blast sending economic rewards skyrocketing to the top of the income and wealth ladders.

Financial policy after 2010 and then again in 2020 rescued markets at the expense of millions, ended any hope that most Americans could save for the future, turned banks into wealth-management machines, let loose unregulated companies with still less regard for family financial well-being, and even began to redefine money to make it serve the needs of those who already had most of it. Much of financial policy's cause and inequality effect has never been shown before, but that's not enough.

This book has to do one more thing: it must do as Theodore Roosevelt urged a nation a century ago confronting inequities born of Gilded Age oligarchs. It must craft a course of positive change that is also politically plausible to put the economic inequality engine into reverse. In the last chapter, I detailed an action plan for federal financial regulators to realign rules for equality and to redefine financial institutions to advance it still farther. In this chapter, I show not just what the Fed should do, but also what it quickly can do to recognize regulatory realities as they are and should be and then to ensure that monetary policy does them one better by making America still more equal.

In both chapters, it is clear that equitable financial policy can be immediately crafted without risk of economic chaos or renewed financial crisis. In sum, change not only should, but also can come.

Turning the Fed into a Force for Good

When one walks into the heavily guarded fortress that is the Federal Reserve Board's executive office in Washington, DC, one passes from a grand lobby into a capacious multistory open room flanked by dual ascending staircases the architect could only have modeled after ancient ziggurats. These triumphal staircases meet far overhead in an open balcony from which generations of Fed chairs must surely have been tempted to throw dollar bills to waiting hordes. Built during the Great Depression, the building was meant to awe the mortals who enter with its power and so it still does now after one first traverses the homeless encampment next door.

Because of both its architecture and its growing omnipotence, some have likened the Fed to a secretive temple.[1] Paul Volcker was said to have saved the US economy singlehandedly when he took over the Fed in 1979 and, under Alan Greenspan in the 1980s and 1990s, it became both a powerful political force and, for the first time, also a mover and even maker of markets. Under Ben Bernanke in the wake of the 2008 great financial crisis and then under his successor, Janet Yellen, the Fed took full charge of regulating the largest US banks and marshalled trillions first to rescue and then to prop up financial markets not just in the US, but also across the globe.

In 2020 under Jerome (Jay) Powell, the Federal Reserve mobilized all these powers and obtained still more. It became not just the dominant force in US and even global monetary and regulatory policy, but also the nation's single most formidable fiscal force. With trillions of self-printed dollars, the US Federal Reserve became the largest player in both government and corporate bonds and – less directly but still almost omnipotently – even in stocks.

But for all the Fed's powers, its results proved not only far, far less than unprecedented central-bank interventions should have evoked, but also counterproductive for all but the wealthiest households with the biggest stakes in financial markets. To be sure, financial markets would have crashed in March 2020 just as they would have crashed in 2008 without Fed intervention. However, it is also certain that the Fed's interventions in both cases were solely focused on markets, lasted too long, and left too many too far behind.

As the Fed itself has said, wealth increases "because of the feedback effect on higher incomes from the returns generated by accumulated assets"[2] – that is, you can no longer work hard and get ahead; now, you have to have the income on hand to put it into the markets to do so. The Fed's post-2010 recovery may have been the longest in US history as Fed officials like to say,[3] but it was also the weakest in modern US history.[4] The Fed also increasingly presided over financial crises that grew ever more destructive even as America became increasingly unequal.

The combination of weak growth with high inequality followed by financial crisis wasn't a sudden manifestation of new macroeconomic or market phenomena. As we saw clearly in Chapter 4, unequal economies grow far more slowly than equal ones and lead more frequently also to financial crises. It thus turns out that equitable financial policy is also sound – indeed, essential – financial policy.

The Fed's Failings

First to the Fed's failings and then to fixes for them. The Fed didn't mean to make US economic growth not just slow, but also inequitable. It of course also didn't mean for there to be another financial crisis so soon and so severe after the ill-effects of the 2008 debacle – also in part the result of failed Fed policy – had begun to fade. How could a central bank with such good intentions – and these are genuinely good intentions – go so wrong?

First, the Fed failed to see how economically unequal America had become. Persuaded by old models and historical experience that more of the same, upward-focused policy would somehow create shared prosperity, the Fed made its second mistake: it failed to understand that unconventional monetary policy, powered as it was only by market gains, couldn't work. If trickle-down policy led to strong recovery, then post-crisis policy could be deemed something of a success even if post-2010 monetary policy left income and wealth distributions as they were or even made them just a bit more inequitable. Instead, a decade of Fed policy led not just to unprecedented inequality, but also to a weak recovery precipitating the Fed's third mistake: failing to understand that inequality breeds financial-system fragility.

The tornado that struck the US in 2020 was thus the result of years of Fed-fueled market gains, inexorable increases in economic inequality, still more market-boosting policies, still less equality, a national economy with no resilience, and then yet another and even more shattering financial crisis. Short-circuiting this doom loop is far easier than it may seem.

The Fed's Equality Toolkit

Once the Fed knows how the economic engine generates inequality, the Fed has tools readily on hand with which to repair it. Most of these are clearly within the Fed's immediate reach under current law. Table 11.1

Table 11.1 Monetary-Policy Tools to Repair the Inequality Engine

Tool	Action	Impact
Forward Guidance	Statements re inequality, policy options at each FOMC meeting Policy-focused research Official speeches, etc. Official reports	• Transparency • Accountability • Leadership focus • Averts Unintended Consequences • End to aggregate data • Equality-focused policy targets • New, better policy options • Leadership incentives for institutional equality commitment • Ongoing assessment/measurement of equality in relation to financial stability • Ongoing assessment/measurement of inequality on monetary-policy effectiveness • Early warning of emerging risks
Fed Portfolio	Gradually shrink to only operational level Increase under stress only for illiquid regulated companies, households, small business Identify new tools for nonbank finance Focus facilities on macro need, not market support	• Restores market risk premiums, reducing risk of asset-price bubbles • Forces markets to rely on value, not Fed price supports • Allows natural market corrections, increasing discipline • Ends bailouts and hope of bailouts • Encourages ground-up growth, restoring equality • Reduces creation of financialized economy • Newly-effective policy • Increased Macro resilience, enhanced equality • Political accountability
Interest Rates	Gradual increase to positive real margin	• Market correction followed by heightened stability • Enhanced ability to save for the future • Return of regulated retail finance • Secure retirement savings

summarizes the equality tools in the Fed's kit and what wielding them would do for whom.[5]

The First Fix: Understanding America as It Is

The Fed thought the US economy was in a "good place" in 2020 because its decision-makers and the models on which they relied sat in the first-class lounge. Looking throughout the station and seeing multitudes holding second- and third-class tickets and still more hopeful passengers just standing in line won't get everyone on the economy's train, but it will start the policy locomotive essential to doing so.

For all its banality, better data that show America as it is would be a remarkably powerful tool with which the Fed could redirect the inequality engine. It's not for nothing that self-help mantras start with an admonition to acknowledge the problem. The Fed can't do so unless or until it realizes that the America it helped to build after 2010 was an unequal, unhappy, and ultimately angry place.

As we saw in Chapter 7, the Fed needs little, if any, new law to mend its ways. The Fed can and should measure performance under its "maximum employment" mandate by using modern measures of full employment that look not only at who files unemployment claims, but also at who is underemployed, underpaid, and underworked. The Fed could never have persuaded itself that the US economy was in a good place up to the moment it collapsed in March 2020 if it had better understood how truly unemployed America as a whole was at the time.

Second, it should judge price stability not by economic-derived "baskets" of selected goods and services, but by what it costs most Americans to feed their families, obtain safe housing, secure an education, and get medical care. From 2010 to 2020, affordable housing became ever scarcer across the nation, with the cities that seemed the most prosperous in fact the least affordable for all but upper-income, established households.[5] Even middle-class Americans skipped medical care to save money[6] and were so mired in student loans that repayment compared to income sometimes seems little more than a mirage; the average loan-to-income ratio for middle-class millennials with student debt was greater than 70 percent in 2016[7] and, when added together with other loan payments and mortgage bills or rent, this student debt meant that most middle-class borrowers with student loans – which was most of those without wealthy parents – had far more debt than income. When income dropped or died in 2020, these households plunged into economic crisis.

These increasingly high true costs of living aren't "price stability" if one measures prices not by models, but instead by what it costs to get by. Throughout the decade after 2010, the Fed was flummoxed by why inflation failed to grow as its models suggested it should, given how high employment was said to be. It turned out that the Fed was wrong on both counts: employment was far less robust when correctly judged and inflation was a lot higher for anyone trying to live what used to be called a middle-class life.

Further, interest rates will only meet the law's "moderate" objective if the savings average families set aside for long-term goals provide an effective engine for wealth accumulation. As we have seen, ultra-low and even negative real rates just make Americans who try to save even poorer for the sacrifices they make to do so. They also drive banks away from making loans to securities trading and other business lines that sustain profitability at cost to macroeconomic growth and financial-market stability.

Finally, blinded by all its post-crisis rules governing the nation's banks, the Fed failed to see that the US had been transformed into a nonbank financial system with an enormous risk buildup that blew in just one or two days under unforeseen stress. Financial stability depends in part on all of the rules we reviewed in the last chapter, which as we saw are joined inseparably with the Fed's monetary policy to make the US still more unequal and crash-prone.

The Second Fix: Set an Equality Plan and Say So

The first express monetary-policy tool is the easiest to wield: forward guidance. While the Fed's other tools are complex and sometimes cost trillions, clear statements from Fed leadership about a new policy premised on enhanced equality would have immediate impact on both markets and the central bank without precipitating undue volatility if clearly and carefully phrased with appropriate transition deadlines.

As we saw in Chapter 6, the Fed uses forward guidance to signal the market about its intentions. This, it is thought, ensures that markets rachet down or up gradually as the Fed prefers instead of shuddering to dangerous halts or revving up out of control.

However, forward guidance has gone over time from a safety catch on other tools to a major implement with which the Fed has made it indisputably clear to financial markets that the Fed has their backs. The Fed has been as good as its word – forward guidance promising market stability has been obeyed every time even a minor market correction threatened. Just one case in point: on June 16, 2020, equity markets feared a COVID second wave and dropped sharply when trading opened; at 2 p.m., the Fed announced a new version of one of its corporate-rescue facilities and markets returned to positive territory by the end of the day even as COVID case counts continued to rise.

However, ever-higher financial markets not only accelerate wealth inequality, but also play a strong role in turning the US economy into an increasingly "financialized" one in which making the most of money, not building factories or opening stores, is the surest path to personal affluence. The more financialized an economy, the more unequal it is due to the barriers to employment facing persons with less education or even just no interest in finance.

Equitable financial policy thus starts with an understanding of who has and owes how much and proceeds to public statements from the Fed that, while it seeks market stability, it cannot and indeed will not guarantee it. Instead, the Fed's priorities should be stated clearly in forward guidance and other official pronouncements as law demands: full employment for all; price stability not just for investors, but also for consumers; and moderate interest rates rewarding savers and encouraging sound lending. This forward guidance would go beyond the dutiful repetition of what the Fed insists is only its "dual-mandate" to adhere to law and then also to explain each time the Fed pronounces how each of its missions will be met, not just for markets, but the nation as a whole.

The Third Fix: A Far Smaller Fed Portfolio

The Fed's next equality tool – and it's a very big one – is its portfolio. The Fed has promised to "normalize" the portfolio since 2013 but proved so frightened of markets that the portfolio still grew and grew each time correction threatened. As we have seen, the portfolio ballooned in late 2019 when the Fed rescued the repo market[8] and then exploded to once unimaginable proportions when COVID called the market's high-flying bluff. Although the Fed's portfolio was set in early April to grow to as much as 60 percent of US GDP by year-end 2020,[9] the Fed throughout the COVID crisis made it clear that it would print even more money and buy still more billions of assets as it thought necessary to backstop financial markets.[10] Nowhere, though, did the Fed express anything but rhetorical good wishes to the millions and millions of American households and very small businesses devastated by COVID's macroeconomic shock waves.

The Fed's formidable portfolio power thus went not for full employment or price stability or moderate rates, but instead for the Fed's preferred definition of financial stability: financial markets that never go down more than wealthy investors would like or high-risk companies can endure. As one very successful investor noted, "In this monetary policy regime, no bet seems unwise, even buying the shares of bankrupt rental car companies after they already have risen 1,000% in a week."[11] The *Wall Street Journal* remarked on this and other amazing market feats: "The Federal Reserve now apparently has the power to raise ... the dead."[12]

Often, companies took advantage of Fed facilities to raise money in a market sure of Fed backstops only then to turn around and fire workers facing unemployment at the height of the pandemic's economic shock.[13] At the same time the Fed opened these programs, 41 percent of Black-owned small businesses had closed their doors under COVID's inexorable macroeconomic stress.[14] Women were also disproportionately hard-hit – the number of female business owners dropped 25 percent from just February to March 2020.[15] Shuttered businesses such as child care, retail, hospitality, and health care have disproportionately high levels of lower-paid female workers, most of whom were sent home with thoroughly uncertain prospects of ever returning.[16] White male traders on Wall Street had no such worries – they headed to their home offices, logged in, and started to profit from all the Fed's programs.

In 2008, it might have made sense for the Fed to throw trillions into the financial system since, at least at the start, the 2008 great financial crisis was, as its name suggests, born of high-risk finance unable to sustain itself after the shock without Fed supports or even bailout. In 2020, the financial markets were fragile due to inequality, but they collapsed only because the novel coronavirus brought the US and global economies to a screeching halt. The more the Fed supported markets, the more markets rallied, but none of this did anything to help the millions of Americans – almost 50 percent by some counts[17] – and the thousands of businesses the Fed acknowledged might never reopen.[18]

The third tool for equitable financial policy thus goes to the heart of the inequality impact of the Fed's giant 2008 portfolio and then its redoubled portfolio bet in 2020. The tool is a new portfolio policy setting the Fed's balance sheet as small as possible under ordinary conditions and allowing growth only under acute stress and then only in a manner that benefits the economy as a whole, not just financial markets.

The third fix also ensures that the Fed complies with the strict injunction of Section 13(3) of the Federal Reserve Act.[19] As we have seen, the law stipulates that Fed support must be broadly based, go out only in "unusual and exigent" circumstances, and then also only to entities that are demonstrably solvent that may need short-term liquidity support. The Fed's trillions and trillions in holdings year in, year out not only go principally to support the have-a-lots, but also do so in violation of express statutory injunction.

It's true that the Fed's facilities were indeed broad-based, going to classes of financial instruments or companies, not to single entities, as was the case in 2008. However, this broadly based support actually took over the market instead of only supporting it *in extremis*, as the law's intent clearly requires. After COVID's initial shock toppled financial markets, they recovered not only due to all the Fed's massive interventions, but also growing hope for a COVID vaccine, reassuring macroeconomic numbers, and even the occasionally reassuring tweet from the White House. As we have seen, equity markets roared backed, recovering far faster than ever seen in all of the market data going back before the Great Depression. By mid-June, markets reached heights not seen since well before the beginning of the year, up 47 percent since its March intraday low.[20] Bond markets also recovered so much of their mojo that many, including Senate Republicans, questioned why the Fed was continuing to prop up the corporate-bond market.[21] Although the Fed's facilities also restricted borrowers to those who could not find credit elsewhere,[22] this "no-credit-elsewhere" criterion was actually defined not to mean absolutely no credit was to be had, but only that the borrower didn't like the terms on which it was offered. The Fed was, as I said, not supporting the market *in extremis*; it instead became the market even though conditions improved so much that the highest-risk assets regained all the pricing advances regardless of risk that characterized the run-up to COVID's crash.[23]

Not only do Fed facilities contravene key, express injunctions in the federal law meant to limit them, but they also wholly undermine the law's goal of forcing financial markets to rely on their own knowledge in order to prevent their own losses. Now, the taxpayer by way of the Fed has stepped in to create not just a series of safety nets, but also a trampoline – as even a Fed insider has come to believe, all the Fed's 2020 actions make another round of even bigger bailouts even more likely than before, when odds were already high given all the Fed's policies up to that point.[24] The 13(3) restrictions demanded by the Dodd-Frank Act in 2010 were supposed to end moral hazard; as the Fed interprets them, moral hazard is made still more certain.

Instead of bailing out markets, a new, equality- and growth-focused portfolio policy dictates that the Fed's portfolio will be deployed for emergency ground-up economic recovery, not permanent trickle-down market largesse. Instead of trillions for markets that thus never go down, the Fed can and should invest the far fewer billions it would take from time to time to support equal, sustainable, and secure macroeconomic growth.

For example, the Fed could open what I call a Family Financial Facility to aid solvent families experiencing sudden income loss and do the same for small businesses forced to shut their doors.[25] This facility would, for example, provide bank-account holders with the funds needed to prevent high-cost overdrafts or, far more costly, to help them avoid payday loans by providing liquidity to banks through which they could fund short-term, small-dollar loans. A liquidity facility backing home-equity lines of credit would also have allowed families with positive home values to tap into them under stress to make ends meet. I am not alone in suggesting a realignment of Fed facilities – the head of the Bank for International Settlements, the proverbial central bank of central banks – did the same in 2020.[26]

The new portfolio policy must also identify institutions that support equitable and sustainable growth such as state and local governments and nonprofit institutions. The Fed in 2020 did open a liquidity facility for hard-pressed states, cities, and counties,[27] but it did so grudgingly, with tight limits, and initially only to the largest cities and counties. This was like the Main Street facility – a big-city-centered approach that, before the Fed was forced to think better of it, left out the 35 most heavily African American cities.[28] Many municipalities live above their means and perhaps needed tough love.

However, the Fed's decision to pick its customers by size, not fiscal restraint, suggests that the Fed was focused on operational efficiency instead of equity. The small children who need to go to a decent school, the fragile elderly people dependent on supportive housing and food assistance, and so many other vulnerable citizens are innocent bystanders of municipal excess, as are most of the rest of us who just need to get our garbage picked up and our streets maintained. Nowhere is it more clear that aid is needed and thus nowhere was it more essential for the Fed to do what it could to the greatest extent possible. The Fed bent the law to aid giant corporations,[29] but was extraordinarily literal-minded when it came to state and local governments.

The same is true for the nonprofits that provide urgent community and civic services; when the Fed proposed its nonprofit backstop,[30] it did so only because Congress demanded it. Even then, the Fed offered support only to giant foundations, museums, or the few other nonprofit entities able to demonstrate ability to repay a loan that could be no less than $250,000, but as much as $300 million. The Fed did say that a foundation's endowment could be no more than $3 billion, thus excluding the giant foundations set up by the Zuckerbergs and other new-wealth titans, but many of the nonprofits established to advance candidates or political causes by wealthy donors were still eligible. Virtually all of the biomedical, community-service, and social-justice groups on which many depend were far too small for the Fed to bother with.

The Fed didn't intend to be anti-equality, anti-justice, or anti–pretty much anything when it set up its emergency rescue facilities for financial markets and those who did well by them. It favored the few because helping the many is operationally complex and, depending on how it's done, a bit risky, but that's no excuse. As we have seen, economic equality is not just a moral imperative, but also essential for economic growth and for financial stability. The Fed thus not only should, but also must, mend the way it uses its giant portfolio. Governing law not only allows an equality-focused portfolio; it requires it.

The Fourth Fix: Normal, Moderate Interest Rates

The Fed's fourth policy tool is interest rates, set through the various "corridors" we explored in Chapter 6. As we have seen, interest rates hovered barely above zero from 2008 through 2020, when COVID's costs persuaded the Fed to drive them down to levels once as unimaginable as the size of the Fed's portfolio. Under conventional monetary policy (see Chapter 5), low, "accommodative" interest rates stoke growth because the middle class follows the Fed's lead and takes out lower-cost loans to buy homes, goods, and services that then restore macroeconomic growth. After 2008, the Fed's thoroughly unconventional policy was premised on this same expectation but, as we have seen, it faltered after 2010 and then failed in 2020 largely because the US no longer has a robust, resilient middle class.

As a result, the Fed's ultra-low rates led to the yield-chasing that propelled financial markets ever higher even as regulated financial institutions changed their business model from taking deposits and making loans to average households to one betting on stocks and offering loans and other services to wealthy households, financial markets, and giant corporations. Ultra-low rates failed to trickle down to low-, moderate-, and even middle-income households who, as we saw, were mired in high-cost debt that often came directly or indirectly from unregulated companies. Mortgage rates did fall when the Fed lowered rates after 2010, but the US homeownership rate nonetheless fell to record lows in 2016 and has barely hovered above this bottom ever since.[31]

Ultra-low rates fundamentally eviscerate the ability of all but the wealthy to gain an economic toehold; instead, they lead investors to drive up equity and other asset prices to achieve their return-on-investment objectives, but average Americans hold little, if any, stock or investment instruments. Instead, they save what they can in bank accounts. The rates on these have been so low for so long that these thrifty, prudent households have in fact set themselves back with each dollar they save. Pension funds are just as hard-hit, meaning not only that average Americans can't save for the future, but also that the instruments on which they count for additional security are unlikely to meet their needs. Retirement savings and related resources in the US are thus at an all-time low – average American retirement account balances fell below even $100,000 in the first quarter of 2020,[32] very little even with the added benefit of Social Security to fund housing, health care, food, and perhaps even a bit of fun for households likely to live on for years after wages end. And, like all averages, this one – small though it is –overstates how retirement-ready most Americans are likely to be.

As a result, the Fed should thus turn its fourth tool – interest rates – in a new direction. Instead of driving rates ever lower in an ineffectual search for economic recovery, the Fed must gradually raise rates to levels that ensure a positive real return -- that is, make money in the bank turn into money for the future. As we have seen, US interest rates long hovered around 5 percent – now, a determined increase first to 1 and then to 2 and then to 3 percent or more should be resolutely pursued.

In a conventional construct, raising rates would "tighten" the economy and reduce growth, but America is no longer a country in which conventional monetary policy applies. The combination of post-2008 Fed policy and the rapid growth in economic inequality helped to make the US economy one in which only a new but still unconventional toolkit will make both an equality and an economic difference. Ultra-low rates combined with the Fed's huge portfolio to ensure markets rise ever higher and investors do as well or better than ever before, but that's of course only until the next crash comes along.

The Final Fix: Ensuring Financial Stability

Each of the fixes described above meets the Fed's triple mandate for full employment, stable prices, and moderate interest rates with equitable results, a sharp contrast to the Fed's current construct. If it does not change its ways and enhance equality via monetary policy and all the regulatory and payment-system changes we have explored, then the Fed will not only fall far short of its triple monetary-policy mandate, but it will also fail its fourth mandate: ensuring financial stability.

Inequality and instability are inexorably intertwined. This is evident from all the research marshalled elsewhere in this book. This includes compelling research from the Federal Reserve Bank of San Francisco.[33] This paper deploys exhaustive research across decades in 17 countries based on statistical correlations of inequality, productivity, credit growth, and crises. Although productivity has a strong impact on crisis risk, a widening income share for the top 1 percent is the most predictive antecedent to a crash even when controlling for an array of other possible causes, including the asset-price bubbles the Fed fuels with its persistent market rescues. More theoretical research from elsewhere in the Fed shows a link not just to inequality, but also to continued slow growth – essentially inequality fires up its own engine, overpowering any macroeconomic signals the Fed tries to send.[34]

However, we don't need research to prove the inequality/instability nexus. The world has lived this in crisis after crisis since the 1980s. Those in the United States include the savings and loan (S&L) crisis of the 1980s, the banking crisis of the early 1990s, and the international-financial crisis of the mid-1990s, followed in short-order by the near-systemic collapse of a huge hedge fund. These financial crises paralleled growing US inequality, but inequality was just beginning its upward march and other causes took precedence over it as the sparks in these systemic debacles. These crises were followed by another financial crisis – 9/11 – which had little to do with inequality and everything to do with financial-system operational fragility and a payment system already outmoded in 2001. The dot-com bust that followed 2001 in short order never proved systemic, although it exacerbated the Fed's tendency to alter policy to suit the markets, not the nation as a whole. The next crisis – 2008 – was of course a broad-based systemic disaster caused by the confluence of anti-equality monetary policy; rates were at unprecedented lows even then and moral hazard had by then come to rule the markets. The Fed's solutions to 2008 exacerbated US inequality – indeed, they singlehandedly made it worse. This brings us to 2020, the next crash and its still more profoundly unequalizing impact.

Ending the Doom Loop

Ever since 2008, financial-market theory has included what is ominously called the "doom loop." It is usually associated with the inexorable link between countries that issue more debt than they can honor or take other unsustainable risks and large bank investments in the sovereign debt of high-risk countries. National macroeconomic or financial stress would be bad enough on its own, but because banks are often also huge investors in their home country's debt, banks suddenly become fragile or even fail. This then weakens the national economy still more, adversely affecting even the banks with smaller holdings of sovereign debt. Sound banks then follow weaker ones into severe stress, with the financial sector as a whole essentially shutting down, starving the economy of services, and making the macroeconomic situation still worse. In short, bad goes to worse and then from worse to awful and from awful to economically disastrous.

A "doom loop" also aptly describes the relationship between post-2008 US monetary policy and economic fragility. Here, the loop goes from a large Fed portfolio and ultra-low rates to ever-upward financial markets along with ever-downward economic equality. This triggers speculative, increasingly fragile finance and weak macroeconomic growth that then destroys household financial resilience for all but the wealthiest. This fragility and vulnerability cannot be corrected by the Fed's current toolkit so the Fed just doubles down, increasing its portfolio and dropping rates until the crisis that its policy helps precipitate causes a crash. Then the Fed deploys the only tools it's come to know – its portfolio and ultra-low rates – varying the playbook only to use its portfolio to still greater effect for all but those who need it the most.

Thus the doom loop reverberates all over again, just louder and still more dangerously. This isn't theory – it's what happened between 2008 and 2020 and seems set to happen again given what the Fed continues to do.

The doom loop is not just a macroeconomic and financial-system problem; it is also embedded in the economic-inequality engine. To break it, the Fed must break with its past. Although it has long pursued what is widely called unconventional monetary policy, the fundamental assumptions underlying post-2008 actions are the same, conventional ones that have long been the basis of central-bank thinking: the best way to make economies grow or to slow them down is to rely on central-bank signals sent through banks that in turn lower or raise borrowing costs to stimulate or quash growth. Financial regulation has yet to go as unconventional as I propose in Chapter 10; instead, it's mired in old thinking. This has it that financial systems depend on banks so financial-system stability also depends on banks that, if regulated toughly enough, ensure systemic stability. As we have seen, this logic depends on middle-class nations with bank-centric financial systems that power up productive – not financialized – economies.

The US is, though, now a most unequal and financialized nation with a hollowed-out middle class and a nonbank-centric financial system. Thus, Fed policy since 2008 faltered after the crisis ebbed in 2010, floundered for the next decade, and failed spectacularly in 2020.

The right way to cut the doom loop is conventional in one sense – central banking steps back from both market-making and fiscal policy – and highly unconventional in others. This new policy construct integrates monetary and regulatory policy first so that financial markets know that the Federal Reserve will not rescue their wildest and worst bets, bets instead constrained by a combination of hard-learned market discipline and like-kind rules on financial institutions taking like-kind bets backed by implicit or even explicit taxpayer guarantees such as FDIC insurance.

New policy continues with a very small Fed portfolio that increases only under stress and then only for ground-up backstops instead of trickle-down market bailouts. New policy recognizes that higher interest rates stoke growth because they skewer the "zombie" companies that live only because interest rates are so low that investors are willing to fund their debt secure in the knowledge that the Fed will never let equity or bond markets go down more than might be temporarily inconvenient.[35] Ending companies that exist largely to profit private-equity firms and overpaid CEOs and instead increasing the number of truly productive companies would boost sustained and equitable growth. Higher interest rates also make saving for the future not just virtuous, but successful, giving families with growing wages in a more productive economy a better chance for wealth accumulation, intergenerational mobility, and a secure retirement.

The Future of Equitable Finance

In 2020, the Fed pulled the US economy and financial system off the brink just as it successfully did in 2008. However, by pursuing the same policies the Fed then prolonged after 2010 and indeed by going them one bigger, although not better, the Fed has set the stage for another decade of weak growth, high-risk finance, low wages, negative savings, and lost hope.

My new framework for US monetary and regulatory policy may seem radical, but it's actually far less revolutionary than what's likely to happen if the Federal Reserve fails to reform itself. When the people get angry enough to do it on their own, change may come faster, but it's not at all clear it will be better. Economic equality is absolutely essential for financial stability and, without financial stability, there is neither stable macroeconomic growth nor constructive social consensus.

Notes

Introduction

1. Karen Shaw Petrou, "Income Inequality: The Battlefield Casualty of Post-Crisis Financial Policy" (speech, Chicago, November 3, 2020), available at https://fedfin.com/images/stories/press_center/speeches/Income%20 Inequality-The%20Battlefield%20Casualty%20of%20Post-Crisis%20Financial %20Policy_Speech.pdf.
2. Karen Shaw Petrou, "The Inexorable Will of the Financial Market: Profit Imperatives and Financial-Policy Design" (speech, New York, March 1, 2018), available at https://fedfin.com/images/stories/press_center/speeches/Karen %20Petrou%20Remarks%20Prepared%20for%20Distinguished%20Speaker %20Lecture%20Federal%20Reserve%20Bank%20of%20New%20York.pdf.
3. Thomas Piketty, *Capital in the Twenty-First Century*, translated by Arthur Gold-hammer (Cambridge: Belknap Press of Harvard University Press, 2014).
4. Irving Kristol, "'When virtue loses all her loveliness' – some reflections on capitalism and 'the free society,'" *Public Interest* 8 (Fall 1970), available at https://www.nationalaffairs.com/storage/app/uploads/public/58e/1a4/afc/ 58e1a4afc4eee090463739.pdf.

Chapter 1

1. Federal Deposit Insurance Corporation (FDIC) Chair Jelena McWilliams, "Remarks to the Institute of International Finance (IFF)-Bank Policy Institute (BPI) Cross Border Resolution & Regulation Colloquium" (speech, London,

July 1, 2019), available at https://www.fdic.gov/news/news/speeches/spjul 0119.html.

2. Board of Governors of the Federal Reserve System (FRB) Chair Jerome H. Powell, "Opening Remarks" (speech, Kansas City, MO, October 9, 2019), available at https://www.federalreserve.gov/newsevents/speech/powell20191009a.htm.

3. Carlotta Balestra and Richard Tonkin, "Inequalities in household wealth across OECD countries: Evidence from the OECD Wealth Distribution Database," *Organization for Economic Co-operation and Development (OECD) Working Paper No. 88*, 14–15 (June 20, 2018), available at http://www.oecd.org/officialdocuments/publicdisplaydocumentpdf/?cote=SDD/DOC(2018)1&docLanguage=En.

4. James Mackintosh, "Why Mr. Market Ignores a World in Turmoil," *Wall Street Journal*, June 4, 2020, available at https://www.wsj.com/articles/why-mr-market-ignores-a-world-in-turmoil-11591272919.

5. Tyler Clifford, "Jim Cramer: The pandemic led to 'one of the greatest wealth transfers in history,'" *CNBC*, June 4, 2020, available at https://www.cnbc.com/2020/06/04/cramer-the-pandemic-led-to-a-great-wealth-transfer.html.

6. FRB Gov. Lael Brainard, "Is the Middle Class within Reach for Middle-Income Families?" (speech, Washington, DC, May 10, 2019), FRB, available at https://www.federalreserve.gov/newsevents/speech/brainard20190510a.htm.

7. FRB Chair Jerome H. Powell, "Welcoming Remarks" (speech, Washington, DC, May 9, 2019), FRB, available at https://www.federalreserve.gov/newsevents/speech/powell20190509a.htm.

8. Binyamin Appelbaum, "Janet Yellen Gives an Economic Short Course, Beyond Interest Rates," *New York Times*, January 12, 2017, available at https://www.nytimes.com/2017/01/12/business/janet-yellen-interest-rates.html.

9. Heather Long and Andrew Van Dam, "The black-white economic divide is as wide as it was in 1968," *Washington Post*, June 4, 2020, available at https://www.washingtonpost.com/business/2020/06/04/economic-divide-black-households/.

10. Bruce Springsteen, "Glory Days," April 3, 1982, track #10 on *Born in the U.S.A.*, Columbia, June 4, 1984, studio album.

11. Vice President George H.W. Bush, "Address Accepting the Presidential Nomination at the Republican National Convention in New Orleans" (speech, New Orleans, August 18, 1988), available at https://www.presidency.ucsb.edu/documents/address-accepting-the-presidential-nomination-the-republican-national-convention-new.

12. David McCullough, *Truman* (New York: Simon & Schuster, 1992), 663.

13. Ali Alichi, Rodrigo Mariscal, and Daniela Muhaj, "Hollowing Out: The Channels of Income Polarization in the United States," *IMF Working Paper WP/17/244* (November, 2017), available at https://www.imf.org/en/Publications/WP/Issues/2017/11/15/Hollowing-Out-The-Channels-of-Income-Polarization-in-the-United-States-45375.

14. Chuck Collins and Josh Hoxie, "Billionaire Bonanza 2018: Inherited Wealth Dynasties of the United States," *Institute for Policy Studies* 3 (October 30, 2018), available at https://ips-dc.org/wp-content/uploads/2018/11/Billionaire-Bonanza-2018-Report-October-2018-1.pdf.

15. FRB, "Report on the Economic Well-Being of U.S. Households in 2019, Featuring Supplemental Data from April 2020," 25 (May 14, 2020), available at https://www.federalreserve.gov/publications/files/2019-report-economic-well-being-us-households-202005.pdf.

16. FRB, "2016 Survey of Consumer Finances Chartbook," 7 (October 16, 2017), available at https://www.federalreserve.gov/econres/files/BulletinCharts.pdf.

17. Emmanuel Saez, "Striking It Richer: The Evolution of Top Incomes in the United States" (updated March 2, 2019), available at https://eml.berkeley.edu/~saez/saez-UStopincomes-2017.pdf.

18. FRB, "Report on the Economic Well-Being of U.S. Households," 21.

19. Ibid.

20. Joseph C. Sternberg, *The Theft of a Decade: How the Baby Boomers Stole the Millennials' Economic Future* (New York: PublicAffairs, 1999).

21. Kasey M Lobaugh, Bobby Stephens, and Jeff Simpson, "The consumer is changing, but perhaps not how you think," *Deloitte Insights*, May 29, 2019, available at https://www2.deloitte.com/insights/us/en/industry/retail-distribution/the-consumer-is-changing.html.

22. Andrew Van Dam, "The unluckiest generation in U.S. history," *Washington Post*, May 27, 2020, available at https://www.washingtonpost.com/business/2020/05/27/millennial-recession-covid/.

23. Merrill Edge, "Spring 2019 Merrill Edge Report" (June 14, 2019), available at https://olui2.fs.ml.com/Publish/Content/application/pdf/GWMOL/Merrill_Edge_Report_Spring_2019.pdf.

24. Jung Hyun Choi, Alanna McCargo, Michael Neal, Laurie Goodman, and Caitlin Young, "Explaining the Black-White Homeownership Gap, Urban Institute" (October 2019, updated November 2019), available at https://www.urban.org/sites/default/files/publication/101160/explaining_the_black-white_homeownership_gap_1.pdf.

25. Lisa J. Dettling, Joanne W. Hsu, Lindsay Jacobs, Kevin B. Moore, and Jeffrey P. Thompson, "Recent Trends in Wealth-Holding by Race and Ethnicity:

Evidence from the Survey of Consumer Finances," *FRB FEDS Note*, September 27, 2017, available at https://www.federalreserve.gov/econres/notes/feds-notes/recent-trends-in-wealth-holding-by-race-and-ethnicity-evidence-from-the-survey-of-consumer-finances-20170927.htm.

26. FRB Chair Janet L. Yellen, "Normalizing Monetary Policy: Prospects and Perspectives (speech, San Francisco, March 27, 2015), available at https://www.federalreserve.gov/newsevents/speech/yellen20150327a.htm.

27. Michael S. Derby, "Fed's Williams: Economy May Be Bottoming as Fed Weights Yield-Curve Control," *Wall Street Journal*, May 27, 2020, available at https://www.wsj.com/articles/feds-williams-economy-may-be-bottoming-as-fed-weighs-yield-curve-control-11590594508.

28. Valerie Wilson and Janelle Jones, "Working harder or finding it harder to work," *Economic Policy Institute*, February 22, 2018, available at https://www.epi.org/publication/trends-in-work-hours-and-labor-market-disconnection/.

29. FRB Gov. Lael Brainard, "Is the Middle Class within Reach for Middle-Income Families?" (speech, Washington, D.C., May 10, 2019), available at https://www.federalreserve.gov/newsevents/speech/brainard20190510a.htm.

30. U.S. Bureau of Economic Analysis, "Real Gross Domestic Product," retrieved from Federal Reserve Economic Data (FRED), Federal Reserve Bank of St. Louis on July 19, 2019, *FRED Economic Data Series GDPC1*, available at https://fred.stlouisfed.org/series/GDPC1.

31. Michael R. Strain, "Americans May Be Strapped, But the Go-To Statistic Is False," *Bloomberg*, June 4, 2019, available at https://www.bloomberg.com/opinion/articles/2019-06-04/the-400-emergency-expense-story-is-wrong?srnd=opinion.

32. Aparna Mathur, "Poor Work Incentives in Disability: What to Do," *Forbes*, September 22, 2016, available at https://www.forbes.com/sites/aparnamathur/2016/09/22/poor-work-incentives-in-disability-what-to-do/#34a3ca8b3a14.

33. See for example: Phil Gramm and John F. Early, "The Myth of American Inequality," *Wall Street Journal*, August 9, 2018, available at https://www.wsj.com/articles/the-myth-of-american-inequality-1533855113.

34. Brainard, "Is the Middle Class within Reach for Middle-Income Families?"

35. Moritz Kuhn, Moritz Schularick, and Ulrike Steins, "Income and Wealth Inequality in America, 1949-2016," *FRB-Minneapolis Opportunity & Inclusive Growth Institute Working Paper 9*, (June, 2018), available at https://www.minneapolisfed.org/institute/working-papers-institute/iwp9.pdf.

36. Brainard, "Is the Middle Class within Reach for Middle-Income Families?"

37. Milton Friedman, *Capitalism and Freedom: Fortieth Anniversary Edition* (Chicago: University of Chicago Press, 2002), 133.

38. Henning Hesse, Boris Hofmann, and James Weber, "The Macroeconomic Effects of Asset Purchases Revisited," *Bank for International Settlements (BIS) Working Paper No. 680* 4 (December 2017), available at https://www.bis.org/publ/work680.pdf.

39. FRB, "Distribution of Household Wealth in the U.S. since 1989: Corporate equities and mutual fund shares," *FRB DFA: Distributional Financial Accounts* (2018:Q4), accessed June 5, 2019, available at https://www.federalreserve.gov/releases/z1/dataviz/dfa/distribute/table/#quarter:117;series:Corporate%20equities%20and%20mutual%20fund%20shares;demographic:networth;population:all;units:shares.

40. Michael Batty, Jesse Bricker, Joseph Briggs, Elizabeth Holmquist, Susan McIntosh, Kevin Moore, Eric Nielsen, Sarah Reber, Molly Shatto, Kamila Sommer, Tom Sweeney, and Alice Henriques Volz, "Introducing the Distributional Financial Accounts of the United States," *FRB Finance and Economic Discussion Series (FEDS) 2019-17* (March, 2019), available at https://www.federalreserve.gov/econres/feds/files/2019017pap.pdf.

41. David Willetts, "Intergenerational warfare: Who stole the millennials' future?" *Financial Times*, July 3, 2019, available at https://www.ft.com/content/0c2a575a-8c4b-11e9-b8cb-26a9caa9d67b.

42. Alex J. Pollock, *Finance and Philosophy: Why We're Always Surprised* (Philadelphia: Paul Dry Books, 2018), available at https://books.google.com/books?id=7DmqDwAAQBAJ&pg=PT88&lpg=PT88&dq=Alex+Pollock+trillion+from+savers&source=bl&ots=HmHZvstfmO&sig=ACfU3U0pFdc5g3_n6EtwPv3evRNMrw-J_A&hl=en&ppis=_e&sa=X&ved=2ahUKEwiJwdDUz_7nAhXMlnIEHbH4BTAQ6AEwAXoECAoQAQ#v=onepage&q=2.4&f=false.

43. Jeanna Smialek, "Powell Says Federal Reserve Crossed Red Lines to Help Economy," *New York Times*, May 29, 2020, available at https://www.nytimes.com/2020/05/29/business/economy/powell-federal-reserve-economy-coronavirus.html.

44. BIS, "Annual Economic Report 2019," 56 (June 20, 2019), available at https://www.bis.org/publ/arpdf/ar2019e.pdf.

45. Libra, "Introducing Libra: A simple global currency and financial infrastructure that can empower billions of people," Libra.org, June 23, 2019, available at https://libra.org/en-US/wp-content/uploads/sites/23/2019/06/IntroducingLibra_en_US.pdf.

46. Tom Wheeler, "Who makes the rules in the new Gilded Age? Lessons from the industrial age inform the information age," *Brookings Institution Center for*

Technology Innovation, December 12, 2018, available at https://www.brookings
.edu/research/who-makes-the-rules-in-the-new-gilded-age/.

47. Jonathan Fisher, David Johnson, Timothy Smeeding, and Jeffery Thompson, "Estimating the Marginal Propensity to Consume Using the Distributions of Income, Consumption, and Wealth," *FRB-Boston Working Papers No. 19-4* (February 2019), available at https://www.bostonfed.org/publications/research-department-working-paper/2019/estimating-the-marginal-propensity-to-consume-using-the-distributions-income-consumption-wealth.aspx.

48. Cynthia L. Doniger, "Do Greasy Wheels Curb Inequality?" *FRB FEDS 2019-021* (March 12, 2019), available at https://www.federalreserve.gov/econres/feds/files/2019021pap.pdf.

49. Council of Inspectors General on Financial Oversight, U.S. Department of Treasury, *Annual Report of the Council of Inspectors General on Financial Oversight* 43 (July 2012), available at https://www.treasury.gov/about/organizational-structure/ig/Documents/CIGFO%20Document/508_CIGFO%20Annual%20Report.pdf.

50. John Kenneth Galbraith, "A Journey Through Economic Time," Interview by Brian Lamb, Booknotes C-SPAN, November 13, 1994, available at https://www.c-span.org/video/?60409-1/a-journey-economic-time.

Chapter 2

1. Board of Governors of the Federal Reserve System (FRB), "Distribution of Household Wealth in the U.S. since 1989," *DFA: Distributional Financial Accounts*, updated December 23, 2019, available at https://www.federalreserve.gov/releases/z1/dataviz/dfa/distribute/chart/.

2. Alina K. Bartscher, Moritz Kuhn, Moritz Schularick, and Ulrike I. Steins, "Modigliani Meets Minsky: Inequality, Debt, and Financial Fragility in America, 1950–2016," *Federal Reserve Bank of New York Staff Report No. 924* (May 2020), available at https://www.newyorkfed.org/medialibrary/media/research/staff_reports/sr924.pdf.

3. Joint Center for Housing Studies of Harvard University (JCHS Harvard), "The State of the Nation's Housing 2019," 11 (June 25, 2019), available at https://www.jchs.harvard.edu/sites/default/files/Harvard_JCHS_State_of_the_Nations_Housing_2019.pdf.

4. Federal Reserve Bank of New York (FRBNY) Research and Statistics Group, "Quarterly Report on Household Debt and Credit 2019: Q4," *FRBNY Center for Microeconomic Data*, 3 (February 2020), available at https://www.newyorkfed.org/medialibrary/interactives/householdcredit/data/pdf/HHDC_2019Q4.pdf.

5. FRB, "Report on the Economic Well-Being of U.S. Households in 2019, Featuring Supplemental Data from April 2020," 21 (May 14, 2020), available at https://www.federalreserve.gov/publications/files/2019-report-economic-well-being-us-households-202005.pdf.

6. Ibid., 22.

7. Bruce D. Meyer and James X. Sullivan, "Consumption and Income Inequality in the U.S. Since the 1960s," *AEI Economics Working Paper 2017-16* (August 2017), available at http://www.aei.org/publication/consumption-and-income-inequality-in-the-us-since-the-1960s/.

8. Jonathan Fisher, David Johnson, Timothy Smeeding, and Jeffrey P. Thompson, "Estimating the Marginal Propensity to Consume Using the Distributions of Income, Consumption, and Wealth," *Federal Reserve of Boston Department Working Paper 19-4* (February 2019), available at https://www.bostonfed .org/publications/research-department-working-paper/2019/estimating-the-marginal-propensity-to-consume-using-the-distributions-income-consumption-wealth.aspx.

9. Jonathan Fisher, David Johnson, Timothy Smeeding, and Jeffrey Thompson, "Inequality in 3-D: Income, Consumption, and Wealth," *FRB Finance and Economics Discussion Series (FEDS) 2018-001,* available at https://www .federalreserve.gov/econres/feds/files/2018001pap.pdf.

10. Jesse Bricker an Alice Henriques Volz, "Wealth concentration levels and growth: 1989–2016," *FEDS Notes*, FRB (February 20, 2020), available at https:// www.federalreserve.gov/econres/notes/feds-notes/wealth-concentration-levels-and-growth-1989-2016-20200220.htm.

11. FRB, "Report on the Economic Well-Being of U.S. Households in 2019," 11.

12. FRB Gov. Lael Brainard, Speech at "Renewing the Promise of the Middle Class," 2019 Federal Reserve System Community Development Research Conference, Washington, DC: Is the Middle Class within Reach for Middle-Income Families? (May 10, 2019), available at https://www .federalreserve.gov/newsevents/speech/brainard20190510a.htm.

13. Census Bureau, "Table H-3. Mean Household Income Received by Each Fifth and Top 5 Percent," *Historical Income Tables: Income Inequality*, accessed February 27, 2020, available at https://www.census.gov/data/tables/time-series/demo/income-poverty/historical-income-inequality.html.

14. Ibid.

15. Ibid.

16. Census Bureau, "Table H-2. Share of Aggregate Income Received by Each Fifth and Top 5 Percent of Households," *Historical Income Tables: Income Inequality*, accessed February 27, 2020, available at https://www.census.gov/

data/tables/time-series/demo/income-poverty/historical-income-inequality
.html.

17. Facundo Alvaredo, Lucas Chancel, Thomas Piketty, Emmanuel Saez, and Gabriel Zucman, "World Inequality Report 2018," *World Inequality Lab,* 80 (December 2017), available at https://wir2018.wid.world/files/download/wir2018-full-report-english.pdf.

18. Ibid.

19. Ibid.

20. Congressional Budget Office (CBO), "Projected Changes in Distribution of Household Income, 2016-2021," 5 (December 2019), available at https://www.cbo.gov/system/files/2019-12/55941-CBO-Household-Income.pdf.

21. Ibid.

22. Juliana Menasce Horowitz, Ruth Igielnik, and Rakesh Kochhar, "Most Americans Say there Is Too Much Economic Inequality in the U.S., But Fewer than Half Call It a Top Priority" (January 9, 2020), available at https://www.pewsocialtrends.org/2020/01/09/trends-in-income-and-wealth-inequality/.

23. Ibid.

24. Ibid.

25. Emily Dohrman and Bruce Fallick, "Is the Middle Class Worse Off than It Used to Be?" *Federal Reserve Bank of Cleveland Economic Commentary 2020-03* (February 12, 2020), available at https://www.clevelandfed.org/en/newsroom-and-events/publications/economic-commentary/2020-economic-commentaries/ec-202003-is-middle-class-worse-off.aspx.

26. FRB, "Distribution of Household Wealth in the U.S. since 1989."

27. Ibid.

28. Ibid.

29. Kuhn, Schularick, and Steins, "Income and Wealth Inequality in America, 1949–2016," 33.

30. Ibid.

31. Ibid.

32. Jonathan Heathcote, Fabrizio Perri, and Giovanni L. Violante, "The Rise of US Earnings Inequality: Does the Cycle Drive the Trend?" *Federal Reserve Bank of Minneapolis Staff Report No. 604* (June 2020), available at https://www.minneapolisfed.org/research/staff-reports/the-rise-of-us-earnings-inequality-does-the-cycle-drive-the-trend.

33. Bruce Stokes, "A Decade After the Financial Crisis, Economic Confidence Rebounds in Many Countries," *Pew Research Center* (September 18, 2018), available at http://www.pewglobal.org/2018/09/18/a-decade-after-

the-financial-crisis-economic-confidence-rebounds-in-many-countries/?
mod=article_inline.

34. William R. Emmons, Ana H. Kent, and Lowell R. Ricketts, "The Demographics of Wealth: How Education, Race and Birth Year Shape Financial Outcomes," *FRB St. Louis The Demographics of Wealth 2018 Series* 5 (February 2018), available at https://www.stlouisfed.org/~/media/Files/PDFs/HFS/essays/HFS_essay_1-2018.pdf?la=en.

35. Organization for Economic Cooperation and Development (OECD), *A Broken Social Elevator? How to Promote Social Mobility,* 27 (June 15, 2018), available at https://www.oecd.org/social/soc/Social-mobility-2018-Overview-MainFindings.pdf.

36. Moritz Kuhn, Moritz Schularick, and Ulrike I. Steins, "Income and Wealth Inequality in America, 1949–2016," *Federal Reserve Bank of Minneapolis Opportunity and Inclusive Growth Institute Working Paper 9* (June 2018), available at https://www.minneapolisfed.org/institute/working-papers-institute/iwp9.pdf.

37. Lisa J. Dettling, Joanne W. Hsu, Lindsay Jacobs, Kevin B. Morre, and Jeffrey P. Thompson, "Recent Trends in Wealth-Holding by Race and Ethnicity: Evidence from the Survey of Consumer Finances," *FEDS Notes,* FRB (September 27, 2017), available at https://www.federalreserve.gov/econres/notes/feds-notes/recent-trends-in-wealth-holding-by-race-and-ethnicity-evidence-from-the-survey-of-consumer-finances-20170927.htm.

38. Jung Hyun Choi, "Breaking Down the Black-White Homeownership Gap," *Urban Institute* (February 21, 2020), available at https://www.urban.org/urban-wire/breaking-down-black-white-homeownership-gap.

39. Census Bureau, "Quarterly Residential Vacancies and Homeownership, Fourth Quarter 2019," *Census Bureau Release No. CB20-05* (January 30, 2020), available at https://www.census.gov/housing/hvs/files/currenthvspress.pdf.

40. Ibid.

41. FRB, "Distribution of Household Wealth in the U.S. since 1989."

42. Census Bureau, "Quick Facts: United States," accessed February 24, 2020, available at https://www.census.gov/quickfacts/fact/table/US/PST045218.

43. National Urban League, *Save Our Cities: Powering the Digital Revolution: State of Black America 2018*, 42nd edition, 5 (May 2, 2017), available at http://www.ncbw-qcmc.org/uploads/1/0/2/9/102980742/nul-soba2018-executive_summary.pdf.

44. François Bourguignon, *The Globalization of Inequality*, translated by Thomas Scott-Railton (Princeton: Princeton University Press, 2015).

45. Alvaredo et al., "World Inequality Report," 131.

46. Ibid., 156.

47. Ibid., 70.

48. Mary C. Daly, Joseph H. Pedtke, Nicolas Petrosky-Nadeau, and Annemarie Schweinert, "Why Aren't U.S. Workers Working?" *FRB San Francisco Economic Letter 2018-24* (November 13, 2018), available at https://www.frbsf.org/economic-research/publications/economic-letter/2018/november/why-are-us-workers-not-participating/?utm_source=frbsf-home-economic-letter-title&utm_medium=frbsf&utm_campaign=economic-letter.

49. FRB, "Report on the Economic Well-Being of U.S. Households in 2019," 15.

50. Jacob Fun Kirkegaard, "Is Denmark the new 'American dream'?" *Peterson Institute for International Economics Realtime Economic Issues Watch* (February 21, 2020), available at https://www.piie.com/blogs/realtime-economic-issues-watch/denmark-new-american-dream#_ftn1.

51. FRB "Median value of before-tax family income for families with holdings by percentile of income," *2016 Survey of Consumer Finances Chart Book*, 7 (September 2017), available at https://www.federalreserve.gov/econres/files/BulletinCharts.pdf.

52. FRB, "Median value of net worth for families with holdings by percentile of income," *2016 Survey of Consumer Finances Chart Book*, 43 (September 2017), available at https://www.federalreserve.gov/econres/files/BulletinCharts.pdf

53. FRB, "Median value of before-tax family income."

54. Ibid.

Chapter 3

1. Glenn Loury, "Why Does Racial Inequality Persist? Culture, Causation, and Responsibility, Manhattan Institute" (May 7, 2019), available at https://media4.manhattan-institute.org/sites/default/files/R-0519-GL.pdf.

2. Kevin Williamson, "The White-Minstrel Show," *National Review* (October 20, 2017), available at https://www.nationalreview.com/2017/10/white-working-class-populism-underclass-anti-elitism-acting-white-incompatible-conservativism/.

3. Jonah Goldberg, "Politics In The News: Tax Bill Implications and Russia Probe," NPR Morning Edition (December 18, 2017), available at https://www.npr.org/2017/12/18/571579648/politics-in-the-news-tax-bill-implications-and-russia-probe.

4. Walter Scheidel, *The Great Leveler: Violence and the History of Inequality from the Stone Age to the Twenty-First Century* (Princeton: Princeton University Press, 2017).

5. Mark Hosenball, "U.S. senators launch bill to broaden shell companies' disclosures," *Reuters* (June 10, 2019), available at https://www.reuters

.com/article/us-usa-congress-shell-companies/us-senators-launch-bill-to-broaden-shell-companies-disclosures-idUSKCN1TB26J.

6. Bureau of Economic Analysis, "Interactive Access to Industry Economic Accounts Data: GDP by Industry (Historical) and GDP by Industry, Value Added by Industry as a Percentage of GDP" (October 29, 2019), available at https://apps .bea.gov/iTable/iTable.cfm?reqid=147&step=2&isuri=1; https://apps.bea .gov/iTable/iTable.cfm?ReqID=51&step=1.

7. Facundo Alvaredo, Lucas Chancel, Thomas Piketty, Emmanuel Saez, and Gabriel Zucman, "World Inequality Report 2018," World Inequality Lab, 89 (December 14, 2017), available at http://wir2018.wid.world/files/download/ wir2018-full-report-english.pdf.

8. FRB Gov. Ben S. Bernanke, "Money, Gold, and the Great Depression" (speech, Lexington, VA, March 2, 2004), available at https://www .federalreserve.gov/boarddocs/speeches/2004/200403022/default.htm.

9. Alvaredo et al., "World Inequality Report 2018."

10. David Altig, Alan J. Auerback, Laurence J. Kotlikoff, Elias Ilin, and Victor Ye, "Marginal Net Taxation of Americans' Labor Supply," *NBER Working Paper No. 27164* (May 2020), available at https://www.nber.org/papers/w27164.

11. GAO, Retirement Security: Income and Wealth Disparities Continue through Old Age, GAO-19-587 (August 2019), available at https://www.gao.gov/ assets/710/700836.pdf.

12. Ibid.

13. OECD, "Preventing Ageing Unequally," OECD, Paris (October 2017) http:// www.oecd.org/social/soc/preventing-ageing-unequally-9789264279087-en .htm.

14. Tara Siegel Bernard, "'Too Little Too Late': Bankruptcy Booms Among Older Americans," *New York Times* (August 5, 2018), available at https:// www.nytimes.com/2018/08/05/business/bankruptcy-older-americans.html.

15. Federal Reserve Bank of New York (FRB-NY), Research and Statistics Group, "Quarterly Report on Household Debt and Credit 2020: Q1," *FRBNY Center for Microeconomic Data* (May 2020), available at https://www.newyorkfed.org/ medialibrary/interactives/householdcredit/data/pdf/HHDC_2020Q1.pdf.

16. Diana Farrell, Fiona Greig, and Amar Hamoudi, "Deferred Care: How Tax Refunds Enable Healthcare Spending," *JP Morgan Chase & Co. Institute*, 2 (January 8, 2018), available at https://www.jpmorganchase.com/corporate/ institute/document/institute-tax-refunds-healthcare-report.pdf.

17. L. Randall Wray, *Modern Money Theory: A Primer on Macroeconomics for Sovereign Monetary Systems,* 2nd ed. (Palgrave Macmillan, 2016).

18. See, for example, U.S. Bureau of Labor Statistics, "Education still pays," *Career Outlook* (September 2014), available at https://www.bls.gov/careeroutlook/2014/data-on-display/education-still-pays.htm.

19. Tax Policy Center, "Tax Policy Center Briefing Book: Key Elements of the U.S. Tax System," 65 (2017), available at http://www.taxpolicycenter.org/sites/default/files/briefing-book/tpc-briefing-book_0.pdf.

20. FRB-NY Research and Statistics Group, "Quarterly Report," 3.

21. Bureau of Labor Statistics, U.S. Department of Labor, "College tuition and fees increase 63 percent since January 2006," *Economics Daily* (August 30, 2016), available at https://www.bls.gov/opub/ted/2016/college-tuition-and-fees-increase-63-percent-since-january-2006.htm.

22. Alvaredo et al., "World Inequality Report 2018," 270.

23. Raji Chakrabarti, Andrew Haughwout, Donghoon Lee, Joelle Scally, and Wilbert van der Klaauw, "Press Briefing on Household Debt, with Focus on Student Debt," Federal Reserve Bank of New York, 28 (April 3, 2017), available at https://www.newyorkfed.org/medialibrary/media/press/PressBriefing-Household-Student-Debt-April32017.pdf#page=28.

24. Valentin Lang and Marina Mendes Tavares, "The Distribution of Gains from Globalization," *IMF Working Paper No. 18/54* (March 13, 2018), available at https://www.imf.org/en/Publications/WP/Issues/2018/03/13/The-Distribution-of-Gains-from-Globalization-45722.

25. Natalija Novta and Evgenia Pugacheva, "Manufacturing Jobs and Inequality: Why Is the U.S. Experience Different?" *IMF Working Paper No. 19/191* (September 13, 2019), available at https://www.imf.org/en/Publications/WP/Issues/2019/09/13/Manufacturing-Jobs-and-Inequality-Why-is-the-U-S-47001.

26. Lang and Tavares, The Distribution of Gains from Globalization."

27. Philipp Heimberger, "Does Economic Globalisation Affect Income Inequality? A Meta-analysis," *wiiw Working Papers 165*, Vienna Institute for International Economic Studies (October 2019), available at https://wiiw.ac.at/does-economic-globalisation-affect-income-inequality-a-meta-analysis-dlp-5044.pdf.

28. John Murphy, "How Closing the Southern Border Would Slam the U.S. Economy," U.S. Chamber of Commerce (April 4, 2019), available at https://www.uschamber.com/series/above-the-fold/how-closing-the-southern-border-would-slam-the-us-economy.

29. United Nations General Assembly, "Transforming our world: The 2030 Agenda for Sustainable Development" (September 25, 2015), available at http://www.un.org/ga/search/view_doc.asp?symbol=A/RES/70/1&Lang=E.

30. G20 Leaders' Declaration, "Shaping an interconnected world" (July 8, 2017), available at http://www.g20.utoronto.ca/2017/2017-G20-leaders-declaration.pdf.

31. European Council, "The Charlevoix G7 Summit Communique" (June 9, 2018), available at https://www.consilium.europa.eu/en/press/press-releases/2018/06/09/the-charlevoix-g7-summit-communique/.

32. Simon Zadek and Tillman Bruett, "Harnessing Digitalization in Financing the Sustainable Development Goals," United Nations Secretary-General's Task Force on Digital Financing of the Sustainable Development Goals (September, 2019), available at https://digitalfinancingtaskforce.org/wp-content/uploads/2019/09/Task-Force-CoChair-Interim-Report.pdf.

Chapter 4

1. Aristotle, *Politics,* Book IV, Part XII (350 BCE), translated by Benjamin Jowett, Digireads.com Publishing (December 26, 2017), available at https://classicalwisdom.com/greek_books/politics-by-aristotle-book-iv/4/.

2. Pablo Fajnzylber, Daniel Lederman, and Norman Loayza, "Inequality and Crime," *Journal of Law and Economics,* 45 (April 2002), available at https://siteresources.worldbank.org/DEC/Resources/Crime%26Inequality.pdf.

3. Steven Woolf and Heidi Schoomaker, "Life Expectancy and Mortality Rates in the United States, 1959-2017," *JAMA* (November 26, 2019), available at https://jamanetwork.com/journals/jama/article-abstract/2756187.

4. David C. Radley, Sara R. Collins, and Susan L. Hayes, "2019 Scorecard on State Health System Performance," *Commonwealth Fund,* 4 (June 2019), available at https://scorecard.commonwealthfund.org/files/Radley_State_Scorecard_2019.pdf.

5. Raj Chetty, Michael Stepner, Sarah Abraham, Shelby Lin, Benjamin Scuderi, Nicholas Turner, Augustin Bergeron, and David Cutler, "The Association Between Income and Life Expectancy in the United States, 2001–2014," *JAMA,* 315(16): 1750–1766 (April 2016), available at https://jamanetwork.com/journals/jama/article-abstract/2513561?redirect=true.

6. Anne Case and Angus Deaton, *Deaths of Despair and the Future of Capitalism* (Princeton: Princeton University Press, 2020).

7. APM Research Lab Staff, "The Color of Coronavirus: COVID-19 Deaths by Race and Ethnicity in the U.S.," *APM Research Lab* (updated June 10, 2020), available at https://www.apmresearchlab.org/covid/deaths-by-race.

8. Ibid.

9. Center for Medicare & Medicaid Services, "Preliminary Medicare COVID-19 Data Snapshot: Medicare Claims and Encounter Data: Services January 1 to May 16, 2020, Received by June 11, 2020" (June 23, 2020), available at

https://www.cms.gov/files/document/medicare-covid-19-data-snapshot-fact-sheet.pdf.

10. See, for example, Tina Nguyen, "'Army of Trump' prepares at CPAC to battle socialism," *Politico* (February 27, 2020), available at https://www.politico.com/news/2020/02/27/cpac-trump-socialism-117974.

11. Philip Stephans, "Populism is the true legacy of the global financial crisis," *Financial Times,* available at https://www.ft.com/content/687c0184-aaa6-11e8-94bd-cba20d67390c.

12. Joshua Green, "The Biggest Legacy of the Financial Crisis Is the Trump Presidency," *Bloomberg Businessweek* (August 30, 2018), available at https://www.bloomberg.com/news/articles/2018-08-30/the-biggest-legacy-of-the-financial-crisis-is-the-trump-presidency.

13. Lydia Saad, "Socialism as Popular as Capitalism Among Young Adults in U.S.," *Gallup* (November 25, 2019), available at https://news.gallup.com/poll/268766/socialism-popular-capitalism-among-young-adults.aspx.

14. Pew Research Center, "Public Trust in Government: 1958–2019" (April 11, 2019), available at https://www.people-press.org/2019/04/11/public-trust-in-government-1958-2019/.

15. Juliana Menasce Horowitz, Ruth Igielnik, and Rakesh Kochhar, "Most Americans Say There Is Too Much Economic Inequality in the U.S., but Fewer than Half Call it a Top Priority: 2. Views of economic inequality," *Pew Research Center* (January 9, 2020), available at https://www.pewsocialtrends.org/2020/01/09/views-of-economic-inequality/.

16. Manuel Funke, Moritz Schularick, and Christoph Trebesch, "Going to extremes: Politics after financial crises, 1870–2014," *CESifo Working Paper Series No. 5553* (October 2015), available at https://papers.ssrn.com/sol3/papers.cfm?abstract_id=2688897.

17. John F. Helliwell, Richard Layard, Jeffrey D. Sachs, and Jan-Emmanuel De Neve, World Happiness Report 2020, Figure 2.1: Ranking of Happiness 2017–2011, 20 (2020), available at https://happiness-report.s3.amazonaws.com/2020/WHR20.pdf.

18. Emmie Martin, "Nearly 70% of Americans consider themselves middle-class—here's how many actually are," *CNBC* (September 26, 2018), available at https://www.cnbc.com/2018/09/26/how-many-americans-qualify-as-middle-class.html.

19. Jonathan Rauch, "Why Prosperity Has Increased but Happiness Has Not," *New York Times* (August 21, 2018), available at https://www.nytimes.com/2018/08/21/opinion/happiness-inequality-prosperity-.html.

20. Board of Governors of the Federal Reserve System (FRB) Vice Chair Richard Clarida, "U.S. Economic Outlook and Monetary Policy" (speech, 36th

Annual NABE Economic Policy Conference, Washington, DC, February 25, 2020), available at https://www.federalreserve.gov/newsevents/speech/files/clarida20200225a.pdf.

21. Michael S. Derby, "Fed's Williams: Economy May Be Bottoming as Fed Weighs Yield-Curve Control," *Wall Street Journal* (May 27, 2020), available at https://www.wsj.com/articles/feds-williams-economy-may-be-bottoming-as-fed-weighs-yield-curve-control-11590594508.

22. See, for example, Joseph Stiglitz, *Inequality and Economic Growth* (July 2016), available at https://www8.gsb.columbia.edu/faculty/jstiglitz/sites/jstiglitz/files/Inequality%20and%20Economic%20Growth.pdf; and Council of Economic Advisors Chairman Alan Krueger, "The Rise and Consequences of Inequality in the United States" (speech, Center for American Progress, Washington, DC, January 12, 2012), available at https://obamawhitehouse.archives.gov/sites/default/files/krueger_cap_speech_final_remarks.pdf.

23. Paul Krugman, "For Whom the Economy Grows," *New York Times* (August 30, 2018), available at https://www.nytimes.com/2018/08/30/opinion/economy-gdp-income-inequality.html?smtyp=curtw-nytopinion.

24. International Monetary Fund (IMF), "United States: 2017 Article IV Consultation-Press Release; Staff Report," Country Report No. 17/239, 14 (July 2017), available at https://www.imf.org/en/Publications/CR/Issues/2017/07/27/United-States-2017-Article-IV-Consultation-Press-Release-Staff-Report-45142.

25. Andrew G. Berg and Jonathan D. Ostry, "Inequality and Unsustainable Growth: Two Sides of the Same Coin?" *IMF Staff Discussion Note 11/08* (April 8, 2011), available at https://www.imf.org/external/pubs/ft/sdn/2011/sdn1108.pdf.

26. Federico Cingano, "Trends in Income Inequality and Its Impact on Economic Growth," *OECD Social, Employment and Migration Working Paper No. 163* (December 2014), available at http://www.oecd.org/els/soc/trends-in-income-inequality-and-its-impact-on-economic-growth-SEM-WP163.pdf.

27. Jonathan D. Ostry, Andrew Berg, and Siddharth Kothari, *Growth-Equity Trade-offs in Structural Reforms*, *IMF Working Paper No. 18/5* (January 2018), available at http://www.imf.org/en/Publications/WP/Issues/2018/01/05/Growth-Equity-Trade-offs-in-Structural-Reforms-45540.

28. Glen-Marie Lang, Quentin Wodon, and Kevin Carey, "The Changing Wealth of Nations 2018: Building a Sustainable Future," World Bank Group (January 2018), available at https://openknowledge.worldbank.org/bitstream/handle/10986/29001/9781464810466.pdf?sequence=4&isAllowed=y.

29. World Economic Forum, "The Inclusive Development Index 2018: Summary and Data Highlights," 3 (January 22, 2018), available at http://www3.weforum.org/docs/WEF_Forum_IncGrwth_2018.pdf.

30. IMF, *U.S. 2017 Article IV Consultation*.

31. FRB, "Report on the Economic Well-Being of U.S. Households in 2019, Featuring Supplemental Data from April 2020," 21 (May 14, 2020), available at https://www.federalreserve.gov/publications/files/2019-report-economic-well-being-us-households-202005.pdf.

32. Facundo Alvaredo, Lucas Chancel, Thomas Piketty, Emmanuel Saez, and Gabriel Zucman, "World Inequality Report 2018," *World Inequality Lab,* 217 (December 14, 2017), available at http://wir2018.wid.world/files/download/wir2018-full-report-english.pdf.

33. Abi Adams-Prassl, Teodora Boneva, Marta Golin, and Christopher Rauh, "Inequality in the Impact of the Coronavirus Shock: Evidence from Real Time Surveys," *CESifo Working Paper 8265* (April 2020), available at https://www.cesifo.org/DocDL/cesifo1_wp8265.pdf.

34. Pierre Monnin, "Monetary Policy, Macroprudential Regulation and Inequality," *CEP Discussion Note 2017/2* (April 2017), available at https://papers.ssrn.com/sol3/papers.cfm?abstract_id=2970459.

35. Pascal Paul, "Historical Patterns of Inequality and Productivity around Financial Crises," Federal Reserve Bank of San Francisco, *Working Paper 2017-23* (March 2020), available at https://www.frbsf.org/economic-research/files/wp2017-23.pdf.

36. Isabel Cairo and Jae Sim, "Income Inequality, Financial Crises, and Monetary Policy," *Federal Reserve Finance and Economics Discussion Series Working Paper 2018-048* (May 2018), available at https://www.federalreserve.gov/econres/feds/files/2018048pap.pdf.

Chapter 5

1. Jonathan Burton, "Ray Dalio: Rising debt, income inequality and political polarization are a recipe for a nasty downturn," *MarketWatch* (September 14, 2018), available at https://www.marketwatch.com/story/the-next-financial-crisis-will-threaten-capitalism-and-democracy-ray-dalio-warns-2018-09-13.

2. Ortenca Aliaj, "Ray Dalio: Tackle inequality or face a violent revolution," *Financial Times* (November 5, 2019), available at https://www.ft.com/content/66fd4626-ffe4-11e9-b7bc-f3fa4e77dd47.

3. Matthew Goldstein and Kate Kelly, "Some Big Investors Are Stockpiling Cash to Prepare for Whatever Comes Next," *New York Times* (March 20, 2020), available at https://www.nytimes.com/2020/03/20/business/coronavirus-hedge-funds-stocks.html.

4. Bureau of Economic Analysis, Interactive Access to Industry Economic Accounts Data: GDP by Industry (Historical) and GDP by Industry, Value Added by Industry as a Percentage of GDP, available at https://apps.bea.gov/

iTable/iTable.cfm?reqid=147&step=2&isuri=1; https://apps.bea.gov/iTable/iTable.cfm?ReqID=51&step=1.

5. Andrew J. Filardo and Pierre L. Siklos, "The Cross-Border Credit Channel and Lending Standards Surveys: Implications for the International Transmission of Monetary Policies," *BIS Working Paper No. 723*, 9 (May 2018), available at https://www.bis.org/publ/work723.pdf.

6. Board of Governors of the Federal Reserve (FRB), "Federal Reserve to review strategies, tools, and communications practices it uses to pursue its mandate of maximum employment and price stability" (November 15, 2018), available at https://www.federalreserve.gov/newsevents/pressreleases/monetary20181115a.htm.

7. Dodd-Frank Wall Street Reform and Consumer Protection Act (Dodd-Frank), Pub. L. No. 111-203, 124 Stat. 1376 (July 21, 2010), available at https://www.gpo.gov/fdsys/pkg/PLAW-111publ203/pdf/PLAW-111publ203.pdf.

8. Financial Stability Board (FSB), "Evaluation of the effects of too-big-to-fail reforms," Consultation Report (June 28, 2020), available at https://www.fsb.org/wp-content/uploads/P280620-1.pdf.

9. Office of the Comptroller of the Currency (OCC), "Policy Statement on Financial Technology Companies' Eligibility to Apply for National Bank Charters" (July 31, 2018), available at https://www.occ.gov/publications/publications-by-type/other-publications-reports/pub-other-occ-policy-statement-fintech.pdf.

10. FRB, "Financial Stability Report" (November 15, 2019), available at https://www.federalreserve.gov/publications/files/financial-stability-report-20191115.pdf.

11. FRB, "Transcript of Chair Powell's Press Conference October 30, 2019," accessed April 16, 2020, available at https://www.federalreserve.gov/mediacenter/files/FOMCpresconf20191030.pdf.

12. FRB, "Transcript of Chair Powell's Press Conference Call March 15, 2020," accessed April 7, 2020, available at https://www.federalreserve.gov/mediacenter/files/FOMCpresconf20200315.pdf.

13. FRB St. Louis, "Total unemployed, plus all marginally attached workers plus total employed part time for economic reasons," *FRED Economic Data Series U6RATE*, accessed February 1, 2019, available at https://fred.stlouisfed.org/series/U6RATE

14. Elise Gould and Heidi Shierholz, "Average wage growth continues to flatline in 2018, while low-wage workers and those with relatively lower levels of educational attainment see stronger gains," *Economic Policy Institute Working Economics Blog* (July 18, 2018), available at https://www.epi.org/blog/average-wage-growth-continues-to-flatline-in-2018-while-low-wage-workers-and-

those-with-relatively-lower-levels-of-educational-attainment-see-stronger-gains/.

15. Sarah A. Donovan and David H. Bradley, "Real Wage Trends, 1979 to 2017," *Congressional Research Service Report R45090*, available at https://fas.org/sgp/crs/misc/R45090.pdf.

16. Bank for International Settlements (BIS) Committee on the Global Financial System (CGFS) Markets Committee, "*Regulatory change and monetary policy,*" *CFGS Paper No. 54* (May, 2015), available at https://www.bis.org/publ/cgfs54.pdf.

Chapter 6

1. Richard W. Stevenson, "Tracking the Wealth Effect," *New York Times* (February 24, 2000), available at https://archive.nytimes.com/www.nytimes.com/library/financial/fed/022400fed-greenspan.html.

2. Janet Yellen, "From Adding Accommodation to Scaling It Back," 10 (speech, Chicago, March 3, 2017), Board of Governors of the Federal Reserve System (FRB), available at https://www.federalreserve.gov/newsevents/speech/yellen20170303a.htm.

3. FRB Chair Powell, "Monetary Policy and the Economy," CSPAN, at 1:03:50 (February 20, 2020), available at https://www.c-span.org/video/?469082-1/monetary-policy-economy.

4. Mark Carney, "The Specter of Monetarism" (speech, Liverpool, UK, December 5, 2016), Bank of England, available at https://www.bankofengland.co.uk/-/media/boe/files/speech/2016/the-spectre-of-monetarism.pdf.

5. Henry Kaufman, "US capitalism has been shattered," *Financial Times* (June 25, 2020), available at https://www.ft.com/content/e7baaac4-b66e-4c87-8d77-ff5135a0f20c.

6. Ibid.

7. Lex, "Fed's $2.3tn bailout: Fielding fallen angels," *Financial Times* (April 9, 2020), available at https://www.ft.com/content/86e2fdc5-0f8c-463b-8d90-8f9f8944b168.

8. Chuck Mikolajczak, "S&P 500 ends best quarter since 1998 on a high note," Reuters (June 30, 2020), available at https://www.reuters.com/article/us-usa-stocks/sp-500-ends-best-quarter-since-1998-on-a-high-note-idUSKBN2411QH.wa

9. FRB, Minutes of the Federal Open Market Committee, June 9–10, 2020 (July 1, 2020), available at https://www.federalreserve.gov/monetarypolicy/files/fomcminutes20200610.pdf.

10. "In light of global economic and financial developments and muted inflation pressures, the Committee will be patient as it determines what future

adjustments to the target range for the federal funds rate may be appropriate." FRB Chair Powell, "Transcript of Chairman Powell's Press Conference January 30, 2019," FRB, 2 (January 30, 2019), available at https://www.federalreserve .gov/mediacenter/files/FOMCpresconf20190130.pdf.

11. Seeking Alpha, "The Fed Is Your Best Friend and The Proof Is In The Balance Sheet Pudding," Chart 4 (January 6, 2020), available at https:// seekingalpha.com/article/4315463-fed-is-your-best-friend-and-proof-is-in-balance-sheet-pudding.

12. Narayana Kocherlakota, "'Absurd' for Fed to leave its policy framework unchanged," University of Rochester (December 9, 2019), available at https://www.rochester.edu/newscenter/rochester-economist-absurd-for-the-fed-to-leave-its-policy-framework-unchanged-410272/.

13. Federal Reserve Bank of St. Louis, "Assets: Total Assets: Total Assets (Less Eliminations From Consolidation): Wednesday Level," FRED Economic Data Series WALCL, accessed July 6, 2020, available at https://fred.stlouisfed.org/ series/WALCL.

14. Bill Nelson, "A former Fed insider explains the internal debate over QE3," *Financial Times* (February 16, 2018), available at https://ftalphaville.ft .com/2018/02/16/2198845/guest-post-a-former-fed-insider-explains-the-internal-debate-over-qe3/.

15. Chris Anstey and Gowri Gurumurthy, "One Last Hurrah? US Junk Bond Premium Hits Lowest Since 2007," Bloomberg News, October 3, 2018, available at https://www.bloomberg.com/news/articles/2018-10-03/a-last-hurrah-u-s-junk-bond-premium-hits-lowest-since-07?sref=BSO3yKhf.

16. Frédéric Boissay and Russell Cooper, "The Collateral Trap," *BIS Working Paper No. 565* (May 2016), available at https://www.bis.org/publ/work565 .pdf.

17. Karen Petrou, "Repo ructions highlight failure of post-crisis policy making," *Financial Times* (November 5, 2019), available at https://www.ft.com/content/ fe562cbe-feee-11e9-b7bc-f3fa4e77dd47.

18. FRB, "Federal Reserve issues FOMC Statement" (March 15, 2020), available at https://www.federalreserve.gov/newsevents/pressreleases/ monetary20200315a.htm.

19. Henning Hesse, Boris Hofmann, and James Weber, "The Macroeconomic Effects of Asset Purchases Revisited," *BIS Working Paper No. 680,* 4 (December 2017), available at https://www.bis.org/publ/work680.pdf.

20. David Greenlaw, James D. Hamilton, Ethan S. Harris, and Kenneth D. West, "A Skeptical View of the Impact of the Fed's Balance Sheet" (February, 2018), available at https://research.chicagobooth.edu/-/media

/research/igm/docs/2018-usmpf-report.pdf?la=en&hash=D8BE7A0F78D72 A6762918282D5A56A2E76349AED.

21. John Kandrac and Bernd Schlusche, "Quantitative easing and bank risk taking: Evidence from lending," FRB Finance and Economics Discussion Series 2017-125 (October 12, 2017), available at https://www.federalreserve.gov/econres/feds/files/2017125pap.pdf.

22. Isabel Cairó and Jae Sim, "Income Inequality, Financial Crises and Monetary Policy," FRB Finance and Economics Discussion Series 2018-048 (May 2018), available at https://www.federalreserve.gov/econres/feds/files/2018048pap.pdf.

23. Robert Kurtzman, Stephan Luck, and Tom Zimmermann, "Did QE lead banks to relax their lending standards? Evidence from the Federal Reserve's LSAPs," FRB Finance and Economics Discussion Series (FEDS) 2017-093 (July 19, 2017), available at https://www.federalreserve.gov/econres/feds/files/2017093pap.pdf.

24. See Jerome H. Powell, "The Case for Housing Finance Reform" (speech, Washington, DC, July 6, 2017), FRB, available at https://www.federalreserve.gov/newsevents/speech/powell20170706a.htm; and Federal Reserve Bank of New York (FRB-NY), 2016 Small Business Credit Survey Report on Employer Firms (April 2017), available at https://www.newyorkfed.org/medialibrary/media/smallbusiness/2016/SBCS-Report-EmployerFirms-2016.pdf.

25. FRB, "Transcript of Chair Powell's Press Conference October 30, 2019," accessed April 16, 2020, available at https://www.federalreserve.gov/mediacenter/files/FOMCpresconf20191030.pdf.

26. Alex J. Pollock, Testimony before the Subcommittee on Monetary Policy and Trade of the Committee on Financial Services: The Federal Reserve's Impact on Main Street, Retirees, and Savings (June 28, 2017), available at https://financialservices.house.gov/uploadedfiles/hhrg-115-ba19-wstate-apollock-20170628.pdf.

27. FRB, "Historical Table 6: Family Holdings of Financial Assets, by Selected Characteristics of Families and Type of Asset, 1989–2016 Surveys," 2016 Survey of Consumer Finances, (September 2017), available at https://www.federalreserve.gov/econres/scfindex.htm.

28. Bank of America, "Millennial Report Winter 2020," *Better Money Habits,* 3 (January 2020), available at https://about.bankofamerica.com/assets/pdf/2020-bmh-millennial-report.pdf.

29. Kathi Schlepper, Heiko Hofer, Ryan Riordan, and Andreas Schrimpf, "Scarcity effects of QE: A transaction-level analysis in the Bund market," *BIS Working Paper No. 625* (April 2017), available at https://www.bis.org/publ/work625.pdf.

30. Pension Benefit Guarantee Corporation, "PBGC Projections: Multiemployer Program Likely Insolvent by the end of 2025; Single-Employer Program Likely to Eliminate Deficit by 2022," PBGC Press Release No. 17-04 (August 3, 2017), available at https://www.pbgc.gov/news/press/releases/pr17-04.

31. Fidelity Investments, "Fidelity Q4 Retirement Analysis: Increased Savings Rates, Enhancements to Employer Savings Plans and Positive Market Performance Help Drive Account Balances to Record Levels" (February 13, 2020), available at https://www.fidelity.com/bin-public/060_www_fidelity_com/documents/press-release/quarterly-retirement-trends-021320.pdf.

32. Transamerica Center for Retirement Studies, "Employers: The Retirement Security Challenge," *19th Annual Transamerica Retirement Survey,* 21 (October 19, 2019), available at https://transamericacenter.org/docs/default-source/retirement-survey-of-employers/tcrs2019_sr_employer_survey_retirement_security_challenge.pdf.

33. Jesse Bricker, Kevin B. Moore, and Jeffrey P. Thompson, "Trends in Household Portfolio Composition," FEDS 2019-069 (September 2019), available at https://www.federalreserve.gov/econres/feds/files/2019069pap.pdf.

34. Emily Barrett, "Upside-Down World of Negative Rates Is Coming for U.S. Savers," *Bloomberg News* (March 17, 2020), available at https://www.bloomberg.com/news/articles/2020-03-17/upside-down-world-of-negative-rates-is-coming-for-u-s-savers?sref=BSO3yKhf.

35. Michael Brei, Claudio Borio, and Leonard Gambacorta, "Bank intermediation activity in a low interest rate environment," *BIS Working Paper No. 807* (August 2019), available at https://www.bis.org/publ/work807.pdf.

36. Kurtzman, Luck, and Zimmermann, "Did QE lead banks to relax their lending standards?"

37. FRB, Financial Stability Report (November 2019), available at https://www.federalreserve.gov/publications/files/financial-stability-report-20191115.pdf.

38. Michael Howell, "The Federal Reserve is the cause of the bubble in everything," *Financial Times* (January 15, 2020), available at https://www.ft.com/content/bc83fda6-3702-11ea-a6d3-9a26f8c3cba4.

39. Claudio Borio and Leonardo Gambacorta, "Monetary policy and bank lending in a low interest rate environment: Diminishing effectiveness?" *BIS Working Paper No. 612* (February 2017), available at https://www.bis.org/publ/work612.pdf.

40. FRB Chairman Powell, "Testimony before the Joint Economic Committee of Congress: The Economic Outlook" (November 13, 2019), available at https://www.federalreserve.gov/newsevents/testimony/powell20191113a.htm. Alex J. Pollock, "Testimony before the Subcommittee on Monetary

Policy and Trade of the Committee on Financial Services: The Federal Reserve's Impact on Main Street, Retirees, and Savings" (June 28, 2017), available at https://financialservices.house.gov/uploadedfiles/hhrg-115-ba19-wstate-apollock-20170628.pdf

41. Bricker, Moore, and Thompson, "Trends in Household Portfolio Composition."

42. Aaron Brown, "The Next Credit Crisis Will Hit Consumers Hardest," *Bloomberg* (November 21, 2018), available at https://www.bloomberg.com/opinion/articles/2018-11-21/households-are-not-positioned-well-for-the-next-credit-crisis.

43. Lauren Lambie-Hanson and Carolina Reid, "Stuck in Subprime? Examining the Barriers to Refinancing Mortgage Debt," Federal Reserve Bank of Philadelphia, *Working Paper No. 17-39* (November 2017), available at https://www.philadelphiafed.org/-/media/research-and-data/publications/working-papers/2017/wp17-39.pdf?la=en.

44. Joint Center for Housing Studies of Harvard University (JCHS Harvard), "The State of the Nation's Housing 2019," 21 (June 2019), available at https://www.jchs.harvard.edu/sites/default/files/Harvard_JCHS_State_of_the_Nations_Housing_2019.pdf.

45. Katherine Di Lucido, Anna Kovner, and Samantha Zeller, "Low Interest Rates and Bank Profits," Liberty Street Economics, FRB-NY (June 21, 2017), available at http://libertystreeteconomics.newyorkfed.org/2017/06/low-interest-rates-and-bank-profits.html.

46. Reid Wilson, "Coronavirus recession will hit low-wage workers hardest," *The Hill,* March 31, 2020, available at https://thehill.com/homenews/state-watch/490429-coronavirus-recession-will-hit-low-wage-workers-hardest.

47. Heather Long, "U.S. now has 22 million unemployed, wiping out a decade of job gains," *Washington Post* (April 16, 2020), available at https://www.washingtonpost.com/business/2020/04/16/unemployment-claims-coronavirus/.

48. René Chalom, Fatih Karahan, Brendan Moore, and Giorgio Topa, "Is the Tide Lifting All Boats? A Closer Look at the Earnings Growth Experiences of U.S. Workers," FRBNY Liberty Street Economics Blog (March 4, 2020), available at https://libertystreeteconomics.newyorkfed.org/2020/03/is-the-tide-lifting-all-boats-a-closer-look-at-the-earnings-growth-experiences-of-us-workers.html.

49. Bureau of Labor Statistics (BLS), "Labor Force Statistics from the Current Population Survey," BLS Databases, Tables & Calculators by Subject, available at https://data.bls.gov/timeseries/LNS11300000.

50. National Public Radio (NPR)/Marist Institute for Public Opinion (MIPO), "1/22: Employment Poll Findings," Poll Results January 2018: Picture of Work, 1 (January 22, 2018), available at http://maristpoll.marist.edu/wp-content/misc/usapolls/us171204_KoC/NPR/NPR_Marist%20Poll_National%20Nature%20of%20the%20Sample%20and%20Tables_January%202018.pdf.

51. United States Census Bureau, "Historical Income Table H-12: Household by Number of Earners by Median and Mean Income," available at https://www.census.gov/data/tables/time-series/demo/income-poverty/historical-income-households.html.

52. Josh Eidelson, "U.S. Income Inequality Hits a Disturbing New Threshold," *Bloomberg News* (March 1, 2018), available at https://www.bloomberg.com/news/articles/2018-03-01/america-s-wage-growth-remains-slow-and-uneven.

53. FRB Gov. Lael Brainard, "Why Persistent Employment Disparities Matter for the Economy's Health" (speech, Washington, DC, September 26, 2017), FRB, available at https://www.federalreserve.gov/newsevents/speech/brainard20170926a.htm.

54. Bricker, Moore, and Thompson, "Trends in Household Portfolio Composition," 9.

55. Ibid., 10.

56. Edward N. Wolff, "National Report Card: Wealth Inequality, Stanford Center on Poverty and Inequality" (2014), available at https://inequality.stanford.edu/sites/default/files/media/_media/pdf/pathways/special_sotu_2014/Pathways_SOTU_2014_Wealth_Inequality.pdf.

57. JCHS Harvard, "The State of the Nation's Housing 2017," 11 (June 2017), available at http://www.jchs.harvard.e'du/sites/jchs.harvard.edu/files/harvard_jchs_state_of_the_nations_housing_2017.pdf.

58. Moritz Kuhn, Moritz Schularick, and Ulrike I. Steins, "Income and Wealth Inequality in America, 1949–2016," FRB Minneapolis Institute, *Working Paper 9,* 40 (June 2018), available at https://www.minneapolisfed.org/institute/working-papers-institute/iwp9.pdf.

59. JCHS Harvard, "America's Rental Housing 2020," 1 (January 31, 2020), available at https://www.jchs.harvard.edu/sites/default/files/Harvard_JCHS_Americas_Rental_Housing_2020.pdf.

60. Kuhn, Schularick, and Steins, "Income and Wealth Inequality in America, 1949–2016," 22.

61. FRB, "Distribution of Household Wealth in the U.S. since 1989," DFA: Distributional Financial Accounts (updated June 19, 2020), available at https://www.federalreserve.gov/releases/z1/dataviz/dfa/distribute/chart/.

62. Based on a comparison of data gathered from Treasury International Capital
    System (TIC) Table 1D: U.S. Long-Term Securities Held by Foreign Resi-
    dents in October 2017, available at http://ticdata.treasury.gov/Publish/slt1d
    .txt; and FRB Statistical Release H.4.1: Factors Affecting Reserve Balances of
    Depository Institutions and Condition Statement of Federal Reserve Banks
    (release date September 13, 2018), available at https://www.federalreserve
    .gov/releases/h41/20180913/.

63. FRB, "Federal Reserve Board announces Reserve Bank income and expense
    data and transfers to the Treasury for 2019" (January 10, 2020), available at
    https://www.federalreserve.gov/newsevents/pressreleases/other20200110a
    .htm.

64. See Chapter 9 for a discussion of modern-day money and how the Fed prints
    it.

65. Coronavirus Aid, Relief, and Economic Security (CARES) Act §4003, Pub.
    L. No. 116-136, 134 Stat. 281, 470 (March 27, 2020), available at https://
    www.congress.gov/116/bills/hr748/BILLS-116hr748enr.pdf.

66. Stephanie Kelton, *The Deficit Myth: Modern Monetary Theory and the Birth of the
    People's Economy* (New York: PublicAffairs, 2020).

67. Deniz Igan, Hala Moussawi, Alexander F. Tieman, Aleksandra Zdzienicka,
    Giovanni Dell'Ariccia, and Paolo Mauro, "The Long Shadow of the
    Global Financial Crisis: Public Interventions in the Financial Sector," *IMF
    Working Paper 19/164* (July 30, 2019), available at https://www.imf.org/en/
    Publications/WP/Issues/2019/07/30/The-Long-Shadow-of-the-Global-
    Financial-Crisis-Public-Interventions-in-the-Financial-Sector-48518.

Chapter 7

1. FRB, "Federal Reserve Board announces it is expanding the scope and eligibility for the Main Street Lending Program" (April 30, 2020), available at https://
   www.federalreserve.gov/newsevents/pressreleases/monetary20200430a.htm.

2. Ben S. Bernanke, "Testimony before the Joint Economic Committee:
   The Economic Outlook" (November 8, 2007), available at https://www
   .federalreserve.gov/newsevents/testimony/bernanke20071108a.htm.

3. Janel L. Yellen, "The U.S. Economy and Monetary Policy" (speech, Washington, DC, October 15, 2017), available at https://www.federalreserve.gov/
   newsevents/speech/yellen20171015a.htm.

4. Board of Governors of the Federal Reserve System (FRB), "Minutes of the
   Federal Open Market Committee: January 28–29, 2020," 15 (February 11,
   2020), available at https://www.federalreserve.gov/monetarypolicy/files/
   fomcminutes20200129.pdf.

5. Ibid., 14.

6. Ibid.

7. Ibid., 16.

8. Ibid.

9. Ibid.

10. FRB, *Financial Stability Report* (November, 2019), available at https://www
    .federalreserve.gov/publications/files/financial-stability-report-20191115
    .pdf.

11. George Whitney Martin, *Madam Secretary, Frances Perkins* (Boston: Houghton
    Mifflin, 1976).

12. Amir Sufi, "Out of Many, One? Household Debt, Redistribution and Mon-
    etary Policy during the Economic Slump" (June 2015), available at https://
    www.bis.org/events/agm2015/sp150628.pdf.

13. Ibid., 1.

14. Ibid., 2.

15. Spencer Soper and Sophie Alexander, "Jeff Bezos Sets Record With $165
    Million Beverly Hills Home Purchase," *Bloomberg* (February 13, 2020), avail-
    able at https://www.bloomberg.com/news/articles/2020-02-12/bezos-sets-
    record-with-165-million-beverly-hills-home-purchase?sref=BSO3yKhf.

16. ATTOM Staff, "U.S. Home Sellers Realized Average Price Gain of $67,100
    in First Quarter of 2020," *ATTOM Data Solutions* (April 30, 2020), avail-
    able at https://www.attomdata.com/news/market-trends/home-sales-prices/
    attom-data-solutions-q1-2020-u-s-home-sales-report/.

17. Jonathan Spicer, "Mortgage, Groupon and card debt: How the bottom
    half bolsters U.S. economy," *Reuters* (July 23, 2018), available at https://
    www.reuters.com/article/us-usa-economy-consumers-insight/mortgage-
    groupon-and-card-debt-how-the-bottom-half-bolsters-u-s-economy-
    idUSKBN1KD0EM.

18. Raj Chetty, John N. Friedman, Nathaniel Hendren, and Michael Stepner,
    "How Did COVID-19 and Stabilization Policies Affect Spending and Employ-
    ment? A New Real-Time Economic Tracker Based on Private Sector Data,"
    Opportunity Insights (June 17, 2020), available at https://opportunityinsights
    .org/wp-content/uploads/2020/05/tracker_paper.pdf.

19. Edward N. Wolff, "Household Wealth Trends in the United States, 1962 to
    2016: Has Middle Class Wealth Recovered?" *NBER Working Paper No. 24085*,
    50 (November 2017), available at http://www.nber.org/papers/w24085.

20. Bureau of Economic Analysis, "Table 6.6D. Wages and Salaries per Full-Time
    Equivalent Employee by Industry," *National Income and Product Accounts*,
    accessed May 1, 2020, available at https://apps.bea.gov/iTable/iTable.cfm?
    reqid=19&step=2&isuri=1&1921=survey.

21. Courtney Connley, "62% of federal workers say they used up all or most of their savings during the government shutdown," *CNBC* (February 15, 2019), available at https://www.cnbc.com/2019/02/15/62percent-of-federal-workers-spent-most-of-their-savings-during-the-shutdown.html.

22. See, for example: FRB Chair Powell, "Monetary Policy and the Economy," *CSPAN*, at 1:03:50 (February 20, 2020), available at https://www.c-span.org/video/?469082-1/monetary-policy-economy.

23. Federal Reserve Reform Act of 1977, Pub. L. No. 95-188, 91 Stat. 1387 (November 16, 1977), available at https://fraser.stlouisfed.org/scribd/?title_id=1040&filepath=/files/docs/historical/congressional/federal-reserve-reform-1977.pdf.

24. Aaron Steelman, "The Federal Reserve's 'Dual Mandate': The Evolution of an Idea," *FRB Richmond Economic Brief 11-12* (December 2011), available at https://www.richmondfed.org/-/media/richmondfedorg/publications/research/economic_brief/2011/pdf/eb_11-12.pdf.

25. Daniel L. Thornton, "The Dual Mandate: Has the Fed Changed Its Objective?," *Federal Reserve Bank of St. Louis Review 94*, no. 2 (March 2012), available at https://research.stlouisfed.org/publications/review/2012/03/01/the-dual-mandate-has-the-fed-changed-its-objective/.

26. George A. Kahn and Lisa Taylor, "Evolving Market Perceptions of Federal Reserve Policy Options," *Federal Reserve Bank of Kansas City Economic Review 99*, no. 1 (Q1 2014), available at https://www.kansascityfed.org/MTnUd/publicat/econrev/pdf/14q1Kahn-Taylor.pdf.

27. Employment Act of 1946, Pub. L. No. 79-304, 60 Stat. 23, 23 (February 20, 1946), available at http://www.legisworks.org/congress/79/publaw-304.pdf.

28. Full Employment and Balanced Growth Act of 1978, Pub L. No. 95-523, 92 Stat. 1887 (October 27, 1978), available at https://www.gpo.gov/fdsys/pkg/STATUTE-92/pdf/STATUTE-92-Pg1887.pdf.

29. Frederic S. Mishkin, "Monetary Policy and the Dual Mandate" (speech, Bridgewater, VA, April 10, 2007), available at https://www.federalreserve.gov/newsevents/speech/mishkin20070410a.htm.

30. FRB, "Federal Reserve to review strategies, tools, and communication practices it uses to pursue its mandate of maximum employment and price stability" (November 15, 2018), available at https://www.federalreserve.gov/newsevents/pressreleases/monetary20181115a.htm.

31. Dodd-Frank Wall Street Reform and Consumer Protection Act (Dodd-Frank) § 165, 124 Stat. 1376, 1423 (July 21, 2010), available at https://www.gpo.gov/fdsys/pkg/PLAW-111publ203/pdf/PLAW-111publ203.pdf.

32. FRB, *Financial Stability Report*, 1 (November 2019), available at https://www
.federalreserve.gov/publications/files/financial-stability-report-20191115
.pdf.

33. Walter Bagehot, *Lombard Street: A Description of the Money Market* (London:
Henry S. King & Co., 1873).

34. Federal Reserve Act § 13(3), 12 U.S.C. § 343 (2018), available at https://
www.govinfo.gov/content/pkg/USCODE-2018-title12/pdf/USCODE-
2018-title12-chap3-subchapIX-sec343.pdf.

35. Dodd-Frank § 1101, 124 Stat. 1376, 2113 (July 21, 2010), available at https://
www.gpo.gov/fdsys/pkg/PLAW-111publ203/pdf/PLAW-111publ203.pdf.

36. Coronavirus Aid, Relief, and Economic Security (CARES) Act §
4003(c)(3)(b), Pub. L. No. 116-136, 134 Stat. 281, 472 (March 27, 2020),
available at https://www.congress.gov/116/bills/hr748/BILLS-116hr748enr
.pdf.

37. Federal Reserve, Secondary Market Corporate Credit Facility Term Sheet
(March 23, 2020), available at https://www.federalreserve.gov/newsevents/
pressreleases/files/monetary20200323b2.pdf.

38. Federal Reserve, Secondary Market Corporate Credit Facility Term Sheet
(April 9, 2020), available at https://www.federalreserve.gov/newsevents/
pressreleases/files/monetary20200409a2.pdf.

39. Jim Bianco, "The Fed's Cure Risks Being Worse Than the Disease," *Bloomberg*
(March 27, 2020), available at https://www.bloomberg.com/opinion/
articles/2020-03-27/federal-reserve-s-financial-cure-risks-being-worse-
than-disease?sref=BSO3yKhf.

40. Mark DeCambre and Andrea Riquier, "Dow, S&P 500 end last session in
April lower, but notch best monthly gains since 1987," *MarketWatch* (April
30, 2020), available at https://www.marketwatch.com/story/dow-futures-
rise-as-market-watches-for-jobless-claims-and-quarterly-results-from-apple-
others-2020-04-30.

41. Based on an analysis of: Federal Deposit Insurance Corporation (FDIC),
"Quarterly Banking Profile: Fourth Quarter 2019: 2019 Summary of Deposits
Highlights," *FDIC Quarterly* 14(1), 5 (March 11, 2020), available at https://
www.fdic.gov/bank/analytical/quarterly/2020-vol14-1/fdic-v14n1-4q2019
.pdf; and National Credit Union Administration (NCUA), *2019 Annual
Report*, 6 (March 20, 2020)

42. Bureau of Economic Analysis (BEA), "Gross Domestic Product, 1st Quarter
2020 (Advance Estimate)" (April 29, 2019), available at https://www.bea.gov/
news/2020/gross-domestic-product-1st-quarter-2020-advance-estimate.

43. Dave Michaels, "Investors Eye Fed Emergency Lending Program That Brought
Rich Returns in 2009," *Wall Street Journal* (April 25, 2020), available at

https://www.wsj.com/articles/investors-eye-fed-emergency-lending-program
-that-brought-rich-returns-in-2009-11587807001.

44. Peter Eavis, Niraj Chokshi, and David Gelles, "Take Government Aid?
We'll See, Some Businesses Say," *New York Times* (April 3, 2020), available
at https://www.nytimes.com/2020/04/03/business/economy/coronavirus-
business-bailouts.html.

45. Brian Chappatta, "Fed Is Getting Awfully Close to Backing Apple Stock,"
Bloomberg News (July 6, 2020), available at https://www.bloomberg.com/
opinion/articles/2020-07-06/covid-fed-gets-close-to-backing-apple-stock-
by-buying-its-bonds?sref=BSO3yKhf.

46. Sarah Bloom Raskin per Robert Kuttner, "The Bailout, the Fed, and the Aftermath," *American Prospect* (April 21, 2020), available at https://prospect.org/
economy/the-bailout-the-fed-and-the-aftermath/.

47. Sam Long and Alexander Synkov, "The Fed Punishes Prudence," *Wall Street
Journal* (April 26, 2020), available at https://www.wsj.com/articles/the-fed-
punishes-prudence-11587930994.

48. Karen Petrou, "Nothing to suggest trickle-down monetary policy will
suddenly work," *American Banker* (March 20, 2020), available at https://www
.americanbanker.com/opinion/nothing-to-suggest-trickle-down-monetary-
policy-will-suddenly-work.

49. The Fed Up Coalition, "Fed Up Coalition Priorities," Center for Popular
Democracy and Action for the Common Good, available at https://drive
.google.com/file/d/0B4cNN9sfL5mIMDYtVjJCVmY4OGs/view.

50. Lawrence Summers, "My views and the Fed's views on secular stagnation,"
Financial Times (December 22, 2015), available at https://www.ft.com/
content/7d222674-f1f4-3f0d-84fd-c154ebdf80ce.

51. Ibid.

52. John Taylor, *Testimony before the Subcommittee on Monetary Policy and Trade Committee on Financial Services U.S. House of Representatives: Sound Monetary Policy*
(March 16, 2017), available at https://republicans-financialservices.house.gov/
uploadedfiles/hhrg-115-ba19-wstate-jtaylor-20170316.pdf.

53. Kevin Warsh, "Fed Tightening? Not Now," *Wall Street Journal* (December
16, 2018), available at https://www.wsj.com/articles/quantitative-tightening-
not-now-11544991760.

54. Adair Turner, "Debt, Money and Mephistopheles: How Do We Get Out of
This Mess?" (speech, Cass Business School), February 6, 2013, available at
http://www.observatorio.unr.edu.ar/wp-content/uploads/2016/04/Debt-
Money-and-Mephistopheles.pdf.

55. Ben Bernanke, "What tools does the Fed have left? Part 3: Helicopter money,"
Brookings Institution (April 11, 2016), available at https://www.brookings.edu/

blog/ben-bernanke/2016/04/11/what-tools-does-the-fed-have-left-part-3-helicopter-money/

56. Bernie Sanders, "Bernie Sanders: To Rein In Wall Street, Fix the Fed," *New York Times* (December 23, 2015), available at https://www.nytimes.com/2015/12/23/opinion/bernie-sanders-to-rein-in-wall-street-fix-the-fed.html.

57. Greg Ip, "Green New Deal Won't Enjoy a Free Lunch at the Fed," *Wall Street Journal* (February 20, 2019), available at https://www.wsj.com/articles/green-new-deal-wont-enjoy-a-free-lunch-at-the-fed-11550658601.

58. Network for Greening the Financial System, *Origin and Purpose*, accessed May 1, 2020, available at https://www.ngfs.net/en/about-us/governance/origin-and-purpose.

59. James Bullard and Riccardo DiCecio, "Optimal Monetary Policy for the Masses," *FRB St. Louis Working Paper 2019-009C* (April 2019), available at https://s3.amazonaws.com/real.stlouisfed.org/wp/2019/2019-009.pdf.

Chapter 8

1. Federal Financial Analytics, Inc. (FedFin), "A New Framework for Systemic Financial Regulation: Simple, Transparent, Enforceable and Accountable Rules to Reform Financial Markets" (November 2011), available at http://www.fedfin.com/images/stories/client_reports/complexityriskpaper.pdf.

2. Karen Shaw Petrou, *The Not-So Normal New: The Assault on Bank Franchise Value and Its Policy Impact* (May 8, 2014), available at http://www.fedfin.com/images/stories/client_reports/The%20Not-So%20Normal%20New%20-%20May%202014.pdf.

3. Federal Reserve Bank of New York (FRB-NY), *Quarterly Report on Household Debt and Credit 2020:Q1*, 3 (May 2020), available at https://www.newyorkfed.org/medialibrary/interactives/householdcredit/data/pdf/HHDC_2020Q1.pdf.

4. Bureau of Labor Statistics, "U-3 Total unemployed, as a percent of the civilian labor force (official unemployment rate)," *Table A-15. Alternative measures of labor underutilization*, accessed May 8, 2020, available at https://www.bls.gov/news.release/empsit.t15.htm.

5. Andrew Haughwout, Donghoon Lee, Joelle Scally, and Wilbert van der Klaauw, "U.S. Consumer Debt Payments and Credit Buffers on the Eve of COVID-19," *Liberty Street Economics* (May 5, 2020), available at https://libertystreeteconomics.newyorkfed.org/2020/05/us-debt-payments-and-credit-buffers-on-the-eve-of-covid-19.html.

6. Ibid.

7. Board of Governors of the Federal Reserve System (FRB), *Report on the Economic Well-Being of U.S. Households in 2019, Featuring Supplemental Data from April* 2020, 23 (May 14, 2020), available at https://www.federalreserve .gov/publications/files/2019-report-economic-well-being-us-households-202005.pdf.

8. Atif Mian, Ludwig Straub, and Amir Sufi, "The Saving Glut of the Rich and the Rise in Household Debt" (November 2019), available at https:// www.rba.gov.au/publications/workshops/research/2019/pdf/rba-workshop-2019-sufi.pdf.

9. Neil Bhutta, Steven Laufer, and Daniel R. Ringo, "The Decline in Lending to Lower-Income Borrowers by the Biggest Banks," *FEDS Notes* (September 28, 2017), available at https://www.federalreserve.gov/econres/notes/feds-notes/the-decline-in-lending-to-lower-income-borrowers-by-the-biggest-banks-20170928.htm.

10. FRB-NY, *Quarterly Report on Household Debt and Credit 2020:Q1.*

11. Tom Quinn, "The 850 FICO Score," *FICO Blog* (September 17, 2019), available at https://www.fico.com/blogs/850-fico-score.

12. FRB-NY, *Quarterly Report on Household Debt and Credit 2020:Q1.*

13. U.S. Government Accountability Office, "Millennial Generation: Information on the Economic Status of Millennial Households Compared to Previous Generations," *GAO-20-194* (December 2019), available at https://www.gao.gov/ assets/710/703222.pdf.

14. FRB-NY, "Non-Housing Debt Balance," *Quarterly Report on Household Debt and Credit 2020:Q1 Interactive Data* (May 2020), available at https://www .newyorkfed.org/medialibrary/interactives/householdcredit/data/xls/HHD_ C_Report_2020Q1.xlsx.

15. Andrew Haughwout, Donghoon Lee, Joelle Scally, and Wilbert van der Klaauw, "Just Released: Auto Loans in High Gear," *FRB-NY Liberty Street Economics Blog* (February 12, 2019), available at https://libertystreeteconomics .newyorkfed.org/2019/02/just-released-auto-loans-in-high-gear.html.

16. Christopher Maloney and Adam Tempkin, "America's Middle Class Is Addicted to a New Kind of Credit," *Bloomberg* (October 29, 2019), available at https://www.bloomberg.com/news/articles/2019-10-29/america-s-middle-class-is-getting-hooked-on-debt-with-100-rates.

17. Tara Siegel Bernard and Karl Russell, "The Middle-Class Crunch: A Look at 4 Family Budgets," *New York Times* (October 3, 2019), available at https:// www.nytimes.com/interactive/2019/10/03/your-money/middle-class-income.html.

18. Christopher Maloney and Adam Tempkin, "America's Middle Class Is Addicted to a New Kind of Credit."

19. Ibid.

20. Alina K. Bartscher, Moritz Kuhn, Moritz Schularick, and Ulrike I. Steins, "Modigliani Meets Minsky: Inequality, Debt, and Financial Fragility in America, 1950–2016," *Institute for New Economic Thinking (INET) Working Paper No. 124* (April 28, 2020), available at https://www.ineteconomics.org/uploads/papers/WP_124-Schularik-et-al-Debt.pdf.

21. Lauren Lambie-Hanson, Carolina Reid, "Stuck in Subprime? Examining the Barriers to Refinancing Mortgage Debt," *Federal Reserve Bank of Philadelphia Working Paper No. 17-39* (November 2017), available at https://www.philadelphiafed.org/-/media/research-and-data/publications/working-papers/2017/wp17-39.pdf?la=en.

22. Hannah Levitt, "Wells Fargo Stops Accepting Home Equity Credit Line Applications," *Bloomberg News* (April 30, 2020), available at https://www.bloomberg.com/news/articles/2020-04-30/wells-fargo-stops-accepting-home-equity-credit-line-applications?sref=BSO3yKhf.

23. Adam Tempkin and Christopher Maloney, "Expensive Loans to Desperate People Built This $90 Billion Industry," *Bloomberg* (February 14, 2019), available at https://www.bloomberg.com/news/articles/2019-02-14/expensive-loans-to-desperate-people-built-this-90-billion-industry.

24. Heather Long, "Personal loans are 'growing like a weed,' a potential warning sign for the U.S. economy," *Washington Post* (November 21, 2019), available at https://www.washingtonpost.com/business/2019/11/21/personal-loans-are-growing-like-weed-potential-warning-sign-us-economy/.

25. Ibid.

26. Thomas L. Hogan, "What Caused the Post-crisis Decline in Bank Lending?" Rice University's Baker Institute for Public Policy, *Issue Brief No. 01.10.19*, 1 (January 10, 2019), available at https://www.bakerinstitute.org/media/files/files/97fc7f24/bi-brief-011019-cpf-banklending.pdf.

27. FDIC, "Statistics At A Glance: As of December 31, 2017," available at https://www.fdic.gov/bank/statistical/stats/2017dec/industry.pdf.

28. FDIC, "Statistics At A Glance: As of December 31, 2019," available at https://www.fdic.gov/bank/statistical/stats/2019dec/industry.pdf.

29. Hogan, "What Caused the Post-crisis Decline in Bank Lending?" 4.

30. FDIC, "Fourth Quarter 2019," *FDIC Quarterly Banking Profile* 14(1), 5 (February 2020), available at https://www.fdic.gov/bank/analytical/quarterly/2020-vol14-1/fdic-v14n1-4q2019.pdf.

31. Peter Atwater, "US bank earnings show the wealthy are gorging on credit," *Financial Times* (October 18, 2018), available at https://www.ft.com/content/98c00ade-d2ba-11e8-9a3c-5d5eac8f1ab4.

32. Lex, "UBS: Wealth of Nations," *Financial Times* (October 22, 2018), available at https://www.ft.com/content/f488bb68-d607-11e8-ab8e-6be0dcf18713.

33. Shahien Nasiripour, "Banks That Shun Risky Borrowers Offer Rosy View of U.S. Consumer," *Bloomberg* (January 17, 2020), available at https://www.bloomberg.com/news/articles/2020-01-17/banks-that-shun-risky-borrowers-offer-rosy-view-of-u-s-consumer.

34. Ibid.

35. Brenna Hughes Neghaiwi and Simon Jessop, "Coronavirus crisis a window of opportunity for bankers to the rich," *Reuters* (May 14, 2020), available at https://www.reuters.com/article/us-global-banking-wealth-analysis/coronavirus-crisis-a-window-of-opportunity-for-bankers-to-the-rich-idUSKBN22Q1UB.

36. FRB, Consumer Financial Protection Bureau (CFPB), Federal Deposit Insurance Corporation (FDIC), National Credit Union Administration (NCUA), and OCC, *Joint Statement Regarding Responsible Small-Dollar Lending in Response to COVID-19* (March 26, 2020), available at https://www.federalreserve.gov/newsevents/pressreleases/files/bcreg20200326a1.pdf.

37. OCC, FRB, FDIC Regulatory Capital Rule: Money Market Mutual Fund Liquidity Facility, 85 Fed. Reg. 16232 (March 23, 2020) (to be codified at 12 C.F.R. §§ 3, 217 & 324), available at https://www.govinfo.gov/content/pkg/FR-2020-03-23/pdf/2020-06156.pdf.

38. Financial Stability Oversight Council (FSOC), *2019 Annual Report*, 42 (December 4, 2019), available at https://home.treasury.gov/system/files/261/FSOC2019AnnualReport.pdf.

39. Housing Finance Policy Center, "Housing Finance at a Glance: August 2019," *Urban Institute* (August 27, 2019), available at https://www.urban.org/sites/default/files/publication/100866/august_chartbook_2019_0.pdf.

40. Ibid., 44.

41. Housing Finance Policy Center, "Housing Finance at a Glance: A Monthly Chart Book," *Urban Institute*, 6 (November 2019), available at https://www.urban.org/sites/default/files/publication/101389/november_chartbook_2019_1.pdf.

42. Mortgage Bankers Association (MBA), *MBA Statement on FHFA's Announcement on Advance Obligation Limits for Loans in Forbearance* (April 21, 2020), available at https://www.mba.org/2020-press-releases/april/mba-statement-on-fhfas-announcement-on-advance-obligation-limits-for-loans-in-forbearance.

43. FRB, FDIC, OCC, *Interagency Guidance on Leveraged Lending* (March 21, 2013), available at https://www.federalreserve.gov/supervisionreg/srletters/sr1303a1.pdf.

44. Comptroller of the Currency Joseph M. Otting, "Remarks by Joseph M. Otting, Comptroller of the Currency, Special Seminar on International Finance" (speech, Tokyo, JP, November 14, 2018), available at https://www.occ.gov/news-issuances/speeches/2018/pub-speech-2018-120.pdf.

45. FRB, *Financial Stability Report*, 9 (November 2019), available at https://www.federalreserve.gov/publications/files/financial-stability-report-20191115.pdf.

46. FRB, *Term Sheet: Primary Market Corporate Credit Facility*, 1 (April 9, 2020), available at https://www.federalreserve.gov/newsevents/pressreleases/files/monetary20200409a5.pdf.

47. International Monetary Fund (IMF), *Global Financial Stability Report: Lower for Longer*, 36 (October 2019), available at https://www.imf.org/en/Publications/GFSR/Issues/2019/10/01/global-financial-stability-report-october-2019.

48. Securities and Exchange Commission (SEC) Financial Responsibility Rules for Broker-Dealers, 78 Fed. Reg. 51824 (August 21, 2013) (to be codified at 17 C.F.R. § 240), available at https://www.govinfo.gov/content/pkg/FR-2013-08-21/pdf/2013-18734.pdf.

49. FRB, "Federal Reserve Board broadens program of support for the flow of credit to households and businesses by establishing a Money Market Mutual Fund Liquidity Facility (MMLF)" (March 18, 2020), available at https://www.federalreserve.gov/newsevents/pressreleases/monetary20200318a.htm.

50. Katy Burne, "J.P. Morgan to Exit Part of Its Government Securities Business," *Wall Street Journal* (July 21, 2016), available at https://www.wsj.com/articles/j-p-morgan-to-exit-part-of-its-government-securities-business-1469135462.

51. Myles Udland, "The Composition of the Trillion-Dollar Repo Market Is Shifting in an Unsettling Way," *Business Insider* (June 1, 2014), available at https://www.businessinsider.com/repo-market-shifting-to-non-banks-2014-6.

52. Federal Reserve Bank of St. Louis (FRB-StL), "Deposits, All Commercial Banks," *Federal Reserve Economic Data Series DPSACBW027SBOG*, accessed July 13, 2020, available at https://fred.stlouisfed.org/series/DPSACBW027SBOG.

53. FRB-StL, "Bank Credit, All Commercial Banks," *Federal Reserve Economic Data Series TOTBKCR*, accessed July 13, 2020, available at https://fred.stlouisfed.org/series/TOTBKCR.

54. Garrett Watson, "Unequal Tax Treatment Is Contributing to Rising Debt Levels for Entrepreneurs," *Tax Foundation* (December 13, 2018), available at https://taxfoundation.org/unequal-tax-treatment-debt-levels-entrepreneurs/.

55. Richard J. Herring, *The Evolving Complexity of Capital Regulation*, The Wharton School at the University of Pennsylvania (January 23, 2018), available at https://fic.wharton.upenn.edu/wp-content/uploads/2018/07/Evolution-of-Complexity-in-Cap-Rega-1.23.18.pdf.

56. OCC, FRB, FDIC Changes to Applicability Thresholds for Regulatory Capital and Liquidity Requirements, 84 Fed. Reg. 59230 (November 1, 2019) (to be codified at 12 C.F.R. §§ 3, 50, 217, 249, 324 & 329), available at https://www.govinfo.gov/content/pkg/FR-2019-11-01/pdf/2019-23800.pdf.

57. FRB Amendments to the Regulatory Capital, Capital Plan, and Stress Test Rules (proposed March 4, 2020) (to be codified at 12 C.F.R. §§ 217, 225 & 252), available at https://www.federalreserve.gov/newsevents/pressreleases/files/bcreg20200304a2.pdf.

58. Diana Olick, "Here's why it's suddenly much harder to get a mortgage, or even refinance," *CNBC* (April 13, 2020), available at https://www.cnbc.com/2020/04/13/coronavirus-why-its-suddenly-much-harder-to-get-a-mortgage-or-even-refinance.html.

59. Khristopher J. Brooks, "Nearly 50 million Americans just had their credit card limits cut," *CBS News* (May 4, 2020), available at https://www.cbsnews.com/news/credit-card-limits-reduced-canceled-50-million-americans/.

60. Sarah Silbert, "Thanks to credit card enhancements from issuers like American Express and Citi, it's easier than ever to earn and redeem points during quarantine," *Business Insider* (July 2, 2020, available at https://www.businessinsider.com/personal-finance/new-credit-card-rewards-options-quarantine-2020-4,

61. Colleen Baker, Christine Cumming, and Julapa Jagtiani, "The Impacts of Financial Regulations: Solvency and Liquidity in the Post-crisis Period," *FRB Philadelphia Working Paper No. 17-10*, 12 (April 18, 2017), available at https://philadelphiafed.org/-/media/research-and-data/publications/working-papers/2017/wp17-10.pdf.

62. BIS, "Impact of financial regulations: Insights from an online repository of studies," *BIS Quarterly Review* (March, 5, 2019), available at https://www.bis.org/publ/qtrpdf/r_qt1903f.pdf.

63. BCBS, "Literature Review on integration of regulatory capital and liquidity instruments," *BCBS Working Paper No. 30*, 1 (March 2016), available at https://www.bis.org/bcbs/publ/wp30.pdf.

64. Francisco Covas, "Capital Requirements in Supervisory Stress Tests and their Adverse Impact on Small Business Lending" *Clearing House Staff Working Paper 2017-2* (August 10, 2017), available at https://bpi.com/wp-content/uploads/2018/07/capital-requirements-in-supervisory-stress-tests-and-their-adverse-impact-on-small-business-lending.pdf.

65. FSB, *Vulnerabilities associated with leveraged loans and collateralised loan obligations* (December 19, 2019), available at https://www.fsb.org/wp-content/uploads/P191219.pdf.

66. BIS Committee on the Global Financial System (CGFS) Markets Committee, "Regulatory change and monetary policy," *CFGS Paper No. 54*, 10-11 (May 2015), available at https://www.bis.org/publ/cgfs54.pdf.

67. David Benoit, "How the Discount Window Became a Pain in the Repo Market," *Wall Street Journal* (November 21, 2019), available at https://www.wsj.com/articles/how-the-discount-window-became-a-pain-in-the-repo-market-11574337601.

68. FRB, *Financial Stability Report*, 32–33.

69. Ibid.

70. Alan Moreira and Alexi Savov, "The Macroeconomics of Shadow Banking" (July 2014), available at http://www.newyorkfed.org/research/conference/2014/wholesalefunding/TheMacroeconomicsofShadowBanking_Moreira.pdf; Francesco Ferrante, "A model of endogenous loan quality and the collapse of the shadow banking system" (March 2015), available at http://www.federalreserve.gov/econresdata/feds/2015/files/2015021pap.pdf; Joe Peek and Eric S. Rosengren, "The Role of Banks in the Transmission of Monetary Policy" (September 9, 2013), available at http://bostonfed.org/economic/ppdp/2013/ppdp1305.pdf.

71. Dodd-Frank Wall Street Reform and Consumer Protection Act (Dodd-Frank) Title II, Pub. L. No. 111-203, 124 Stat. 1376, 1442 (July 21, 2010), available at https://www.gpo.gov/fdsys/pkg/PLAW-111publ203/pdf/PLAW-111publ203.pdf.

72. FRB and FDIC Resolution Plans Required, 84 Fed. Reg, 59194 (November 1, 2019) (to be codified at 12 C.F.R. §§ 243 & 381), available at https://www.govinfo.gov/content/pkg/FR-2019-11-01/pdf/2019-23967.pdf.

73. FedFin, *"Are U.S. SIFIs Still TBTF?: An Assessment of the New Resolution Regime for Systemically-Important Financial Institutions"* (October 22, 2012), available at http://www.fedfin.com/images/stories/client_reports/assessment%20of%20resolution%20regime%20for%20sifis.pdf.

74. Dodd-Frank Title X, Pub. L. No. 111-203, 124 Stat. 1376, 1995.

75. "OCC Guidance on Supervisory Concerns and Expectations Regarding Deposit Advance Products," 78 Fed. Reg. 70624 (November 26, 2013), available at https://www.occ.treas.gov/news-issuances/federal-register/2013/78fr70624.pdf.

76. Dodd-Frank § 1075, Pub. L. No. 111-203, 124 Stat. 1376, 2068.

77. Credit Card Accountability Responsibility and Disclosure Act, Pub. L. No. 111-24, 123 Stat. 1734 (May 22, 2009), available at https://www.gpo.gov/fdsys/pkg/STATUTE-123/pdf/STATUTE-123-Pg1734.pdf.

78. Clearing House, "Why Have Banks' Market-to-Book Ratios Declined?" *TCH Research Note* (October 2016), available at https://www.theclearinghouse .org/-/media/action%20line/documents/volume%20vii/20161101_tch_ research_note_market_to_book_ratios_decline%20v2.pdf.

79. Mark Manuszak and Krzysztof Wozniak, "The Impact of Price Controls in Two-sided Markets: Evidence from US Debit Card Interchange Fee Regulation," *FRB Finance and Economic Discussion Series No. 2017-074*, 5 (July 2017), available at https://www.federalreserve.gov/econres/feds/files/2017074pap.pdf.

80. Julia Fonseca, Katherine Strair, Basit Zafar, "Access to Credit and Financial Health: Evaluating the Impact of Debt Collection," *FRB-NY Staff Report No. 814* (May 2017), available at https://www.newyorkfed.org/medialibrary/media/research/staff_reports/sr814.pdf?la=en.

81. For example, see House Financial Services Committee (HFSC), "Hearing on Monetary Policy and the State of the Economy," *HFSC Transcript Serial No. 114-93*, 18–19 (June 22, 2016), available at https://www.govinfo.gov/content/pkg/CHRG-114hhrg25848/pdf/CHRG-114hhrg25848.pdf

82. Franklin Allen, Itay Goldstein, and Julapa Jagtiani, "The Interplay Among Financial Regulations, Resilience, and Growth," *FRB Philadelphia Working Paper No. 18-09* (February 2018), available at https://www.philadelphiafed .org/-/media/research-and-data/publications/working-papers/2018/wp18-09.pdf.

83. Ibid., 22.

84. BIS, "Impact of financial regulations: Insights from an online repository of studies."

85. Rachel Louise Ensign and Coulter Jones, "The Problem for Small-Town Banks: People Want High-Tech Services," *Wall Street Journal* (March 2, 2019), available at https://www.wsj.com/articles/the-problem-for-small-town-banks-people-want-high-tech-services-11551502885.

86. Ibid.

87. FRB, *Perspectives from Main Street: Bank Branch Access in Rural Communities* (November 2019), available at https://www.federalreserve.gov/publications/files/bank-branch-access-in-rural-communities.pdf.

Chapter 9

1. For a thorough explanation of money theory, see: Markus K. Brunnermeier, Harold James, and Jean-Pierre Landau, *The Digitalization of Money* (August 2019), available at https://scholar.princeton.edu/sites/default/files/markus/files/02c_digitalmoney.pdf.

2. Board of Governors of the Federal Reserve System (FRB), "Report on the Economic Well-Being of U.S. Households in 2019, Featuring Supplemental Data from April 2020" (May 14, 2020), available at https://www.federalreserve.gov/publications/files/2019-report-economic-well-being-us-households-202005.pdf.

3. FRB, "Perspectives from Main Street: Bank Branch Access in Rural Communities" (November 2019), available at https://www.federalreserve.gov/publications/files/bank-branch-access-in-rural-communities.pdf.

4. Federal Deposit Insurance Corporation (FDIC), "Third Quarter 2019," *FDIC Quarterly Banking Profile* 13(4), 1 (September 2019), available at https://www.fdic.gov/bank/analytical/qbp/2019sep/qbp.pdf#page=1.

5. M. Szmigiera, "Number of FDIC-insured commercial bank branches in the United States from 2000 to 2018," *Statista* (November 7, 2019), available at https://www.statista.com/statistics/193041/number-of-fdic-insured-us-commercial-bank-branches/.

6. Credit Union National Association (CUNA), "Monthly Credit Union Estimates November 2019," 4 (December 7, 2019), available at https://www.cuna.org/uploadedFiles/Global/About_Credit_Unions/CUMonthEst_Nov19.pdf.

7. Timothy Baxter on behalf of the National ATM Council, "Testimony before the Subcommittee on Financial Institutions and Consumer Credit of the House Financial Services Committee: Examining De-risking and Its Effect on Access to Financial Services" (February 15, 2018), available at https://financialservices.house.gov/uploadedfiles/02.15.2018_timothy_baxter_testimony.pdf.

8. Penny Crosman, "Walmart, Green Dot inching MoneyCard closer to banking look-alike," *American Banker* (May 27, 2020), available at https://www.americanbanker.com/news/walmart-green-dot-inching-moneycard-closer-to-banking-look-alike.

9. Federal Reserve Bank of New York (FRB-NY) Executive Vice President and General Counsel Michael Held, "U.S. Regulations and Approaches to Cryptocurrencies," Speech at the BIS Central Bank Legal Experts' Meeting, Basel (December 12, 2019), available at https://www.newyorkfed.org/newsevents/speeches/2019/hel191212.

10. Wend Matheny, Shaun O'Brien, and Claire Wang, "Preliminary Findings from 2015 *Diary of Consumer Payment Choice*," *Federal Reserve Bank of San Francisco FedNotes* (November 3, 2016), available at https://www.frbsf.org/cash/publications/fed-notes/2016/november/state-of-cash-2015-diary-consumer-payment-choice/.

11. FDIC, "2017 FDIC National Survey of Unbanked and Underbanked Households," 19 (October 2018) available at https://www.fdic.gov/householdsurvey/2017/2017report.pdf.

12. See for example, Payment Choice Act, S. 4145, 116th Cong. (2020), available at https://www.menendez.senate.gov/news-and-events/press/menendez-cramer-introduce-bipartisan-bill-to-protect-cash-as-payment-choice-for-customers-during-the-covid-19-pandemic-and-beyond Payment Choice Act of 2019, H.R. 2650, 116th Cong. (2019), available at https://www.congress.gov/116/bills/hr2650/BILLS-116hr2650ih.pdf.

13. Jonathan Ashworth and Charles Goodhart, "Coronavirus panic fuels a surge in cash demand," *Centre for Economic Policy Research* (June 2020), available at https://cepr.org/active/publications/discussion_papers/dp.php?dpno=14910.

14. Takashi Umekawa, "In cash-loving Japan, banks still busy despite coronavirus emergency," *Reuters* (April 27, 2020), available at https://www.reuters.com/article/us-health-coronavirus-japan-banks/in-cash-loving-japan-banks-still-busy-despite-coronavirus-emergency-idUSKCN229112.

15. Martin Arnold, "Banknote virus fears won't stop Germans hoarding cash," *Financial Times*, March 25, 2020, available at https://www.ft.com/content/7f88763c-6df0-11ea-89df-41bea055720b.

16. Bank for International Settlements (BIS) General Manager Agustín Carstens, "Big tech in finance and new challenges for public policy," Speech at the FT Banking Summit, London (December 4, 2018), available at https://www.bis.org/speeches/sp181205.pdf.

17. Ben Winck, "Alphabet's soaring stock just pushed it above a $1 trillion market cap. Here are the 11 highest-valued public companies," *Business Insider* (January 19, 2020), available at https://markets.businessinsider.com/news/stocks/highest-valued-public-companies-apple-aramco-biggest-market-cap-2020-1-1028827570#10-jpmorgan-chase2.

18. Financial Stability Board (FSB), "Addressing the regulatory, supervisory and oversight challenges raised by "global stablecoin" arrangements" (April 14, 2020), available at https://www.fsb.org/wp-content/uploads/P140420-1.pdf.

19. Bank of England Governor Mark Carney, "The Growing Challenges for Monetary Policy in the Current International Monetary and Financial System" (speech, Jackson Hole, WY, August 23, 2019), available at https://

www.kansascityfed.org/~/media/files/publicat/sympos/2019/governor
%20carney%20speech%20jackson%20hole.pdf?la=en.

20. Markus K. Brunnermeier, Harold James, and Jean-Pierre Landau, "The Digitalization of Money," 2 (August 2019), available at https://scholar.princeton
.edu/sites/default/files/markus/files/02c_digitalmoney.pdf.

21. BIS General Manager Agustín Carstens, "The future of money and the payment system: What role for central banks?" Lecture at the Princeton University, Princeton, NJ (December 5, 2019), available at https://www.bis.org/
speeches/sp191205.pdf

22. Tobias Adrian and Tommaso Mancini-Griffoli, "The Rise of Digital Money,
IMF Fintech Note 19/01 (July 2019), available at https://www.imf.org/
en/Publications/fintech-notes/Issues/2019/07/12/The-Rise-of-Digital-
Money-47097.

23. Brunnermeier, James, and Landau, *The Digitalization of Money*.

24. David Marcus, "Hearing before the United States Senate Committee on Banking, Housing, and Urban Affairs: Testimony of David Marcus, Head of Calibra, Facebook" (July 16, 2019), available at https://www.banking.senate.gov/imo/
media/doc/Marcus%20Testimony%207-16-19.pdf.

25. Penny Crosman, "Is Big Tech's 'for the people' rhetoric legit?" *American Banker*
(November 3, 2019), available at https://www.americanbanker.com/opinion/
is-big-techs-for-the-people-rhetoric-legit.

26. CoinMarketCap.com, "All Cryptocurrencies," accessed March 9, 2020, available at https://coinmarketcap.com/all/views/all/.

27. Basel Committee on Banking Supervision (Basel Committee), "Discussion paper: Designing a prudential treatment for crypto-assets," 1 (December 2019), available at https://www.bis.org/bcbs/publ/d490.pdf.

28. CoinMarketCap.com, "Global Charts: Total Market Capitalization," accessed March 9, 2020, available at https://coinmarketcap.com/charts/.

29. Liaquat Ahamed, *Lords of Finance: The Bankers Who Broke the World* (New York: Penguin Press, 2009).

30. Jeff John Roberts and Nicolas Rapp, "Exclusive: Nearly 4 Million Bitcoins Lost Forever, New Study Says," *Fortune* (November 25, 2017), available at https://
fortune.com/2017/11/25/lost-bitcoins/.

31. Itai Agur, Anil Ari, and Giovanni Dell'Ariccia, "Designing Central Bank Digital Currencies," *IMF Working Paper 19/252* (November 18, 2019), available at https://www.imf.org/en/Publications/WP/Issues/2019/11/18/
Designing-Central-Bank-Digital-Currencies-48739.

32. G7 Working Group on Stablecoins, "Investigating the impact of global stablecoins" (October 2019), available at https://www.bis.org/cpmi/publ/d187
.pdf.

33. Morgan Ricks, John Crawford, and Lev Menand, "Central Banking for All: A Public Option for Bank Accounts," *Great Democracy Initiative* (June 2018), available at https://greatdemocracyinitiative.org/wp-content/uploads/2018/06/FedAccountsGDI.pdf.

34. Banking for All Act, S. 3571, 116th Cong. (2020), available at https://www.congress.gov/116/bills/s3571/BILLS-116s3571is.pdf.

Chapter 10

1. Senate Banking hearing, "The Semiannual Monetary Policy Report to the Congress" (June 16, 2020), available at https://www.banking.senate.gov/hearings/06/08/2020/the-semiannual-monetary-policy-report-to-the-congress.

2. National Commission on Financial Institution Reform, Recovery, and Enforcement (NCFIRRE), "Origin and Causes of the S&L Debacle: A Blueprint for Reform: A Report to the President and Congress of the United States," (July 1993), available at https://babel.hathitrust.org/cgi/pt?id=pur1.32754063100741;view=1up;seq=3.

3. Treasury, "Blueprint for a Modernized Financial Regulatory Structure" (March 2008), available at https://www.treasury.gov/press-center/press-releases/Documents/Blueprint.pdf.

4. Federal Reserve, "Financial Stability Report" (May 15, 2020), available at https://www.federalreserve.gov/publications/files/financial-stability-report-20200515.pdf.

5. Bonnie Sinnock, "Mortgage bankers renew push for a market-wide liquidity facility," *National Mortgage News* (May 20, 2020), available at https://www.nationalmortgagenews.com/news/mortgage-bankers-renew-push-for-a-market-wide-liquidity-facility.

6. Federal Housing Finance Agency (FHFA) Director Mark Calabria, "Testimony Before the U.S. Senate Committee on Banking, Housing, and Urban Affairs" (June 9, 2020), available at https://www.fhfa.gov/Media/PublicAffairs/Pages/Statement-of-Dr-Mark-A-Calabria-FHFA-Director-Before-the-US-Senate-Committee-on-Banking-Housing-and-Urban-Affairs-06092020.aspx.

7. "Treasury, Opportunities and Challenges in Online Marketplace Lending" (May 10, 2016), available at https://www.treasury.gov/connect/blog/Documents/Opportunities%20and%20Challenges%20in%20Online%20Marketplace%20Lending%20vRevised.pdf.

8. Kevin Wack, "Battered by coronavirus crisis, online lenders face reckoning," *American Banker* (May 14, 2020), available at https://www.americanbanker.com/news/battered-by-coronavirus-crisis-online-lenders-face-reckoning.

9. John Reosti, "As PPP deadline approaches, a few lenders make a final push," *American Banker* (June 9, 2020), available at https://www.americanbanker .com/news/as-ppp-deadline-approaches-a-few-lenders-make-a-final-push.

10. FRB, "Regulations Q, Y, and YY: Regulatory Capital, Capital Plan, and Stress Test Rules" (March 18, 2020) (to be codified at 12 C.F.R. §§ 217, 225, and 252), available at https://www.govinfo.gov/content/pkg/FR-2020-03-18/pdf/2020-04838.pdf.

11. FRB, "In the matter of Wells Fargo & Company, Order to Cease and Desist Issued Upon Consent Pursuant to the Federal Deposit Insurance Act, as Amended," Docket No. 18-007-B-HC (February 2, 2018), available at https://www.federalreserve.gov/newsevents/pressreleases/files/ enf20180202a1.pdf.

12. Community Reinvestment Act of 1977 (CRA), Pub. L. No. 95-128, Title VIII, 91 Stat 1147 (October 12, 1977), available at https://www.govinfo.gov/ content/pkg/STATUTE-91/pdf/STATUTE-91-Pg1111.pdf.

13. Dodd-Frank, Pub. L. No. 111-203, 124 Stat. 1376 (July 21, 2010), available at https://www.gpo.gov/fdsys/pkg/PLAW-111publ203/pdf/PLAW-111publ203.pdf.

14. "FSOC Authority to Require Supervision and Regulation of Certain Non-bank Financial Companies," 12 C.F.R § 1310 (2019), available at https://www .govinfo.gov/content/pkg/FR-2019-12-30/pdf/2019-27108.pdf.

15. Dodd-Frank § 120, Pub. L. No. 111-203, 123 Stat. 1376, 1408.

16. "FSOC Authority to Require Supervision and Regulation of Certain Non-bank Financial Companies," 84 Fed. Reg. 71740 (December 30, 2020) (to be codified at 12 C.F.R. § 1310), available at https://www.govinfo.gov/content/ pkg/FR-2019-12-30/pdf/2019-27108.pdf.

17. OCC, "Third-Party Relationships: Frequently Asked Questions to Supplement OCC Bulletin 2013-29," *OCC Bulletin 2020-10* (March 5, 2020), available at https://www.occ.gov/news-issuances/bulletins/2020/bulletin-2020-10.html.

18. FHFA, 2019 Report to Congress (June 15, 2020), available at https://www .fhfa.gov/AboutUs/Reports/ReportDocuments/FHFA_2019_Report-to-Congress.pdf.

19. Ginnie Mae, "Ginnie Mae MBS Outstanding Increases to $2.152 Trillion," available at https://www.ginniemae.gov/newsroom/Pages/ PressReleaseDispPage.aspx?ParamID=200.

20. FRB, OCC, FDIC, CFPB, NCUA, "Interagency Statement on the Use of Alternative Data in Credit Underwriting," December 3, 2019, available at https://www.federalreserve.gov/newsevents/pressreleases/files/ bcreg20191203b1.pdf.

21. Robert Armstrong, "'Resilient' subprime borrowers spread cheer in US debt markets," *Financial Times* (June 10, 2020), available at https://www.ft.com/content/5482b949-3d54-44a2-8713-4efcf07164ea.

22. Ibid.

23. See, for example, James Conklin, W. Scott Frame, Kristopher Gerardi, and Haoyang Liu, "Did Subprime Borrowers Drive the Housing Boom?" *Federal Reserve Bank of New York Liberty Street Economics Blog* (February 26, 2020), available at https://libertystreeteconomics.newyorkfed.org/2020/02/did-subprime-borrowers-drive-the-housing-boom.html; James Conklin, W. Scott Frame, Kristopher Gerardi, and Haoyang Liu, "Villains or Scapegoats? The Role of Subprime Borrowers in Driving the U.S. Housing Boom" *FRB-Atlanta Working Paper 2018-10* (August 2018), available at https://www.frbatlanta.org/-/media/documents/research/publications/wp/2018/10-villains-or-scapegoats-the-role-of-subprime-borrowers-in-driving-the-us-housing-boom-2018-08-28.pdf; Morris Davis, William Larson, Stephen Oliner, and Benjamin Smith, "A Quarter Century of Mortgage Risk," *FHFA Working Paper 19-02* (January 2019), available at https://www.fhfa.gov/PolicyProgramsResearch/Research/PaperDocuments/wp1902.pdf.

24. Adam Levitin and Susan Wachter, *The Great American Housing Bubble: What Went Wrong and How We Can Protect Ourselves in the Future* (Cambridge, MA: Harvard University Press, 2020).

25. FHFA, 2019 Report to Congress, 9.

26. Sarah Burd-Sharps and Rebecca Rasch, "Impact of the US Housing Crisis on the Racial Wealth Gap Across Generations," Social Science Research Council and American Civil Liberties Union (June, 2015), available at https://www.aclu.org/files/field_document/discrimlend_final.pdf.

27. See, for example, David Dayen, "The Housing Recovery Has Skipped Poor and Minority Neighborhoods," *New Republic* (June 29, 2015), available at https://newrepublic.com/article/122202/housing-recovery-has-skipped-poor-and-minority-neighborhoods.

28. Stuart Gabriel, Matteo Iacoviello, and Chandler Lutz, "A Crisis of Missed Opportunities? Foreclosure Costs and Mortgage Modification During the Great Recession," *FRB Finance and Economics Discussion Series Working Paper 2020-053* (July 2020), available at https://www.federalreserve.gov/econres/feds/files/2020053pap.pdf.

29. OCC, FRB, FDIC, Farm Credit Administration (FCA), and FHFA, "Margin and Capital Requirements for Covered Swap Entities," 85 Fed. Reg. 39754 (July 1, 2020), (codified at 24 C.F.R. § 624), available at https://www.govinfo.gov/content/pkg/FR-2020-07-01/pdf/2020-14097.pdf.

30. Brian Browdie, "The bank that watches your every move," *American Banker* (January 1, 2019), at https://www.americanbanker.com/news/the-bank-that-watches-your-every-move-the-rise-of-behavioral-banks.

31. United States Postal Service Office of Inspector General, "Providing Non-Bank Financial Services for the Underserved," *RARC-WP-14-007* (January 27, 2014), available at https://www.uspsoig.gov/sites/default/files/document-library-files/2015/rarc-wp-14-007_0.pdf.

32. Postal Banking Act, S. 2755, 115th Cong. (2018), available at https://www.congress.gov/115/bills/s2755/BILLS-115s2755is.pdf.

33. Board of Governors of the Federal Reserve System (FRB), *Perspectives from Main Street: Bank Branch Access in Rural Communities*, (November 2019), available at https://www.federalreserve.gov/publications/files/bank-branch-access-in-rural-communities.pdf.

34. GAO, "U.S. Postal Service: Congressional Action Is Essential to Enable a Sustainable Business Model," *GAO-20-385* (May 2020), available at https://www.gao.gov/assets/710/706729.pdf.

35. The Coronavirus Aid, Relief, and Economic Security Act (CARES Act) Pub. L. 116–136, (March 27, 2020), available at https://www.govinfo.gov/content/pkg/BILLS-116hr748enr/pdf/BILLS-116hr748enr.pdf.

36. Aimee Picchi, "20 million Americans still waiting for their stimulus checks," *CBS News* (May 15, 2020), available at https://www.cbsnews.com/news/stimulus-check-delays-payment-status-not-available/.

37. GAO, COVID-19: Opportunities to Improve Federal Response and Recovery Efforts, *GAO-20-625*, (June 25, 2020), available at https://www.gao.gov/assets/710/707839.pdf.

38. Tony Romm, "Unemployed workers face new delays and paused payments as states race to stamp out massive nationwide scam," *Washington Post* (June 12, 2020), available at https://www.washingtonpost.com/business/2020/06/12/unemployment-benefits-fraud-delays/.

39. See, for example, Mehrsa Baradaran, "Testimony before the Task Force on Financial Technology of the House Financial Services Committee: Inclusive Banking During a Pandemic: Using FedAccounts and Digital Tools to Improve Delivery of Stimulus Payments" (June 11, 2020), available at https://financialservices.house.gov/uploadedfiles/hhrg-116-ba00-wstate-baradaranm-20200611.pdf; and Morgan Ricks, "Testimony before the Task Force on Financial Technology of the House Financial Services Committee: Inclusive Banking During a Pandemic: Using FedAccounts and Digital Tools to Improve Delivery of Stimulus Payments" (June 11, 2020), available at https://financialservices.house.gov/uploadedfiles/hhrg-116-ba00-wstate-ricksm-20200611.pdf.

40. GAO, "Prolonged Conservatorships of Fannie Mae and Freddie Mac Prompt Need for Reform," *GAO-19-239* (January 18, 2019), available at https://www.gao.gov/assets/700/696516.pdf.

41. Ibid.

42. An Act to establish a Federal Credit Union System, to establish a further market for securities of the United States, and to make more available to people of small means credit for provident purposes through a national system of cooperative credit, thereby helping to stabilize the credit structure of the Unites States (The Federal Credit Union Act, or FCU Act), Pub. L. No. 73-467, 48 Stat. 1216 (June 26, 1934), available at https://www.loc.gov/law/help/statutes-atlarge/73rd-congress/session-2/c73s2ch750.pdf.

43. Federal Financial Analytics, "The Credit-Union Equality Commitment: An Analytical Assessment" (June 25, 2019), available at http://www.fedfin.com/info-services/issues-in-focus?task=weblink.go&id=517.

44. Depository Institutions Deregulation and Monetary Control Act, Pub. L. 96-221, 94 Stat. 13, (March 31, 1980), available at https://fraser.stlouisfed.org/title/depository-institutions-deregulation-monetary-control-act-1980-1032.

45. OCC, Policy Statement on Financial Technology Companies' Eligibility to Apply for National Bank Charters (July 31, 2018), available at https://occ.gov/news-issuances/news-releases/2018/pub-other-occ-policy-statement-fintech.pdf.

46. B Lab, State by State Status of Beneficial Corporation Legislation, accessed June 26, 2020, available at https://benefitcorp.net/policymakers/state-by-state-status.

47. J. Christopher Giancarlo, "Testimony before the Task Force on Financial Technology of the House Financial Services Committee: Inclusive Banking During a Pandemic: Using FedAccounts and Digital Tools to Improve Delivery of Stimulus Payments" (June 11, 2020), available at https://financialservices.house.gov/uploadedfiles/hhrg-116-ba00-wstate-giancarloj-20200611.pdf.

Chapter 11

1. William Greider, *Secrets of the Temple: How the Federal Reserve Runs the Country* (New York: Simon & Schuster Inc., 1987).

2. Lisa J. Dettling, Joanne W. Hsu, Lindsay Jacobs, Kevin B. Moore, and Jeffrey P. Thompson, "Recent Trends in Wealth-Holding by Race and Ethnicity: Evidence from the Survey of Consumer Finances," *FEDS Notes* (September 27, 2017), available at https://www.federalreserve.gov/econres/notes/feds-notes/recent-trends-in-wealth-holding-by-race-and-ethnicity-evidence-from-the-survey-of-consumer-finances-20170927.htm.

3. Federal Reserve Bank of San Francisco (FRBSF) President and CEO Mary C. Daly, "We Can't Afford Not To" (speech, Washington, DC, June 15, 2020), FRBSF, available at https://www.frbsf.org/our-district/press/presidents-speeches/mary-c-daly/2020/june/we-cant-afford-not-to/?utm_source=frbsf-home-president-speeches&utm_medium=frbsf&utm_campaign=president-speeches.

4. See Chapter 6.

5. Joint Center for Housing Studies of Harvard University (JCHS Harvard), *The State of the Nation's Housing 2019*, June 25, 2019, available at https://www.jchs.harvard.edu/sites/default/files/Harvard_JCHS_State_of_the_Nations_Housing_2019.pdf.

6. Board of Governors of the Federal Reserve System (FRB), *Report on the Economic Well-Being of U.S. Households in 2019, Featuring Supplemental Data from April 2020*, 25 (May 14, 2020), available at https://www.federalreserve.gov/publications/files/2019-report-economic-well-being-us-households-202005.pdf.

7. US Government Accountability Office, "Millennial Generation: Information on the Economic Status of Millennial Households Compared to Previous Generations," *GAO-20-194*, 27 (December 2019), available at https://www.gao.gov/assets/710/703222.pdf.

8. Karen Petrou, "Repo ructions highlight failure of post-crisis policymaking," *Financial Times* (November 5, 2019), available at https://www.ft.com/content/fe562cbe-feee-11e9-b7bc-f3fa4e77dd47.

9. Colby Smith, "How big could the Fed's balance sheet get?," *Financial Times* (April 5, 2020), available at https://www.ft.com/content/ec10b41a-84af-4e44-ad3f-5bb86b6e1eaa.

10. FRB, *Federal Reserve Issues FOMC Statement* (June 10, 2020), available at https://www.federalreserve.gov/newsevents/pressreleases/monetary20200610a.htm

11. Jim Bianco, "Blame the Fed for the Disconnect in Markets," *Bloomberg News* (June 11, 2020), available at https://www.bloomberg.com/opinion/articles/2020-06-11/the-fed-has-designed-markets-to-favor-investors?sref=BSO3yKhf.

12. Editorial Board, "The Federal Resurrection Board," *Wall Street Journal* (June 14, 2020), available at https://www.wsj.com/articles/the-federal-resurrection-board-11592167678.

13. Brian Chappatta, "Fed Needs Better Answers on Runaway Markets and Inequality," *Bloomberg News* (June 9, 2020), available at https://www.bloomberg.com/opinion/articles/2020-06-09/fed-needs-better-answers-on-runaway-markets-and-inequality?sref=BSO3yKhf.

14. Robert W. Fairlie, "The Impact of COVID-19 on Small Business Owners: Evidence of Early-Stage Losses from the April 2020 Current Population Survey," *National Bureau of Economic Research (NBER) Working Paper 27309*, 1 (June 2020), available at https://www.nber.org/papers/w27309.pdf.

15. Ibid., 7.

16. Shelly Banjo, "A Decade's Worth of Progress for Working Women Evaporated Overnight," *Bloomberg Businessweek* (June 3, 2020), available at https://www.bloomberg.com/news/articles/2020-06-03/coronavirus-is-disproportionately-impacting-women?sref=BSO3yKhf.

17. Jane Callen, "New Household Pulse Survey Shows Concern Over Food Security, Loss of Income," *United States Census Bureau* (May 20, 2020), available at https://www.census.gov/library/stories/2020/05/new-household-pulse-survey-shows-concern-over-food-security-loss-of-income.html.

18. FRB, *FedListens: Perspectives from the Public*, vii (June 2020), available at https://www.federalreserve.gov/publications/files/fedlistens-report-20200612.pdf.

19. Federal Reserve Act § 13(3), 12 U.S.C. § 343 (2018), available at https://www.govinfo.gov/content/pkg/USCODE-2018-title12/pdf/USCODE-2018-title12-chap3-subchapIX-sec343.pdf.

20. Chappatta, "Fed Needs Better Answers on Runaway Markets and Inequality."

21. Rich Miller, "Powell Plays Down Significance of Move to Buy Corporate Bonds," *Bloomberg News* (June 16, 2020), available at https://www.bloomberg.com/news/articles/2020-06-16/powell-plays-down-significance-of-move-to-buy-corporate-bonds?sref=BSO3yKhf.

22. See, for example, FRB, *Main Street New Loan Facility Borrower Certifications and Covenants Instructions and Guidance*, 8 (June 11, 2020), available at https://www.bostonfed.org/-/media/Documents/special-lending-facilities/mslp/legal/msnlf-borrower-certifications-and-covenants.pdf

23. John Cassidy, "The Coronavirus Is Exposing Wall Street's Reckless Gamble on Bad Debt," *New Yorker* (May 24, 2020), available at https://www.newyorker.com/business/currency/the-coronavirus-is-exposing-wall-streets-reckless-gamble-on-bad-debt.

24. Bill Dudley, "Fed's Coronavirus Rescues Invite Bigger Bailouts," *Bloomberg News* (June 5, 2020), available at https://www.bloomberg.com/opinion/articles/2020-06-05/federal-reserve-s-coronavirus-rescues-invite-bigger-bailouts?sref=BSO3yKhf.

25. Karen Petrou, "Nothing to suggest trickle-down monetary policy will suddenly work," *American Banker* (March 20, 2020), available at https://www.americanbanker.com/opinion/nothing-to-suggest-trickle-down-monetary-policy-will-suddenly-work.

26. Agustín Carstens, "Bold steps to pump coronavirus rescue funds down the last mile," *Financial Times* (March 29, 2020), available at https://www.ft.com/content/5a1a1e9c-6f4d-11ea-89df-41bea055720b

27. FRB, "Term Sheet: Municipal Liquidity" (June 3, 2020), available at https://www.federalreserve.gov/newsevents/pressreleases/files/monetary20200603a1.pdf.

28. Aaron Klein and Camille Busette, "Improving the equity impact of the Fed's municipal lending facility," *Brookings Institution* (April 14, 2020), available at https://www.brookings.edu/research/a-chance-to-improve-the-equity-impact-of-the-feds-municipal-lending-facility/.

29. Brian Chappatta, "Fed Seems to Skirt the Law to Buy Corporate Bonds," *Bloomberg News* (June 18, 2020), available at https://www.bloomberg.com/opinion/articles/2020-06-18/fed-seems-to-skirt-the-law-to-buy-corporate-bonds?sref=BSO3yKhf.

30. FRB, "Federal Reserve Board announces it will be seeking public feedback on proposal to expand its Main Street Lending Program to provide access to credit for nonprofit organizations" (June 15, 2020), available at https://www.federalreserve.gov/newsevents/pressreleases/monetary20200615b.htm.

31. Federal Reserve Bank of St. Louis, "Homeownership Rate for the United States," *Federal Reserve Economic Data Series RHORUSQ156N*, accessed June 19, 2020, available at https://fred.stlouisfed.org/series/RHORUSQ156N.

32. Fidelity Investments, "Fidelity Q1 Retirement Analysis: Retirement Savers 'Stayed the Course' Despite Economic Crisis" (April 24, 2020), available at https://newsroom.fidelity.com/press-releases/news-details/2020/Fidelity-Q1-2020-Retirement-Analysis-Retirement-Savers-Stayed-the-Course-Despite-Economic-Crisis/default.aspx.

33. Pascal Paul, "Historical Patterns of Inequality and Productivity around Financial Crises," Federal Reserve Bank of San Francisco, *Working Paper 2017-23* (March 2020), available at https://www.frbsf.org/economic-research/files/wp2017-23.pdf.

34. Isabel Cairo and Jae Sim, "Income Inequality, Financial Crises, and Monetary Policy," Federal Reserve Finance and Economics Discussion Series, *Working Paper 2018-048* (May 2018), available at https://www.federalreserve.gov/econres/feds/files/2018048pap.pdf.

35. Noah Smith, "If Zombie Companies Don't Die, We'll Pay a Price," *Bloomberg News* (June 17, 2020), available at https://www.bloomberg.com/opinion/articles/2020-06-17/zombie-companies-feasting-on-coronavirus-relief-funds-hurt-growth?sref=BSO3yKhf.

Index